Anatoly and Avital Shcharansky

ANATOLY and AVITAL SHCHARANSKY

The Journey Home

by
THE JERUSALEM POST

Harcourt Brace Jovanovich, Publishers
San Diego   New York   London

Library of Congress Cataloging-in-Publication Data

Anatoly and Avital Shcharansky.

1. Shcharansky, Anatoly. 2. Shcharansky, Avital.
3. Jews—Soviet Union—Biography. 4. Refuseniks—
Biography. 5. Political prisoners—Soviet Union—
Biography. 6. Civil rights—Soviet Union. 7. Israel—
Emigration and immigration—Biography. I. Jerusalem
post.
DS135.R95A113   1986   325'.247'095694   86-14808
ISBN 0-15-106670-1

Designed by G. B. D. Smith

Printed in the United States of America

First edition

A B C D E

Contents

Moscow to Siberia

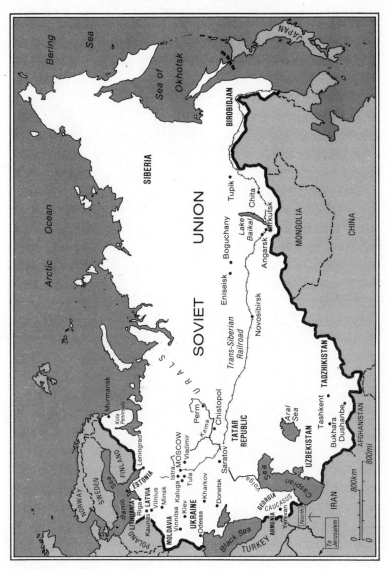

Moscow to Jerusalem

Preface

It is a hard thing to be regarded as a symbol, instead of as a human being. The Kremlin elected to see in Anatoly Shcharansky the embodiment of Russian Jewry's struggle to be free; and it punished him as if by crushing Shcharansky it could wipe out his people's aspirations. The Soviets chose well, in that Shcharansky was a natural leader and did represent much of what the Soviets feared most about the Jewish movement, including its potential alliance with the human rights movement; but they chose badly, in that they could not crush him. Despite the isolation, ill-treatment, and misinformation meted out to him during his nine years of imprisonment, Anatoly Shcharansky understood the significance of the role allotted to him and undertook to live up to it.

Shcharansky was ever a gadfly to the Soviet establishment, stinging them repeatedly while he was free and active, stinging them vicariously after his imprisonment, through the ceaseless campaigning of his wife, Avital, and the relentless struggle of his fellow activists.

To the Western world, Anatoly Shcharansky became a symbol of Soviet Jewry, oppressed but dauntless; and the projection of this image was due in great part to his wife, Avital. Separated for much longer than they were together, Avital and Anatoly seemed to grow closer each year apart. Each said many times that they never felt apart from the other: and strange as the claim seems, it was borne out by their demeanor. Observers of Anatoly in prison spoke of the aura of liberty he exuded; whereas Avital in her mournful freedom seemed always shackled, never truly free.

If Anatoly (renamed Natan in Israel) and Avital thought that his release would allow them to exchange a symbolic for a private life, they were wrong. Within a few weeks of his arrival in Israel, Anatoly was flinching from the pictures of himself plastered throughout the local and foreign press and refusing to read any of the millions of words being written about him and Avital. Everywhere he went, in even the smallest Israeli village, he was recognized; and despite all of his charm, humor, and feeling of inner wholeness, the attention began to wear on him. For many of his thirty-eight years, he had lived in a sea of hate. "Now I have to learn to get accustomed to an ocean of love, and I assure you, it's not easy," he told an audience of students who had worked for his release. Someone asked if he was going to become religious, now that he was free to practice Judaism openly. "Religious freedom is inside you, not external," he replied. "I was a free man in prison in the Soviet Union, and I'll continue to be a free man in Israel."

There's nothing he can do about it: he's more of a symbol than ever, mainly because of the gifts he possesses. Courageous and brilliant, warm and very funny, he's a diminutive man whom everybody looks up to. In a society that is a paranoid's paradise, Shcharansky never lost either his sense of proportion or his sense of humor. Who else, when KGB agents followed him so closely that they even crowded into his taxi, would insist on their splitting the fare? Who else would call KGB headquarters to complain that one of his tails was drunk? Throughout his trial and the years of harsh punishment that followed, Anatoly exhibited a strength that even the nonreligious called God-given—though he himself ascribed much of it to a woman, his wife. If the KGB under-estimated his power of endurance, they completely over-looked hers. Anatoly was denied information about his wife's campaign to free him, but he was always able to gauge its effectiveness by the vehemence of the Soviet attacks on her.

The team of *Jerusalem Post* writers who produced this book has felt privileged to describe the story of a great movement and of two people who have come to personify the Soviet Jewish emigration struggle. It is an important chapter in Jewish history, but it is also something more: Shcharansky's victory represents a triumph of the human spirit over the authoritarian state. He fought for justice and human rights in general and the Jewish people in particular. And though the Kremlin persecuted the leadership of both the Jewish emigration and the dissident movements, it could not crush either movement. Nearly half a million Soviet Jews are seeking to emigrate, and the struggle for human rights continues in the USSR. In their different ways, Anatoly and Avital Shcharansky are inspirational figures, to whom we are all indebted.

With two exceptions, those of us who worked on this book had never been even slightly interested in Soviet Jewry—

an embarrassing admission, coming from Israeli journalists who work for a newspaper with a Zionist point of view. In retrospect we find our own apathy strange, since Russia was the home of grandparents who went to America, or South Africa, or Palestine or who perished during the Second World War; since over 150,000 Soviet Jews have settled in Israel in the last fifteen years; since there are hundreds of thousands of others trying to get through a door that has been almost completely closed. Perhaps we needed a focus, a person who was more than just a name on posters held high at demonstrations. For all of us who worked on this book, the story of Anatoly and Avital has been an eye-opener; and we believe the reader will feel the same way.

The story of Avital and Anatoly is actually many stories, and we have tried to do justice to each. It is the story of the evolution of a movement in which totally assimilated Jews gradually became aware of their identity and fought to express it freely. It tells of two people in adversity, struggling against great odds to attain the simple things that other couples take for granted: a home, a life together, children. There is treachery and a villain with the smile of a Cheshire cat. Finally, it is the story of the perversion of justice in the Soviet Union, of a trial as monumentally unjust as that of Dreyfus, and of life in the Gulag.

The diplomatic efforts that led to Anatoly's freedom are chronicled for the first time in this book, through the reportorial skills of three *Jerusalem Post* correspondents: Wolf Blitzer in Washington, Walter Ruby in New York, and Wladimir Struminski in Bonn. The chapter entitled "The Winding Road to Freedom" includes the first in-depth report on the 1983 offer to release Anatoly on health grounds and why he turned it down. In Jerusalem, the team of Abraham

Rabinovich, Douglas Davis, Robert Rosenberg, and Louis Rapoport wrote *The Journey Home*, which includes a chapter on the Shcharanskys' reunion in Israel. The final draft was edited by Louis Rapoport, who also wrote the epilogue.

Many people have helped us, and we would like to thank in particular Mark Nashpitz, Dina Beilina, Sylva Zalmanson, Hillel Butman, Lev Ulanovsky, Felix Kandel, Yosef Ahs, and Alexander Lunts. Thanks also to Irwin Kotler, Alan Dershowitz, Mark Epstein, Shcharansky biographer Martin Gilbert, David Shipler, Walter Mondale, Zbigniew Brzezinski, Dan Fisher, William Claiborne, Jerry Goodman, Robert Drinan, Richard Pipes, Michael Sherbourne, Glenn Richter, Enid Wurtman, Jerry Stern, Irene Manekofsky, and Israel Radio and Israel Television.

The book would not have been possible without the initiative and hard work of our editor at Harcourt Brace Jovanovich, David Rosenberg, and *Jerusalem Post* editor Ari Rath. The head of the *Post*'s book division, Daphne Raz, and reporter Judy Siegel have also been most helpful. Special thanks are due as well to Barbara Rogan.

Louis Rapoport
JERUSALEM, MAY 1986

1

"See You in Jerusalem"

She had no marriage license. No rabbi. The groom was in jail. But Nataliya Steiglits was undeterred. She was determined that within two weeks she would marry Anatoly Shcharansky.

They had met eight months before, in October 1973, in a crowd of Jews on tree-lined Arkhipova Street opposite Moscow's Great Synagogue, a Greek-style building with ornate Ionic columns. Nataliya had been seeking information about her brother Michael—"Misha"—who had been arrested.

Although it was snowing, the people on the street made no move to enter the warm synagogue. It was a Saturday morning and services were going on inside, but the people outside had come to commune with one another. The focus of their thoughts was, however, identical to that of the devout Jews inside: Jerusalem, and how to get there.

Nataliya stood shyly on the fringes, intimidated by the police who lounged around the sentry booth beside the synagogue steps. KGB men mingled with the crowd, eavesdropping, sometimes openly taking notes. Most of the people had applied to emigrate to Israel, and some were "refuseniks": their applications had been denied. They were without legal recourse, without hope.

All were talking about the Yom Kippur War, which had begun with a surprise Arab attack earlier that month.

"Where are we now?" one asked; another answered, "We're advancing toward Damascus."

These were her brother's friends, not hers. She too was of Jewish origin, but unlike them she knew nothing of the religion, culture, or history of her people. She had not even known until she was twenty that she was Jewish—her staunchly pro-Soviet parents had kept her heritage from her. After leaving home to live with her brother she had learned a little, but Michael, though deeply involved in the Jewish movement, was protective of his young sister and secretive about his activities.

One day, traveling in a bus to the art institute where she studied, Nataliya noticed a large group of people standing in front of the Tass news agency building. All at once they raised placards that read "Visas for Israel," and "Give us visas." Immediately the police rushed in, and as they led the demonstrators away she was shocked to recognize the tall figure of her brother. "Misha!" she screamed, and "Stop the bus!" But the driver drove on to the next stop.

By the time she returned to the site, the demonstrators had been dispersed. Nataliya went home, but Michael did not return. He had given her a scrap of paper with an emergency phone number on it. She called the number and spoke to a man, Arye Liberman, who told her Michael had been detained, and not for the first time. He told her not to worry, that Misha would be all right. Come to Arkhipova Street on Saturday, he said.

Out of the crowd of strangers in front of the Great Synagogue an odd figure emerged: a small man with a big head and broad mutton-chop sideburns, who exuded warmth and vitality. His name, he said, was Anatoly Shcharansky. "Don't worry about your brother," he said. "It's nothing. I was just released myself, after fifteen days in jail."

Nataliya was not comforted. Misha, she explained, was her whole world, her Jewish mother. To distract her, Anatoly turned the conversation to other things: her work, herself. He asked if she planned to go to Israel—he had applied for an exit visa six months before. Nataliya heard herself say, "Yes."

"How's your Hebrew?" he asked.

"How's yours?" she countered.

"About a thousand words."

"That's about my level," she said, stretching the truth. She liked this man, and the attraction was strong, despite her anxiety over Michael. Anatoly was a head shorter than she, pudgy and balding; but he walked tall and moved and spoke with a confidence and freedom rare among Russians. *This*, Nataliya thought, *is what Israelis are like.* Certainly, the life he lived was a world away from the life she had known.

Nataliya had been born in a remote Siberian town, the daughter of officials in the Soviet penal system. Her father, the sole survivor of a large Hasidic family that had lived in Poland, had renounced any identification with his people in favor of Communist fundamentalism. Her mother, a jurist, was a stern person whose primary loyalty was to the state. Just as her parents obscured their own Jewishness, they also omitted it from their children's identity cards. Michael rebelled against his parents and their beliefs by embracing the very heritage they had rejected: he wanted to leave home, to live in Moscow with his maternal grandmother, who kept a traditional Jewish home, though she was not religious.

When Avital was seventeen, her grandmother died and the Steiglits family moved from Siberia to Moscow. Michael left the family home to get away from his parents, and a year later Avital, at eighteen, moved in with him. Their relationship was extremely close, and on his part protective. In a world of secrets, she was particularly vulnerable. So Anatoly's open, joyful embrace of all that had been denied in her own life came as a revelation. Although he too came from an assimilated family, his parents were warm, loving, and accepting.

WHEN BORIS Shcharansky returned home to Odessa after serving in the Red Army as a volunteer during World War II, he discovered that his old job was no longer available. Half a million Jews had served in the Russian army, and 200,000 had died fighting for their country. But the editor of the Odessa newspaper where he had worked was quite open about the problem—his paper had its full quota of Jews. "Try your luck in Stalino," the editor suggested. That city, about three hundred miles from Odessa in the southern Ukraine, was a dreary industrial center where there were few Jews. Boris, who had become a member of the Communist Party during the fight against Fascism, might land a job on the local paper there, the editor said.

It was a constructive suggestion. Donetsk, as Stalino was called before and after Stalin's reign, was a no-nonsense, working-class city that owed its existence to nearby coal mines and the development of large metallurgical and chemical industries. It was also a cultural wasteland. Donetsk was a far cry indeed from Odessa, where both Boris Shcharansky and Ida Milgrom had been born and raised, where they met and married.

Odessa had been a major cultural center of Eastern European Jewry, home of some of the founders of the Zionist movement such as Ahad Ha'am and Vladimir Jabotinsky, and of poets and writers including Sholem Aleichem and Chaim Nahum Bialik. Boris was born in 1904, at a time that pogroms were sweeping the Ukraine and Jabotinsky was organizing the first Jewish self-defense force. Boris's father regarded Jabotinsky, who had declared that the Jews must leave Russia, as a hero and a prophet. One of Boris's three brothers, Shamai, was arrested in 1924 as a member of a Zionist organization and was put aboard a ship for Palestine; but Boris himself was not interested in struggling for a Jewish state. He felt that the Communist movement would improve the life of Jews in the USSR.

Ida Milgrom, who married Boris in 1929, was born into a family deeply immersed in the cultural life of the city. She was an economist, and Boris wrote film scripts before becoming a journalist. But the life they had known before World War II could never be restored. The Germans, who had occupied Odessa and most of the Soviet Union's European territories, had exterminated almost half of the USSR's Jewish population of five million; traditional Jewish settlements and historic cultural centers had been obliterated for all time. Nothing would ever be the same. The Shcharanskys were lucky to be alive. In 1946, after seventeen years of marriage, their first child, Leonid, was born. One year later, Ida and Boris packed up their belongings and headed for their new home. Boris Shcharansky soon got a job as the industrial and labor correspondent on the Donetsk paper, while his wife was appointed chief economist of a major commercial enterprise in the city.

The Shcharanskys—educated, cultured, and relatively

comfortable—never felt at home in Donetsk, where the highlight of the social calendar was the regular arrival of large quantities of beer from a nearby brewery. They were not much safer there than they would have been as members of the Odessa intelligentsia. In 1948, Stalin initiated a virulent campaign against "rootless cosmopolitans," a code name for Jewish intellectuals. The leading Jewish writers and cultural figures in the big cities were rounded up and, later, secretly executed.

On January 20, 1948 Ida Milgrom—who retained her maiden name, as do many Soviet women who achieve a degree of academic distinction—gave birth to her second child, Anatoly, a small baby with a round face and full, rosy lips. It was the year of the state of Israel's birth, an event supported by the Soviet Union and a high point in Soviet–Jewish relations. On the day that the first Israeli ambassador, Golda Meir, arrived in Moscow, she was stunned by her reception—a sea of Soviet Jews came out to greet her. But Stalin's initial support for the establishment of a Jewish state in the Middle East did not signal a lessening of his anti-Semitic campaign at home. In fact, the Jews were becoming his obsession. His daughter Svetlana, whose first husband was a Jew, later recalled that her father's anti-Semitism gradually increased "from political hatred to a racial aversion for all Jews, bar none." Stalin told the American ambassador, Charles "Chip" Bohlen, that he didn't know what to do with the Jews: "I can't swallow them; I can't spit them out; they are the only group that is completely unassimilable."

But most Jews of the Russian and Ukrainian republics—where the bulk of Soviet Jewry resides—were like the Shcharanskys: they wanted nothing more than to be accepted as good, loyal citizens of their beloved motherland. They were not like the Jews of the Baltic republics annexed by the Soviets in 1939 and 1940 or the religious, non-Ashkenazi Jews of the Caucasus and Asian provinces, many of whom were Zionists or were cognizant of Jewish and Hebrew tradition. Paradoxically, the new Zionist movement was initiated mainly by assimilated young Jews of Leningrad and Moscow who had no Zionist background, and many of them were confined in the Soviet Gulag.

In the early 1950s, during the height of the anti-Jewish hysteria created by Stalin's campaign, the newspapermen of Donetsk, including Boris Shcharansky, were summoned to a meeting of the Journalists' Union and told that thenceforth no articles would be published that showed Jews in a positive light. This amounted to the formalization of a policy that had been applied de facto for some years. The two hundred Jews who had become generals in the Red Army during the war were never mentioned as Jews in the Soviet press, although members of other national minorities were identified ethnically. But Jewish army deserters, political deviants, or economic criminals were invariably identified. All Jews remaining in the party leadership had been purged in 1952; and when eleven Jewish leaders of the satellite Czech Communist Party were hanged, the newspapers specified that they were Jews. In July 1952, twenty-four Jewish writers were accused of "espionage on behalf of foreign states," and twenty-three of them were executed. In February 1953, after a small bomb went off outside the Soviet mission in Tel Aviv—perhaps planted by the Soviets themselves—Stalin broke off relations with Israel. Now, the journalists' new directive came with the advent of the "Doctors' Plot."

Early in 1953, nine doctors, six of them Jews, were arrested for allegedly murdering in 1949 two of Stalin's most anti-Semitic lieutenants, Alexander Shcherbakov and Andrei Zhdanov. The doctors "confessed" to a Zionist and CIA plot against the Soviet Union and its guiding pilot, Joseph Stalin. The national newspapers, and official provincial dailies like the one that employed Shcharansky, were filled with caricatures of demonic Jews reminiscent of Nazi publications. After all, Boris Shcharansky and his colleagues were told, if Jewish doctors in Moscow had plotted to poison top Soviet leaders, as Stalin had claimed, then there were surely Jewish doctors in Donetsk who would attempt to poison local officials.

Stalin's long reign of terror had engendered slavish obedience among most of his subjects. Boris Shcharansky, like almost everyone else, had reason to fear. Some Soviet Jews were like the Marranos of Inquisition Spain, who professed the state religion in order to escape persecution. A larger number actually believed in the Communist faith. Boris felt he had to accept the new decree in silence. If he had spoken out, he would have been sent to a camp. During the war, Boris had protested against an anti-Semitic speech by a Soviet officer and gotten into trouble. But now, he had a family to consider, children to raise and educate.

Throughout the Soviet Union, there were hundreds of similar meetings of unions and institute and factory staffs, in which numerous Jews were summarily dismissed. The decree also provided an opportunity to purge non-Jews who were suspiciously intellectual.

It was believed in Moscow that Stalin's plan was to hang the "doctor-murderers" in Red Square at the beginning of March 1953. The aroused populace, egged on by government agents, would commit bloody pogroms. Then

Uncle Joe would step in to save all the Jews by deporting them to Siberia, as he had done with some other Soviet minorities. Two million would be placed in camps, which had already been prepared.

The plan had been partially implemented: almost every Jewish doctor in the USSR had been dismissed; Jewish civil servants, factory supervisors, and officials had been purged; and thousands of Moscow Jews had been transferred to Siberia, including many loyal Communists like the parents of Nataliya Steiglits. Synagogues were closed down. Religious Jews, preparing to celebrate Passover in the coming weeks, learned that they would have to bake their own matzoth and felt that the situation paralleled the biblical events of the Exodus.

When Stalin died suddenly in early March 1953, the Jews regarded their last-minute deliverance as a miracle, especially since Stalin was reportedly stricken on the Jewish holiday of Purim. That festival marks the deliverance of the Jewish people from a Persian despot, Haman, who had planned to exterminate the Jews. Not only the Jews saw divine intervention in the coincidence of Stalin's death. Alexander Solzhenitsyn, in *The Gulag Archipelago*, wrote that Stalin's plot against the Jews was "the first plan of his life to fail. God told him—apparently with the help of human hands—to depart from his rib cage."

The deportation plan was dropped following Stalin's death, and ties with Israel were restored, although a low-key anti-Jewish campaign continued until the end of 1954.

The "Doctors' Plot" had an enormous impact on all those who lived through it, constituting another watershed in the awakening of Soviet Jews that eventually led to the exodus of hundreds of thousands. It also caused a great number of Russian Jews to wish that they had never been born into the Jewish covenant. Many of them, including the Shcharanskys, played down their Jewishness. They did not celebrate Passover or any other Jewish holidays, and even had a Christmas tree in the house. Being too Jewish was simply too dangerous.

To officials in Israel, there was a scent of pogrom in the news sifting through from the Soviet Union in the wake of the allegations against the doctors. Early in 1952, a group of men gathered in a room in Tel Aviv to discuss the situation. Some of them were in government service, others had been in the past. For all of them, including those who had been born in what was now the Soviet Union, the Iron Curtain was almost a physical reality that masked the fate of the third largest Jewish community in the world. How many of the estimated two to three million Soviet Jews indeed still considered themselves Jewish after two generations of assimilation and of isolation from their brethren abroad?

The enthusiastic reception given to Ambassador Golda Meir by Moscow Jews upon her arrival indicated that a strong sense of identity still existed among a portion of the Jewish population. But how big a portion and how substantial the enthusiasm? The embassy itself had not proved an effective instrument in providing the answers. Since that initial reception for Mrs. Meir, the Soviet authorities had kept the embassy personnel isolated from the population, and Soviet Jews had reason to fear seeking contacts with the Israeli diplomatic personnel.

The question put to the participants in the Tel Aviv meeting was whether efforts should be made to establish contact with Soviet Jewry despite the dangers involved. Establishing such contacts in Russia, particularly Stalin's Russia, would be far from simple, and the risks for those involved could be considerable. In the absence of any certainty that Jewish identity of any dimension existed in the Soviet Union, it was not at all clear that the risks would be worth running. After considerable debate, the participants decided that the effort must be made. The instinct of mutual help propagated by the Jewish people during their long Diaspora—of offering assistance to brethren in distress even beyond the seas—had been adopted as a central tenet of the Jewish state.

But the first practical steps toward organizing contacts with Soviet Jewry were made to falter when Moscow suspended diplomatic relations between the two countries. By the time relations were resumed, Stalin was dead and the heavy hand of the central regime had relaxed slightly. Within a few years of the reestablishment of relations, more than half a dozen Israeli diplomats in Moscow would be expelled by the Soviet authorities for passing Jewish and Zionist reading material to Soviet citizens. Charged with undiplomatic activity and distributing literature without authorization, the diplomats were declared persona non grata. In 1955, thirty Soviet Jews were arrested for meeting with the Israeli diplomats, and some were given heavy sentences.

The inflow of material, however, would become a tide the Soviets could not stop. The Israelis had discovered that the spark was there to be kindled. Tourists and businessmen from the West, including non-Jews, brought in Hebrew-Russian dictionaries, prayer books, books on Jewish history, copies of novels like *Exodus*. They also brought religious articles like prayer shawls. Most important, they brought to the Jews of the Soviet Union a sense that they were not alone. To the Soviet Jews, starved for knowledge about their own national and religious identity, the material was a culturally life-giving infusion.

EVEN AS A SMALL child, Anatoly showed a boundless curiosity about people and would talk to them for hours. At an early age, he demonstrated an unbreakable will. Some children are sent into a corner and five minutes later come out tearfully apologizing for their misdemeanor. But not Anatoly. If he believed he was right, he was prepared to stay in the corner all day. His mother, a small woman possessed of a calm, warm temperament and a keen wit, realized that her younger son was stubborn to an extreme.

Tolya, as his parents called him, had his first contact with Soviet police around the time of Stalin's death, when he was just five. His parents had given him a bicycle, with a strict injunction not to ride in the streets. The boy chafed at this display of parental authority, and took to the highway to test his new skill. He was promptly hit by a car. His arm was broken and his bicycle demolished. Passersby, not realizing the extent of the child's injuries, took him directly to a police station. But when the police asked his name in order to call his parents, Anatoly sat in stony silence, stubbornly refusing to answer any questions.

His mother, frantic when her son did not return, called every police station in the city. Finally, she discovered where he was. It was only in his mother's arms that he admitted to the pain he was suffering. But he never explained his refusal to cooperate with the police.

It was the boys' father, Boris, who provided much of the children's nurturing. The couple had become parents late in life, and their overriding fear was that they would not survive to see their sons through university. Ida Milgrom was a workaholic, laboring from early morning to late at night at her relatively well-paid job, while her husband undertook to ensure that the boys had lunch when they returned from school and that they attended their afternoon lessons. Years later, Ida expressed regret that she had devoted so much time to her job instead of to her sons.

Both Leonid and Anatoly were highly intelligent, and although they frequently quarreled in the way that small brothers do, they soon became inseparable. This was natural under the circumstances: for though the Shcharanskys, like many other assimilated Jewish families, claimed the Russian language and culture as their own, their neighbors were less willing to ignore their Jewish roots. They were never fully accepted by their Russian and Ukrainian compatriots. As Yosef Begun, a leading figure in the Jewish renaissance, later wrote, "We know almost nothing of who we are, but we feel it. We do not know what a Jew is, but we know that we are Jews."

From an early age, the Shcharansky boys were strongly encouraged to read. Their parents had accumulated an impressive library—it was their third. The first, in Odessa, was abandoned; the second was destroyed during the war. Each time they started a new life, it was with a library—to which the boys were allowed limitless access. As a child, Anatoly read many volumes of poetry and classics. He showed extraordinary taste in one so young, and his parents were surprised at the extent of his knowledge. The boys went to the local school, where both excelled. Leonid, besides being at the top of his class, was also extremely dexterous; he could make or repair almost anything. Anatoly, by contrast, was utterly hopeless in any task requiring skilled hands. But it was a failing for which he more than compensated by winning the school's top awards for outstanding achievement. He displayed a remarkable ability to solve problems, particularly in mathematics and chess, and his accomplishments, as far as his parents could determine, were achieved with unusual ease. By age fourteen, he was the city and regional chess champion, in a country where chess is king. The Shcharanskys supplemented their children's education with private English lessons and sports instruction.

As the Shcharansky boys entered their teens, they started to become conscious, for the first time, that there was "a Jewish problem" and that they were part of it. Donetsk was a city that gave full expression to the endemic Russian suspicion and hatred of Jews, which stemmed from the belief that the Jews were the killers of Jesus and were unrepentant heretics. Anatoly's moment of truth came at seventeen when some boys he had regarded as friends beat him up. A year later, his best friend called him a "dirty Yid." It was not the sort of chillingly official hatred that he later encountered as a Jewish activist in Moscow, in the KGB prisons, and in labor camps; this raw hatred was much more direct. The second incident came as a particular shock, from someone he felt close to. It was an epiphany of sorts: for at that moment, Anatoly recognized that the Union of Soviet Socialist Republics was not his home.

But Russia, though still riddled with official as well as social anti-Semitism, had changed since Stalin's death. Most Jews no longer lived in constant fear that they would be cut down in the street or whisked away to a secret police dungeon and exterminated in Siberia. Forty years before Anatoly was confronted with anti-Semitism, another sensitive

Jewish youth, the future writer Isaac Babel, had a much harsher lesson of what it meant to be a Jew in the Ukraine. One day a peasant smashed a pigeon into his face. When the boy ran home, covered with blood and bird guts, he discovered that his grandfather had been murdered by other peasants, who had stuffed a fish into his mouth.

Jews first settled in Russia centuries before the Christian era began. They lived in the Caucasus and on the banks of the Don, Dnieper, and Volga rivers. They converted the Khazars, a people of Finnish-Turkish origin, and a Jewish kingdom of great power arose in Russia between the seventh and tenth centuries. In the Middle Ages, the position of Jews in Russia was better than that of their coreligionists in western Europe—they were not ghettoized and lived as free men in the cities. But at the end of the fifteenth century, the czars institutionalized anti-Semitism. Catherine the Great, who ascended the throne in 1762, created the Jewish Pale of Settlement, restricting Russia's Jews to the general region of southwestern Russia and Poland. In the second half of the nineteenth century, Czar Alexander II, who abolished serfdom, eased some restrictions on the Jews. For the first time, a few Jews were allowed to attend Russian schools. Alexander's assassination in 1881 was followed by a new wave of persecution, which was to last until the 1917 revolution. Jews were expelled from Moscow, denied jobs, and strictly confined to the Pale. The mass pogroms encouraged by the government resulted in the emigration of hundreds of thousands of Jews to the United States. A few went to Palestine, establishing the first kibbutz settlements and founding the basic institutions of the Jewish community in Palestine. One who went there in 1914 was Mendel Beilis, who had been tried in the Ukrainian city of Kiev for an alleged ritual murder. His trial had aroused outrage in the West, and Beilis was eventually found not guilty.

Not surprisingly, a great many Jews became involved in the revolutionary movements. The majority of Lenin's first Politburo, three of five members, were Jews, including Trotsky, founder of the Red Army. In the period before the 1905 revolution, Lenin attacked the socialist Jewish Bund and denigrated the Zionist idea as "entirely false and reactionary in its essence." He believed that the only solution to the Jewish problem was total assimilation. The Jews were merely a caste, not a separate people. He attacked anti-Semitism and the pogromists, but said that Jewish national culture was "the slogan of the rabbis and the bourgeoisie, the slogan of our enemies." Stalin, in his prerevolution writings, reiterated Lenin's view that the Jews were not a nationality. He derided the Jewish people's "petrified religious rites and fading psychological relics" and agreed with Lenin's proposals to annihilate Judaism, Zionism, and Hebrew culture.

When the revolution came, Hebrew was declared a reactionary language, and the liquidation of Jewish culture was carried out mainly by the Jews themselves. But in spite of the theory that the Jews were not one of the many national groups living in the Soviet Union, in practice the Jews were treated by the Soviets as a distinct people, a nonterritorial "nationality." In 1934, the Soviets tried to create a territory for Jewish national political autonomy in the barren and desolate Birobidzhan region of the Far East, along the border with China; but it was never economically viable, and only a few thousand Jews went there. Soviet Jews were thoroughly urbanized and the most highly educated of all 104 "nationalities" in the USSR, and they preferred to live in the major cultural centers. In recent years, the Jews, less than 1 percent of the Soviet population—2,150,707 according to the 1970 census—accounted for 23 percent of the country's musicians, 14 percent of all Soviet doctors, and 11 percent of the membership of the Soviet Academy of Sciences. This was achieved despite all of the barriers put in front of them. In two generations, Russian Jewry have experienced a remarkable upward mobility, becoming part of the cultural and scientific classes despite all the ravages of Hitler and Stalin.

DONETSK HAD not been the home of choice for the Shcharansky family; nor did it win their hearts.

When Leonid was ready for higher education, his parents sent him to Moscow, where he studied engineering. Anatoly followed in 1966. Soon afterward, when Boris and Ida were ready to retire, they packed up, bade good-bye to the provincial city where they had lived for two decades, and moved within range of Moscow. They found a small one-bedroom apartment in the township of Istra, about sixty miles from the capital, where they hoped their sons would graduate from the university, get jobs, marry, and settle down.

Anatoly entered the Faculty of General and Applied Physics at the Moscow Institute of Physics and Technology, the Soviet M.I.T., which limited the number of Jewish students to a handful—by the mid-1970s, Jews were excluded altogether. Here, in the capital's Dolgoprudny district, the choice young scientific minds of the Soviet Union were cloistered and pampered. Poets who had not won official Soviet approval were brought to the institute to read their works, in an attempt by the authorities to deflect the students' curiosity from "underground" literature, known as *samizdat*.

Into the highly controlled school environment the administrators even brought approved young women for the amuse-
ment of the male scholars and to save them the time-
consuming necessity of conventional dating.

Anatoly took a standard schedule of courses and did
not engage in any kind of classified work. As a student, he
was noted for his thoroughness, independence of thought,
and consistency in both his views and his behavior. After six
years, he earned his diploma in computer programming, de-
signing computer chess games and endgame systems that had
nothing whatsoever to do with national security.

Even as he pursued his studies, Anatoly was becoming
increasingly conscious of his Jewish heritage. The late sixties
saw the peak of the inordinately high representation of Jews
throughout the scientific and technological professions, in
which there was less ideological pressure than in the arts
and humanities. Many activists and leaders of the Jewish
movement emerged from these ranks.

In Moscow, Anatoly came into contact for the first time
with people who wanted to go to Israel, such as a young
music student named Luba Yershkovich, whom he had
known in school in Donetsk. Luba and her father eventually
succeeded in emigrating to Israel, and she was a definite influence on Anatoly. But what galvanized his thinking, and
that of thousands of other young Soviet Jews, was a crucial
event in Jewish history—the 1967 Six-day War in the Middle East.

There had been a liberalization of certain aspects of Soviet society after Stalin's death, although some Soviet-Jewish intellectuals believed this was an illusion. But although
Nikita Khrushchev released hundreds of thousands of prisoners, including tens of thousands of Jews, he launched a

campaign in the early 1960s against "economic crimes," with Zionists as the primary target. Over one hundred Jews were executed between 1961 and 1964, and since then anti-Semitism had blossomed, fueled by the Soviets' pro-Arab policy in the Middle East and the enduring perception of Jewish otherness. The killings of the Jewish "industrial spies" set off a wave of protests in the West, which led to the founding of the American Jewish Conference on Soviet Jewry (later called the National Conference on Soviet Jewry) and the Student Struggle for Soviet Jewry.

The vituperative Soviet media campaign against Israel climaxed at the outbreak of the Six-day War, with Moscow claiming gleefully that the Israeli "aggressors" were about to be swept into the sea. The Soviet campaign, and the reality of the Israeli victory, had a catalyzing effect on Soviet Jews, even the most assimilated like the Shcharansky family. It was both an earthquake and an illumination, which led to expanded Jewish consciousness and a growing awareness of national identity, especially among the generation that came of age in the sixties. As one Soviet-Jewish activist put it, "The Six-day War transformed Soviet Jewry into one large outsider group." Their lives were not free, but their thoughts were—something had happened, deep inside.

Although the Jewish emigration movement, led by assimilated young Jews who had undergone a process of inner liberation, had a certain revolutionary quality, it was in no way directed against the Soviet system. "We were not trying to undermine the existing order," wrote Edward Pshonik, a Kharkov refusenik. "We had our own goals—to continue on the historic path together with our own people. To do this, we had to leave the country which blocked this path."

The first official meeting of Jewish activists from around

the country was held in Moscow in August 1969, to discuss expansion of activities in various spheres. They planned the establishment of Hebrew-language schools in private apartments and an increase in underground publishing. A newspaper, *Iton* (Hebrew for newspaper), would be published in Riga and would represent the whole movement, comprised of highly diverse groups of Jews wishing to go to Israel. But one iron rule was established: there would be no formal organization, for that would only invite a KGB crackdown. "Each one of us decided his personal fate," wrote one of the older leaders, Vitaly Svechinsky. "And for us justice consisted of our needing to be in Israel, sharing the fate of our nation." Shcharansky heard about the meeting from fellow students, and though not yet committed, was becoming increasingly aware of the Zionist message.

In November 1969 in Israel, Golda Meir read the dramatic plea of eighteen Jewish families from Soviet Georgia, protesting against the Soviet denial of their right to emigrate to their historic homeland. In response, the Soviets launched a campaign to prove that Russian Jews were completely integrated into Soviet society and that they identified with neither Judaism nor Israel. Paradoxically, this campaign created a backlash among Soviet Jews, converting many more to Zionism.

In the summer of 1971, while Anatoly was in his fifth year of study, he told his parents that he had just met a remarkable man, a refusenik named Vladimir Slepak. Slepak, a big, bearded scientist twenty-one years older than Shcharansky, was also the son of a journalist, a devout Communist who worked for Tass. Slepak's apartment on Gorky Street in central Moscow had become a center in the

Jewish renewal movement, and Anatoly was drawn to the activists who met there. He and Slepak became close friends.

Shcharansky, like many other Soviet citizens, listened intently to the Voice of America and the BBC—during those periods when the broadcasts were not jammed—for news of what was happening in the world. The Voice of Israel was also received intermittently in the Soviet Union, and these broadcasts helped fire the Zionist resolve of many Jews. Anatoly found it grating to live in a society where one constantly had to think about what one said and to whom one said it. He told a story about it: A young man walked down a Moscow street humming abrasively. A bystander came up and asked him, "What are you doing?"

"I'm jamming my inner Voice of America," he replied.

By the time Anatoly graduated from university in the summer of 1972, the new wave of the Soviet Jewish emigration movement was three years old. Zionist ideology had already changed his life, and the twenty-four-year-old mathematician was preparing to devote more of himself to the movement's activities. It was a matter of no longer living a lie, no longer being a cog in the totalitarian system. The Jewish renaissance, as well as the emerging dissident movements—religious, national, cultural, reformist—meant standing up, speaking out, and identifying oneself. For most of those who did it, these became the most ennobling moments of their lives.

Anatoly had come to believe in the absolute necessity of repatriation of Soviet Jews to their ancestral homeland. He had chosen to live as a Jew, which meant that there was no place for him but Israel. Jews in safe places, in Western countries, could not really understand what it meant to be a Zionist, he felt, because they were not deprived of their culture, religion, and language.

After completing his studies, Anatoly started working as a computer programmer at the Oil and Gas Research Institute in Moscow. The facility was not involved in secret work and was classified as an open institution.

He began to study Hebrew with the help of self-taught tutors. He read in *Pravda* that every Soviet citizen had the right to learn or teach any language. Hebrew was the single, glaring exception. It was dangerous to distribute books or other media on subjects of Jewish knowledge. But books such as *Exodus, The Source,* and *Last of the Just* appeared in *samizdat,* typed in five to ten copies, then recopied and handed from person to person. While there were basic texts readily available in even the most obscure languages of the USSR, such as Chukchi and Avarian, Hebrew works— whether prayer books, novels, or dictionaries—were not permitted. Shcharansky, like others who were emerging into Jewish activism, began to view the repression of the Jewish national and religious heritage as a deliberate attempt to eradicate a large segment of the world's Jewish population. He saw it as more than just a "Jewish problem." The right to preserve one's national or ethnic language and culture was a basic tenet of international law, which had repeatedly been ratified by the Soviet Union. It was necessary to know that law, as well as to assert its validity by learning Hebrew. "We studied law because we did not want to break it," according to one of Shcharansky's friends. "But knowing the law afforded no protection. The Soviets used the legal system against innocent people. They broke their own laws when they persecuted us."

From his first contacts with the Jewish emigration

movement, Anatoly felt he had at last found an outlet for both his formidable energy and his intellect, and he took part in seminars as well as peaceful demonstrations to protest against the refusal of visas and the treatment of prisoners of conscience. Involvement in the movement was a realization of his own aspirations. The very decision to emigrate was in itself an act of liberation. His friend from the music academy, Luba Yershkovich, emigrated to Israel in 1972. A year later, Luba sent him the required *vyzov*, an affidavit inviting a relation or "fiancé" to join family abroad. In April 1973, Anatoly went to the government emigration office, OVIR, the Visas and Registration Department of the Interior Ministry, which was in close contact with the Defense Ministry and the KGB. He realized as he submitted his request to emigrate to Israel that the decision would radically change his life. That same month, Anatoly joined with other Jewish scientists in a seminar held in the apartment of Professor Alexander Lerner, an eminent member of the Soviet Academy of Sciences until 1971, when he was thrown out after applying to emigrate to Israel. Lerner, in his sixties, immediately felt a kinship with the young mathematician and introduced him to people at the core of the movement.

Anatoly's employers at the Institute for Oil and Gas were growing increasingly unhappy with the young graduate's open identification with the Jewish movement. Although he performed well, his mind was clearly not on his work; and he had committed the unpardonable sin of applying for an emigration permit. Under normal circumstances, Anatoly would have been fired right then; but under the Soviet system, all university graduates were obliged to work at an appointed workplace for a statutory three years and ordinarily could not be dismissed during that period. The job, though unsatisfying and distracting from his real concerns, nevertheless provided him with some legal protection: many Jewish activists had been fired, and, unable to find jobs, they were thus liable to criminal charges of "parasitism."

In the summer of 1973, after hearing nothing from the OVIR office, Anatoly obtained an interview with Lieutenant-Colonel Andrei Verein, the head of the Moscow bureau. Verein assured the young man that the visa application was in order and undoubtedly would be accepted; but months passed without any action.

Anatoly did not believe in keeping a low profile in order to improve his chances for obtaining an exit visa. On the contrary—the more activity, the better, he thought. His activities soon began to draw the attention of the KGB. His aging parents continued to live in Istra, where everyone knew everyone else's business. Boris had suffered three heart attacks in recent years, and Anatoly was concerned that KGB men might interrogate or otherwise harass his father. So, though he continued to visit his parents in the country town, he maintained a distance between them and his political activities and friends. Dina Beilina, a Jewish activist who worked closely with him in Moscow for four years, visited the Shcharanskys' home in Istra only once in the period before Anatoly became a prominent figure in the movement.

Beilina found them a very warm and devoted family. There were a lot of books, pictures on the walls, flowers, and good cooking in the kitchen. The atmosphere in the home was not particularly Jewish, but not pro-Soviet either. Boris no longer had hopes that perhaps the Soviet regime might become more liberal.

But Anatoly could not seal them off hermetically from

his other life. When Soviet citizens of any age apply to emigrate, the State requires the consent of their parents. Anatoly had to ask for his parents' signature.

Boris and Ida knew that if Anatoly left Russia, they might never see him again. Leonid, married, with one child, was in Moscow and not yet prepared to emigrate, but this could not compensate for the loss of their second son. Although they had suffered from anti-Semitism, they themselves were not prepared to follow Anatoly's lead. But they respected his decision and gave their consent, painfully but without hesitation.

IN THE TWO years before the 1967 Six-day War, the Soviets allowed a small number of Jews, about 4,500, to emigrate to Israel. This was the beginning of a turning point in emigration policy. After Khrushchev's leadership ended in 1964, there was a three-year transitional period of collective administration, with Leonid Brezhnev at the head of the troika. He eased the emigration restrictions on the Jews as a gesture to placate world opinion and to create a climate of détente with the United States. Prime Minister Alexei Kosygin formally declared in Paris in December 1966 that Jews could apply to go to Israel to be reunited with families, and this had already been put into practice. "The door is open," he said. The change in policy gave great hope to Soviet Jewry, and large numbers appeared in OVIR emigration offices bearing newspapers with Kosygin's statement. In the next few years, from among the hundred-odd nationalities in the USSR, large numbers of Jews, forty thousand Volga Germans, and a few thousand Armenians were allowed out, mainly on the basis of reunification of families. Wartime refugees from Spain and Poland were allowed to leave in the framework of repatriation agreements. The Soviets were not entirely at peace with this policy—there was concern that concessions to Jewish emigration might open a Pandora's box, that any significant loosening of the reins on human rights could threaten the very structure of the totalitarian state.

In the wake of the 1967 war and the Soviet break in relations with Israel, no exit visas were issued to Jews until September 1968, when five were granted. In early 1969, the Kremlin renewed exploratory probes to promote détente with the United States. Soviet envoys in the United States conferred with representatives of the American Jewish community to enlist Jewish support for the détente effort. When some four hundred Soviet Jews received emigration visas in the ensuing months, many Jews who had feared to apply for exit permits submitted their applications. From September 1968 to early 1970, about 34,000 Soviet Jews began the emigration process, and some 3,500 were allowed out during that period.

As small groups of Soviet Jews arrived in Israel, an increasing amount of programming about the movement was beamed to Jews in the USSR over Israel Radio's Russian-language service. Anatoly, while still at the university, had listened hungrily for information about the country he dreamed of making his home. The radio provided more than just a news service: it told prospective emigrants how to go about applying for exit permits; and it also gave the names of activists in the major cities who would provide moral support and practical assistance in overcoming the labyrinthine bureaucratic hurdles on the way to emigration.

The instructions hanging on the wall of every OVIR office listed the many documents that had to be submitted by an applicant. Besides the parental agreement and the invitation from family abroad, there was a catch-22 proviso requiring character references from house committees and the director of the office or plant where the applicant worked. Since most institute directors felt personally compromised when one of their workers wished to leave, they often refused to provide the documents stating that they were aware an employee had applied to emigrate. On many occasions the directors took the opportunity to denounce the potential emigrant before his colleagues, although this wasn't the case with Shcharansky. (In 1976, the controversial requirement was replaced by an "Information Sheet"—which had precisely the same effect—to be signed by the employer.) Among the required documents were certificates of birth, marriage, divorce, death of relatives, diplomas, a certificate from local authorities, a declaration of the emigrant's wish to leave, and a biography.

The Soviets turned the emigration tap on and off in accordance with foreign policy objectives. In mid-1970, for reasons that remain unclear, the tap was almost completely closed off. In Moscow, the Soviet authorities staged a press conference of Jewish Communist stalwarts who condemned alleged Israeli aggression and the "reactionary" Soviet Jews who had applied to emigrate to the Zionist entity. In this atmosphere, a number of applicants, some of whom had received repeated refusals, grew desperate and planned to seize a small, twelve-passenger airplane and fly it to Sweden and freedom. The KGB, aware of the plan, arrested all those involved and used the opportunity to crack down on activists in Leningrad, Riga, Kishinev, and Vilna. It was another turning point in the history of the exodus movement. Eleven of the conspirators, nine of them Jews, were put on trial in

Leningrad on December 15, 1970. One of the ringleaders was Edward Kuznetsov, an intellectual who had spent seven years in prison for dissident activities. Kuznetsov's father was Jewish and his mother Russian, but he had chosen to be a Jew in an act of defiance against the Soviet system. He told the court: "All I wanted was to live in Israel." Several days later, the severe sentences were announced, including the death penalty for Kuznetsov and Mark Dymshits, a pilot who first conceived the plan and who was to have flown the plane to the West. Kuznetsov's wife, Sylva Zalmanson, was sentenced to ten years. In the first Leningrad trial and the ensuing series of trials in Leningrad and Riga, harsh terms were also meted out to Yosef Mendelevich and Hillel Butman, whose paths were to cross Anatoly Shcharansky's years later in prison. The defendants paid a very high price, but they opened the door for many thousands of Jews.

The first trial, and the harsh sentences, produced an outcry in the West and provoked vigorous protests in the United States, Israel, Britain, France, Italy, and many other countries—including the Soviet Union itself. One of a group of protestors who gathered outside the Supreme Court in Moscow was Elena Bonner, Kuznetsov's relative. A fellow demonstrator whom she met—her future husband—was the eminent Russian physicist Andrei Sakharov, who had recently been among the founders of the Soviet Committee on Human Rights. Sakharov's committee tried to get the USSR to uphold its recognition of the 1948 Universal Declaration of Human Rights and appealed against "the unlawful refusal" to allow Jews to emigrate.

In reaction to the worldwide outcry, which even included protest actions by French and Italian Communists, the Soviets reduced the death penalties to long prison terms.

Instead of dampening the movement, the trials had the opposite effect, sparking an ongoing international movement on behalf of Soviet Jewry and emboldening Soviet Jewish activists. The exodus movement took on a buoyant, rebellious character. In February 1971, a major conference of Jewish leaders from Israel and around the world was held in Brussels. Participants called upon the Soviets to issue exit visas to the growing number of refuseniks and new applicants. The conference evoked a wide public response, and the Kremlin, on the eve of the twenty-fourth Communist Party Congress, which met in March, again eased emigration curbs. The Soviets also hoped to curb growing criticism from the European Communist parties, to promote renewal of arms control talks with the United States, and to promote trade links with the West. In the nine-month period following the congress, over fourteen thousand emigration permits were granted to Soviet Jews, almost all of whom came to Israel. This relatively liberal policy continued, with fluctuations, until the end of the decade.

A large number of those who received exit permits in the early seventies were from communities on the fringes of Soviet Jewry—such as the religious Jews of Georgia (who claim descent from one of the Ten Lost Tribes of Israel); the Asiatic Mountain Jews, who speak a Turkish-related language; and the Jews of Bukhara and Uzbek, who speak a Persian dialect. Many Ashkenazi Jews from Moscow, Leningrad, the Ukraine, and the Baltic states were being turned down.

The Soviets deeply resented the actions of bright young people like Shcharansky who, after years of free higher education, turned their backs on the system that had trained them and sought to abandon the motherland. As the exodus movement grew, public opinion began once again to label Soviet Jewry collectively as "traitors."

There is a certain community of interest between Zionism and anti-Semitism. In prewar Poland, Zionists worked with a government that wanted its Jews to leave for Palestine or anywhere else. Although the Jewish renaissance in the USSR was confined to a relatively small number of Soviet Jews, it affected the entire community. In fact, it was becoming increasingly apparent that an inexorable historical process was at work, which would not end until most of the Jews had left Russia. It wasn't just an ethnic or religious identification that was affecting people like Anatoly Shcharansky. They had a specifically Jewish national goal—the achievement of dignity and a normal existence in a homeland that had been restored to the Jewish people after two thousand years in exile.

The Jews were outsiders both before and after the exodus movement began. Soviet Jews could not serve as ambassadors, Jewish writers were not published, Jewish scientists were barred from attending both foreign and local conferences, and Jews were eliminated from leading positions in the military and excluded from universities. Institute directors became even more reluctant to hire those who were liable to bring discredit upon them when they applied to go to Israel. Newspapers portrayed Jews as hooligans, slanderers, cosmopolitans, parasites, and potential traitors. An officially sanctioned anti-Semitic campaign intensified with the publication of such books as *The Black Web of Zionism*, *Their True Face*, and *Against Zionism and Israeli Aggression*. The latter work, by Soviet writer Dmitri Zhukov, promoted the notion that the Talmud taught Jews to hate gentiles, "to fool them in every way, and, when opportunity arose, to destroy them."

IN THE CLIMATE of Soviet anti-Semitism, most Jews had found it expedient to assimilate. Neither Nataliya Steiglits nor Anatoly Shcharansky had ever celebrated Passover until they did so together, in the Moscow apartment of a refusenik friend in April 1974.

The women covered the table with a gleaming white tablecloth and set out the traditional platters of bitter herbs, which symbolized the bitterness of slavery in Egypt; the matzoth, unleavened bread to recall the haste in which they fled; and the shank bone, representing the Paschal thanksgiving sacrifice to the Lord for passing over the houses of the children of Israel when he smote the Egyptians.

The men donned skullcaps and read in halting Hebrew from the Haggadah, the story of the Exodus. "In every generation, it is the duty of each individual to regard himself as though he himself had gone forth out of Egypt." And this commandment was richly fulfilled that night, for to all the Jews present the story of the Exodus embodied their experience and their hopes.

Nataliya (she took the Hebrew name Avital three months later, upon her arrival in Israel) was by this time fully committed, both to Anatoly and to the Jewish movement. His request for an exit visa had finally been refused the previous November—a month after their meeting on Arkhipova Street and six months after he had applied—on the spurious ground of "access to classified materials." He had not kept a low profile during the six months of waiting but had joined activists like Mark Nashpitz and Yosef Beilin, who felt that it was necessary to stage public demonstrations in order to pressure the authorities to grant more exit permits.

Nataliya's brother was gone—shortly after his release from jail, he had received an exit visa and left for Israel. Anatoly was now her protector and her guide, as well as her lover. They had lived together in a series of rooms and tiny apartments, moving six times in as many months. At one point, they shared an apartment with five families, each of whom had one room. Anatoly brought Avital to Istra to meet his parents. Painfully introverted, she could hardly speak in their presence. Boris Shcharansky exclaimed, "How quiet your voice is—I can't hear it!"

Because she was new to the movement and presumably unknown to the ubiquitous KGB men, Nataliya in her first demonstration had been given the task of gaining entry to a meeting of the Communist Party Central Committee to deliver a letter asking that Soviet Jews be allowed to emigrate.

As she got off the subway at a station near the presidium building, she saw a man staring at her and muttering into the lapel of his coat. Another man said, "Yes, it's her," and the KGB agents instructed two policemen to seize her. They led her to a waiting bus, where she found many of her new friends.

They were driven to one of the detoxification lockups where Moscow's numerous alcoholics were taken to be dried out. Inside, the men and women were separated. After a few hours in the "tank," they were summoned one at a time to be interrogated. It was Nataliya's first such experience, and she didn't want to do anything wrong. Afraid to say too much, she decided to say nothing; she even refused to give her name, but demanded the names of her interrogators. This angered her captors, who sent her back to the tank.

Hours after everyone else had been allowed to leave, a guard threatened that if she didn't divulge her name she would be taken to prison. Terrified, she told them who she was. The interrogator waved his hand and said, "Get out."

It was late at night, and Nataliya had no idea how to get home. She stood alone, trembling on an unfamiliar street. Suddenly, Anatoly emerged out of the darkness. "I've been waiting for you," he said in a comforting voice. "Tell me, what happened?" But she couldn't stop shaking. He took her home and took care of her.

Nataliya delayed submitting a formal application to emigrate, for fear it would be granted. How could she leave Tolya? They had known each other for only a few months, but already it was inconceivable that they should ever part. Nataliya spent whole days sitting on a bench outside the institute where Anatoly worked, in the hope that he would be able to snatch a few moments to spend with her. At night, when he came home from work, they clung to each other as if they'd been apart for weeks or months.

Something in Nataliya—perhaps it was her shyness, or her doelike eyes, or her soft voice—brought out the protective instincts in men. Anatoly could not bear to see Nataliya at risk. They were together at a demonstration on May 15, 1974 in front of the Lebanese Embassy, protesting against Lebanese collusion in the PLO terrorist attack that killed twenty-three Israeli schoolchildren in the border town of Ma'alot. After her second demonstration and brief detention, he urged her not to attend any more protests. He also told her to apply to emigrate. Nataliya agreed.

In hopes of increasing Anatoly's chances of getting out if her application were approved, the lovers sought to register as a married couple with the civil authorities. Permission was denied, apparently because of Anatoly's status as a refusenik. When the couple demanded an explanation, the officials at the bureau of registration mockingly replied, "The age difference is too great." Anatoly, age twenty-six, was three years older than Nataliya.

Although the state did not recognize religious weddings, the couple explored the possibility of marrying in the Great Synagogue—the only other synagogue available to Moscow's quarter of a million Jews was a small one located in a remote part of the capital. Frightened synagogue officials told them that a religious wedding could not be performed there until the civil authorities registered the couple. To do otherwise would be to put the synagogue and its officials in danger.

One day late in June 1974, Anatoly failed to return from work. The next day, Nataliya learned from other movement activists that several refuseniks had been picked up by the KGB. It appeared that the authorities had decided to clear Moscow of possible troublemakers on the eve of an official visit by President Richard Nixon.

Two days later, Nataliya was summoned to the emigration office and given a visa to Israel. It would expire in two weeks, instead of the usual four. "But I can't go now," said Nataliya. "My fiancé has been arrested, and I don't know where he is or when he's getting out."

She pleaded for an extension but was told that if she did not use the permit within fourteen days, she would never see another. Anatoly's mother, Ida, who had grown very fond of Nataliya, urged her to make use of the visa while she could.

But Nataliya was determined to leave for Israel as Anatoly's wife. President Nixon, finding respite from the pressures of Watergate in excursions into high policy, was due in Moscow on June 27 for a one-week summit with Chairman Brezhnev. That meant that the activists under preventive arrest should be freed by July 3 or 4. Nataliya's visa expired after July 5. She scheduled the wedding for July 4, hoping Anatoly would make it. Then she set about finding a rabbi who would marry them.

The religious establishment had turned them down, but Nataliya stubbornly kept going back to the synagogue to seek help among the elders of the congregation. She spoke to a sympathetic man who told her to return the following week. She went back and found the old man deep in prayer, rocking back and forth in a ritual still strange to her. When he had folded his prayer shawl and sat down with her, she poured out the whole story, this time mentioning Anatoly's refusenik status. The elder's eyes clouded over.

"I can't help you," he said sadly.

"All right," she said. "No is no." But she lingered by his side.

The man turned away and began speaking to another worshiper. Suddenly, he came back to Nataliya. "Maybe you have a picture of your fiancé?"

She pulled a snapshot out of her bag and handed it over. The old man's face lit up. "That's Tolya!" he exclaimed. "Why didn't you say so?" Anatoly had often come into the synagogue to engage the elders in conversation and pick up something about Jewish practices, but the worshipers knew only his nickname. "Tolya's a brilliant fellow," he said. "I'll do whatever I can to help you." As she departed, he added: "You're a lucky girl."

For the next two weeks she returned almost daily to Arkhipova Street to meet with the learned elder who had undertaken to become her first religious mentor. Nataliya still knew little about Judaism. She was unfamiliar with the Jewish wedding ceremony or the religious obligations of a Jewish wife. Moreover, she had no proof that she herself was Jewish and therefore entitled to be married in a religious ceremony. Her parents had successfully avoided any such testimony to their origins: her identity card listed her ethnic background as Russian, not Jewish. This designation could never be changed on the internal passport, which every Soviet citizen is required to carry from age sixteen. But it might have been possible for Nataliya to obtain official certification as a Jew on an ancillary document, by using her maternal grandmother as a witness. She chose instead to undergo what amounted to a conversion to Judaism through the intensive instructions she received from the old man.

At the same time, she began preparing for both the wedding and her solitary "honeymoon" in Israel, alternately sewing a wedding dress and packing. She was calm now, possessed of a strength she had never known. When a friend of Anatoly's asked indiscreetly how she could leave while his fate was still unknown, she said quietly, "It's all right. I know what I'm doing."

Anatoly's mother slept over on the night of July 3 and helped Nataliya clean the apartment and prepare food for the wedding. The synagogue elder stopped by with his wife and asked if there would be at least ten men at the ceremony the next day to form a minyan, a religious quorum. He had persuaded an elderly rabbi from Lithuania, retired and living now in Moscow, to perform the ceremony. The rabbi was informed that he would be marrying off a couple whom the civil authorities had refused to register. It was to be a marriage made outside of the Soviet heaven.

Nataliya woke early on the morning of the fourth. She had completed her wedding dress the night before and most of the packing for her journey. The synagogue elder brought the rabbi to check the premises and ensure that a wedding canopy had been prepared. Nataliya went out to phone the guests, to tell them that the ceremony would begin at four o'clock.

"Tolya's home?" friends asked.

"Not yet," replied Nataliya. "He will be."

At ten on the morning of his wedding day, Anatoly was sitting on his bunk, reading a book. A KGB guard threw open the door. "Go home," he barked.

Anatoly looked up indifferently. "I'm not finished with the book," he said, and went on reading. Two hours later, he sauntered out.

Nataliya was still at the post office telephoning guests when he arrived home, exhausted, hungry, and disheveled; but Ida was there. Anatoly looked around the room in amazement.

"Congratulations," said his mother. "You're getting married today and Nataliya is leaving tomorrow for Israel."

Mother and son were sitting close together in a corner of the room, talking quietly, when Nataliya came in. She rushed to Anatoly and he held her close. It was the happiest day of his life, and the saddest. Anatoly showered and shaved, and they hurried out to buy wedding rings.

At the appointed hour the guests started arriving. Many had been released from detention that morning and still had the faintly bewildered look of people who have emerged suddenly from darkness into light. Almost all the guests crowding into the apartment were from their new world of Jewish activists. One of those outside the movement circle was the synagogue elder, who arrived with the rabbi and hugged Anatoly warmly. The cheerful hubbub filling the apartment subsided briefly with the entry of a woman unknown to anyone except Nataliya, who embraced her. It was her mother—the former prosecuting attorney who had hoped to shield her daughter from precisely this kind of ambience. Confronted by the irreversible prospect of the wedding and her daughter's imminent departure, Mrs. Steiglits uncharacteristically allowed her maternal feelings to prevail over her political convictions. Nataliya's father, however, stayed away, pleading illness.

There were uninvited guests as well: KGB men in black Volgas surrounded the building all night.

The wedding canopy was raised and the couple stood beneath it, surrounded by their relatives and friends. The old rabbi intoned the traditional prayers. "If I forget thee, O Jerusalem, let my right hand lose its cunning." Anatoly lifted Nataliya's veil and held a cup of wine to her lips. Then he stamped on a small glass, and the room exploded into shouts of "Mazel tov!" Singing loudly in Hebrew, the guests circled round the couple in a wild hora. "Soon may there be heard," they sang, "in the cities of Judah, in the streets of Jerusalem, the voice of joy and gladness, the voice of the bridegroom and the voice of the bride."

After the singing ended, the synagogue elder spoke of the miracle of Jewish survival. Wonders can happen, he said, if people believe. It was a message of solace to the newlyweds, who were cutting their separate rafts loose into the current. They all prayed fervently that it would carry the two of them speedily to the same shore.

Before dawn, the couple left for the airport, accompanied by members of the wedding party. Anatoly and Nataliya clung to each other, whispering promises. They embraced one last time; then Nataliya, alone, crossed into the departure area. She stopped and looked back. Anatoly was standing pensively, the joy gone out of his face. He looked up, caught her eye, and smiled.

"See you soon in Jerusalem," he said.

2

The Spokesman

*F*rom the moment that Anatoly Shcharansky emerged as a potential leader of the movement in 1974, he was, like many other activists, under constant KGB surveillance: At first he tried to elude the inevitable. On one occasion, he tried changing subway trains in order to dodge two agents. The KGB men stopped him and said that if he tried again, they would throw him under the train.

Later he frequently joked about wagging the tail behind him. The activists grew as accustomed to the presence of the KGB men as the rhino to the egret. Anatoly once wrote to a friend in Israel that his KGB tails were "menacing fellows" who one day threatened to "do me in" and the next day, as he groped for change to make a phone call, gave him a handful of two-kopeck pieces. Another time, Anatoly saw one of his KGB tails slumped over drunk in a parked car. He called KGB headquarters to report the man. But sometimes, even Anatoly couldn't make it funny. He wrote Avital in late December 1974, "Natulya, my beloved: I'm writing you from the telegraph office. Two curious characters are circling around me like sharks before an attack. And although I am not deprived of their company for a minute, I am alone as never before. I haven't received anything from you; I am gradually losing not only the details, but the whole picture of your life. This is terrible and sad."

It was necessary to assume, and was true in many cases,

that the KGB engaged in electronic surveillance of activists' homes. Dina and Yosef Beilin lived together for six years without ever allowing themselves the luxury of quarreling, because, they felt, such quarrels would provide the KGB with possible psychological weapons that could be used against them.

Following Avital's departure in July 1974, Anatoly had let go their little room and taken up a gypsy existence, frequently staying with friends in the movement. For a year, he lived with Alexander Lunts, a noted scientist whom Tolya met in 1972; then with Arkady Poliachuk. He had few possessions and a spartan wardrobe. When Dina first met him in 1973, he was wearing an old, torn coat, the same one he was wearing four years later when he was taken away by the KGB. He never bought anything for himself, no clothes, nothing. Sometimes, foreign tourists would bring him gifts from Avital in Israel, including a very good pair of shoes that lasted him till he went to prison. But he did accumulate Jewish books and other literature, which was running a risk.

Lev Ulanovsky, who graduated one year after Anatoly from the Moscow Institute of Physics and Technology with a masters degree in physics, had been told to consult Shcharansky before making his own formal application to emigrate. Ulanovsky asked Anatoly if he thought his application would be turned down because he was a product of the Soviet Union's most prestigious science academy. Anatoly told him that half of the eight alumni who applied had received exit visas. Ulanovsky admired Shcharansky for not hesitating to take part in demonstrations immediately after he himself had applied to emigrate, despite the effect this might have on his chances. This was a show of bravery and selflessness that profoundly influenced the serious young scientist, who decided to go ahead and apply.

Late one afternoon, Ulanovsky received a phone call from Anatoly, who asked, in unusually agitated tones, if he might come over. "Come at once," Ulanovsky told him. When he arrived, the two communicated on that fixture of every refusenik's apartment, the "magic slate" on which words could be written and immediately erased. The KGB was about to search the room he was staying in, Anatoly wrote, and the *samizdat* literature concealed there could form the basis of a criminal charge against him.

Anatoly carried a well-thumbed copy of the Criminal Code of the USSR in the inside pocket of his tattered coat. As a talisman it was remarkably ineffective: though the KGB made a pretense of going by the book, their actions often seemed dictated by whim. Technically, the KGB could not search the room without serving a warrant, he explained to Ulanovsky, and they had to serve the warrant while he was actually in the room. Serving it in the street would enable them to search only the residence where he was officially registered, his parents' home in Istra. Therefore, he could not return to the room until the illicit material had been removed. Of course Anatoly realized that the KGB on that particular day might not be playing the game according to the rules, so all of this might be a futile exercise.

Ulanovsky immediately agreed that Anatoly should sleep over at his apartment that night, and on the following morning he would go to the room and clear out the material. The next day, Ulanovsky gathered together all the "incriminating material" in Shcharansky's room, put it into two plain bags, and left quickly. Although he did not turn around, he knew he was being followed. He ducked into the subway station, still not looking around but sensing the danger closing in on him.

A train thundered into the station, traveling in the direction he was headed. Ulanovsky boarded the train, staying close to the door that would automatically slide shut as the train was about to pull out. It was an old trick, and he was sure the KGB men would be alert to it, but it was his only chance. The conductor announced the train's imminent departure; the doors hissed as they began to close. At the last possible moment, Ulanovsky inserted his foot, squeezed open the doors and slipped out onto the platform. By the time he looked back, the train was pulling away. A quick look along the length of the waiting platform showed that only one of his KGB tails had been quick enough to follow him. The rest were traveling on.

Ulanovsky was still not safe, but he had improved his odds. He knew that ordinarily a single KGB agent would not make an arrest. He also knew that the agent's walkie-talkie would not work deep underground. Until they emerged into the light of day, his tail would be unable to summon assistance. Ulanovsky waited for a train going in a different direction. The KGB man was literally breathing down his neck: there was no chance of pulling off the same trick twice.

Ulanovsky headed for Dina Beilina's apartment, which was close to a subway station. He knew many people would be gathered there for a scheduled meeting. The proximity of her flat to the station would increase his chances of reaching it before the KGB agent could summon reinforcements; the large crowd would provide him with an opportunity to dispose of the illegal literature.

When the train came to a halt, Ulanovsky dashed out

and did not stop running until he had reached the Beilins' apartment. Among the Jews gathered there were Ida Nudel, Vladimir Slepak, and Anatoly himself, who grinned broadly at his friend. When the refuseniks peered out at the court-yard entrance to the apartment house, they saw, not the cus-tomary handful of KGB agents, but a veritable army of secret-service men swarming out of a fleet of black Volgas.

The forbidden literature was hastily dispersed among the activists. They left the apartment together, each carrying a big bag—Shcharansky's and Ulanovsky's bags contained no incriminating matter. They scattered in different direc-tions; and the KGB men, not knowing whom to stop, did nothing. For the next week, the brigade of KGB men plugged the entrance to Dina's apartment building, but they were locking the proverbial empty stable. Anatoly's *samizdat* ma-terial was never discovered.

Even though the activists suffered constant surveillance and KGB harassment, they stayed on the offensive in exert-ing their rights. In October 1974, Dr. Lunts headed a group of refuseniks who traveled alone or in pairs to various cities to canvass Jewish opinion on the Jackson Amendment and to report on local problems regarding emigration. Shchar-ansky and nineteen-year-old Anatoly Malkin went to Riga and Minsk. The Jews of Minsk, Anatoly found, were fright-ened and living in isolation in a highly anti-Semitic environ-ment. "The worst thing is that the KGB is making people sign pledges that they will have no contact with foreigners and will not try to go abroad," he reported. "Even the women who sell brassieres in the state department store have been made to sign. I cannot imagine what kind of state secrets they are supposed to possess."

MANY OF THE REFUSENIKS continued to say, "Come what may, I will chance it." What sometimes came was prison, or Siberia. Mark Nashpitz, a dentist who was the same age as Anatoly, had been among a group of young refuseniks who wrote to President Nixon in 1972 asking him to help them obtain the right to emigrate. His efforts resulted in imprisonment for four months. When he got out, he met Anatoly at the Moscow OVIR office, and the two became close friends. They were part of a group of militant young activists who believed in constant activity: letters, petitions, demonstrations. Over a period of two years, they were often arrested together, serving ten or fifteen days in jail each time.

On one occasion, a group including Nashpitz and Anatoly went to KGB headquarters on Gorky Street to demand a written explanation of why they were refused the right to emigrate. A KGB official told them to return in two weeks for an answer. On their return, they were met by a KGB general, who explained that they were being denied permission for their own good: life in Israel was very bad, he said. Then, speaking more candidly, the general told them that under the Soviet constitution, all nationalities were equal. If people abroad—Communist parties and trade unions—saw that one nationality, the Jews, wanted to leave the USSR, it would set a dangerous precedent.

The group refused to leave the building until they got an explanation in writing. If they didn't leave, the general replied, they would go to prison. They stayed on. Fifteen minutes later, soldiers burst into the room and took them away to the tank. No one was beaten on this occasion.

The activists halted demonstrations for a few months after this stint in jail because of increasing KGB pressure. Then Anatoly came to Nashpitz and said that it was time to resume the actions. The last demonstration Nashpitz took part in occurred on February 24, 1975. After notifying members of the foreign press to be in the vicinity of the Lenin Library, the largest in the Soviet Union, Shcharansky, Nashpitz, and five others approached the site separately. It was immediately apparent that they were expected—no surprise, in view of the KGB's listening devices in apartment walls, constant tails on key figures, and turncoats within the movement. Police were lined up in front of the building and Black Maria police vehicles waited to carry off detainees. Men with movie cameras stood in the back of a truck overlooking the scene.

At a signal, the group of Jews whipped out banners and placards from under their coats and held them aloft. "Visas, not Prisons" and "Freedom for the Prisoners of Zion" were the principal slogans. The foreign journalists barely had time to read them before police pounced on the demonstrators and hustled them away.

It was the first demonstration since the Soviet Union had renounced its trade agreement with Washington because of the U.S. linkage of trade credits to liberalization of Soviet emigration policies. The Soviets regarded the Stevenson Amendment to the Export-Import Bank Act of 1974, limiting credits to the USSR, as an even greater blow than the earlier Jackson-Vanik Amendment; on January 15, 1975 the Kremlin informed the United States that it would not put the 1972 U.S.–Soviet Trade Agreement into effect. At the last demonstration by Jewish activists, four months before, when Moscow was still weighing the proposed deal, police had let the three participants go free. This time, there was no reason for leniency. Four of the demonstrators, including Anatoly, were given fifteen days. One was allowed to go free. But the other two, Nashpitz and Boris Tsitly-onok, were tried together and given sentences that rocked the movement—five years exile in Siberia. The object was twofold: to intimidate other activists and to show scorn for the American Congress. The Soviets sharply cut Jewish emigration in reaction to the U.S. congressional moves: it fell from 33,500 in 1973 to 20,000 in 1974 to 13,000 in 1975.

Nashpitz, who resembled Anatoly in his cheerful disposition and his fearlessness, believed he knew why he had been targeted for special treatment. A month earlier, he had been visited at home by KGB agents. His application for an emigration visa had encountered difficulties, they told him regretfully. However, if he agreed to cooperate, they would use their influence to help him. "Cooperate how?" Nashpitz asked. They spelled out their need for an informant within the Jewish activist movement. Nashpitz promised he would think about it and let them know.

He had secretly taped the conversation, and told his friends about it. They warned him for his own sake not to publicize it. Nashpitz gave it some thought; then he telephoned foreign correspondents, invited them to his home, and played the tape. The KGB had bugged his apartment, and it seemed only fair to bug the buggers. He knew there would be heavy retribution, but decided to act rather than risk being suspected by his friends of collaborating with the KGB. The demonstration at the Lenin Library gave the authorities the opportunity to act on their displeasure.

Mark Nashpitz's road to hell was cold and long. The prison train that took him into exile was not the Siberian Express—for two months it carried him eastward. He and nineteen other prisoners were locked into a compartment normally allotted to four paying passengers. There were long stopovers at various nodes of the Soviet reeducation system: Sverdlovsk Prison, Novosibirsk Prison, Irkutsk Prison, and other inns for the erring along the route to Siberia.

Nashpitz's journey ended at almost the other end of the Soviet Union in a tiny, two-street village appropriately named Tupik, literally "Dead End." The KGB escort turned him over to the local security chief of the desolate place. The exiled political prisoner from Moscow, in the long tradition of Siberian exiles, was absorbed into the village life as a quasi-prisoner. Tsitlyonok, he learned, had been sent to another region in the great white wasteland.

Nashpitz was assigned a room in a log house inhabited by a local family. Temperatures in winter fell to minus 50 degrees centigrade, but his wood-burning stove kept the room from being an icebox. There was a telephone in the room—even Siberian exile, as terrible as it was, was no longer what it used to be—and his spirits were buoyed by calls from his friends Tolya Shcharansky and Dina Beilina. The telephone was the only sign of normal life—otherwise, Tupik was a prison. Both Anatoly and Dina promised to visit him within a few months.

It was not an empty pledge. Anatoly had begun to travel frequently around the country, visiting prisoners and refuseniks, helping them write complaints to the authorities, carrying messages to relatives and friends. Nashpitz knew Tolya wasn't just being polite when he said he was determined to get to the other end of the continent, to "Dead End" as well. And Dina made the long journey twice.

ALTHOUGH THE JEWISH movement never had a formal structure, the activists nevertheless looked to people like Professor Alexander Lerner, a famed scientist and refusenik since

1971, for guidance and inspiration. The movement was roughly divided into four components: those involved in the public information campaign, a cultural and religious group, a Hebrew-teaching group, and the demonstrators. Many activists participated in several of the groups. By 1974 the Soviet-Jewish movement had split, in essence, into those who wished to live in Israel and those whose aim was settlement in America or other Western countries. The latter had little Jewish or Zionist identity—they just wanted to get out because of growing anti-Semitism, and the door had been opened for them by the Zionist activists. But the split was not yet obvious—people didn't say they were *not* going to Israel.

There was a de facto Soviet-Jewish leadership, including Lerner, Vitaly Rubin, Vladimir Slepak, Ida Nudel, Yosef Begun, Dina Beilina, Alexander Voronel, Alexander Lunts, Victor Brailovsky, Benjamin Fain, Ilya Essas, Mark Azbel, and others. In the spring of 1975 Anatoly Shcharansky's name was being considered by this informal leadership for a key position—the movement's spokesman.

The movement's first spokesman, Kiril Henkin, a former journalist, had received an exit visa, and was replaced in 1973 by Alex Goldfarb, a scientist fluent in English. Two years later, Goldfarb also received an emigration permit, and the search for a replacement began. The spokesman's role was critical. It required fluency in English and much more. The spokesman presented the case for Jewish emigration, detailing the plight of individuals and families who had lost their jobs, were intimidated, suddenly drafted into the army (and thus rendered ineligible to emigrate for at least fifteen years), or brought to trial on trumped-up charges. He had to hold daily meetings with visiting Western politicians, members of the foreign press corps in Moscow, and Jewish tourists who would transmit messages to activists in Israel, Europe, and the United States.

When Shcharansky was first proposed to succeed Goldfarb, Dina Beilina laughed at the idea. She regarded Anatoly, at twenty-seven, as too young; he was a relative lightweight unequal to the challenge. Beilina, an engineer born in 1939, played an important role in the movement: her job was to collect and compile information about refuseniks from all over the Soviet Union and to supply this information to the spokesman, their link to the West. The publicity he generated in the foreign media provided the sustenance for emigration lobbyists and activists abroad. Through their efforts, pressure would be brought to bear on legislators who, in turn, would negotiate with the Soviet authorities to ease curbs on emigration. An important example was the recently passed Jackson-Vanik Amendment to the Free Trade Act of 1974, tying U.S. trade benefits to the Soviet-Jewish emigration issue.

The spokesman had to lend weight to the cause and to keep the foreign correspondents interested, while working within the constraints of a minuscule budget. Beilina felt that while others should demonstrate, Anatoly was too valuable to the movement to be locked away for the customary fifteen days. He participated in demonstrations that lasted less than a minute before they were broken up by the KGB. By getting themselves arrested, demonstrators exposed themselves to the arbitrary will of the Soviet system, which could impose sentences ranging from a few days in jail to a few years of prison or internal exile. Even though the demonstrators, including her husband Yosef as well as Anatoly, were engaged in legal activities, she thought it too dangerous.

Anatoly also seemed to her too quiet, modest, and—at a height of five feet—too short for such a post. However, after participating in some meetings with Shcharansky and foreign visitors, she noticed that even among people twice his age, people with the most impressive credentials, he became the center of attention. He possessed extraordinary physical energy, courage, and charm; his intellectual ability was outstanding, his knowledge encyclopedic. Professor Lerner said of Tolya that the great difference in their ages seemed unimportant because he was amazingly mature and farsighted. Dina recognized that her first impression had been wrong. Tolya was special, "a very gifted man." They became close friends, as well as coworkers. From the moment he took on the spokesman's job, in April 1975, she felt he was irreplaceable.

Vitaly Rubin, a professor of Chinese literature, felt the same way. He first met Anatoly at the May 1974 demonstration in front of the Lebanese Embassy. Despite a twenty-five-year age difference, the two men became close friends. A year later, Tolya joined him as the Jewish representative on the Helsinki Watch Group.

Another refusenik who spoke glowingly of the young Shcharansky was Felix Kandel, a writer. They spent fifteen days together jailed in a barracks after one of the demonstrations, after which Kandel described Anatoly as "perfectly honest, sincere, truthful; a man who is noble; a man able to control his emotions and his actions; a man for whom the struggle is not an obsession or a desire but a reasonable, analyzed necessity; a man who is unselfish, who will never sacrifice his principles for the sake of any benefit." Tolya, moreover, was "gifted with the precise analytical intelligence of a chess player." He had no complexes about being "short and bald from his youth. . . . He managed to win the heart of a beauty, not without reason." Shcharansky's wit and charm won over even the common criminals and drunks in the detoxification tank. One, who worked in a fruit and vegetable store, afterward provided his friend Tolya with a great deal of fresh produce, which was duly distributed among the activists.

WHEN THE THREE YEARS of Anatoly's statutory employment at the Oil and Petroleum Institute ended early in 1975, the young mathematician immediately found himself unemployable. Without a regular job, he was liable to the charge of "parasitism." For Anatoly, though, earning enough money to live on was not difficult. In addition to his time-consuming activities on behalf of the movement, he was soon giving private English lessons to a clutch of pupils, including Professor Yuri Orlov, the Russian dissident leader who was to found the Helsinki Watch Group; and Lyudmilla Alekseeva, another dissident leader. He also tutored students, including Dina Beilina's daughter, in math and physics.

The Soviet authorities, however, refused to acknowledge that he was employed. The Istra township's Finance Department rejected without explanation his application to be registered as a private teacher. Refusenik scientist Yosef Begun, when he tried to register as a private Hebrew teacher, was also turned down and eventually arrested on parasitism charges and exiled to Siberia.

Anatoly's problem was solved when Professor Naum Meiman, a respected, elderly mathematician, persuaded the

Moscow labor bureau that he needed a secretary to assist him with his correspondence, and that the young mathematician was the most suitable candidate.

A delegation of U.S. senators, including Abraham Ribicoff, Gary Hart, Charles Percy, Peter Domenici, and Jacob Javits, arrived in Moscow at the end of June 1975 and held an open meeting with the leadership of the Jewish movement, including Lerner, Rubin, Slepak, Nudel, Azbel, Beilina, and Lunts. Anatoly, well known among the Jewish activists, though less known abroad, acted as translator. The refuseniks told the senators that the Jackson Amendment was effective and helpful but they were less enthusiastic about the Stevenson Amendment, which restricted trade credits with the Soviet Union, resulting in increased KGB harassment of Jews and a sharp cut in emigration permits. This open meeting in a Moscow hotel was presented as evidence of treason at Shcharansky's trial three years later.

A few days after this meeting, Anatoly had another encounter that was also to be used against him. On July 4, 1975, the first anniversary of his marriage to Avital, he attended a gathering at Vitaly Rubin's apartment, where he was introduced to Professor Richard Pipes of Harvard University, a well-known Soviet affairs expert. They talked for about thirty minutes in the presence of a man named Riabsky. Rubin suspected that Riabsky was only feigning interest in emigration and that he was, in fact, a KGB agent, but felt they had nothing to hide: the refuseniks were accustomed to agents or informers hanging around. Pipes told Anatoly that he was going to Israel from the Soviet Union, and offered to call Avital. The innocent conversation later came out in a totally unrecognizable, insidious form.

Anatoly's encounters with visitors from the West became almost a daily occurrence, and several of the people he met later worked assiduously for his freedom and reunification with Avital.

A wealthy New York businessman, Jerome Stern, and his wife Jane met Anatoly two days after Avital's departure for Israel: he acted as their interpreter in talks with various refuseniks. They attended a party celebrating the release that week of about thirty refuseniks, including Anatoly, who had been jailed for fifteen days. There were tearful embraces and people swapping jail stories, laughing, and singing Israeli songs.

The party was still going full swing at about 1:00 A.M. when an insistent knocking sounded on the door. "Police!" they shouted, "Let us in." The celebrants refused to open the door without first seeing a search warrant. Stern was getting more than a little worried by the time Anatoly picked up the phone and, aware that the KGB was listening in, called a *New York Times* correspondent. After explaining the situation, Tolya put Stern on the phone. Stern said he was an American citizen, and asked him to notify the U.S. Embassy if Stern didn't call back in the morning. The correspondent promised to do so. Within minutes, the police were gone. "You see, Jerry," Anatoly said, "it's just as I told you. If you Western Jews are strong, then we are strong. It was the telephone that saved us tonight."

After several days with Anatoly, Stern came away with the impression that beneath his warmth and sense of humor was an iron will. Anatoly knew exactly what he was getting himself into, but he was determined to continue to exert his rights. Stern noticed that Anatoly never appeared without a heavy briefcase; when he asked, the refusenik opened it for him. It contained a huge dictionary, a novel, a heavy sweater, and a toothbrush. "I never know when I'll be arrested again. I swore to myself that never again am I going to let them take me to jail without a sweater to keep warm, without something to read, and without a toothbrush."

Irene Manekofsky, head of the Washington Committee for Soviet Jewry, met Anatoly some six months later in December 1974. He spoke mostly about Avital, saying, "Can you imagine that such a tall, beautiful woman would marry somebody like me?" Manekofsky thought Shcharansky was "a little guy who was like a giant."

IN THE SUMMER OF 1975, thirty-five nations, including the Soviet Union, the Eastern European countries, and the United States, signed the Helsinki accords, a document defining human rights, which both East and West solemnly agreed to uphold. The Conference on Security and Cooperation in Europe, which had begun three years earlier, concluded on August 1, 1975 with President Gerald Ford, Soviet leader Leonid Brezhnev, and British Prime Minister Harold Wilson in attendance. The Soviet aim was to gain recognition of the frontiers of 1945, which meant approval of its annexation of the Baltic countries and parts of Poland. The West sought to establish respect for fundamental freedoms, including freedom of religion and the right to emigrate. The participating countries undertook to contribute to the solution of humanitarian problems pertaining to human rights and national minority rights.

The signing of the final act was a fateful moment, which infused both the Soviet-Jewish and human rights movements with hope. Anatoly wrote to Avital that the international agreement "speaks exactly of us: of the reunification of families and of free emigration. Soon we will be together in Jerusalem." But it was soon evident that the Soviet leaders had no intention of adhering either to the letter or to the spirit of the agreement. The Soviet system is based on the premise that the interests of the state take priority over the rights of man, a principle in direct contrast to the spirit of Helsinki. Nevertheless, and even though the Helsinki accords do not have the status of an international treaty, the USSR incorporated the ten principles of the final act, including freedom of religion, into the Soviet Constitution itself.

In September 1975, after the Soviets ratified the accords, Professor Yuri Orlov, a leading Soviet academic concerned with human rights issues, decided that the time had come to act. At his initiative, the Helsinki Watch Group was formed to monitor Soviet violations of human rights. Andrei Sakharov, the nuclear scientist who later won the Nobel Peace Prize in 1976, was active in the group though not a member of the committee of eleven. His wife, Elena Bonner, was on the committee, as was longtime dissident intellectual Alexander Ginzburg, executor of the Solzhenitsyn Fund for Aid to Political Prisoners. Ginzburg, whose mother was Jewish, followed the Russian Orthodox faith. He took his mother's name as a gesture of defiance against Soviet anti-Semitism.

Anatoly Shcharansky had close ties to important non-Jewish dissident leaders. He was Orlov's English teacher and had also tutored Lyudmilla Alexseeva, the Watch Group's secretary; he had served on occasion as Sakharov's official translator. Now he and Vitaly Rubin were personally invited to join the committee as representatives of the Jewish emigration movement.

The roots of the Soviet dissident movement grew out of the post-Stalin era, when hundreds of thousands of educated Russians were released from the prison camps and many began speaking out. The movement became public after the 1966 trial of two writers, Andrei Sinyavsky and Yuli Daniel, which radicalized many Soviet intellectuals and created a storm of protest in the West. In the late 1960s, Alexander Solzhenitsyn openly joined the critics of the Soviet system, adding a note of renewed Christian spirituality to the dissident movement. Some of the younger and middle-aged Jewish intellectuals, without Jewish education and heavily influenced by Russian culture, felt the Soviet Union was their home, and had closer ties to the liberal dissident movement than to the Jewish emigration movement. Other members of the Jewish intelligentsia joined the emigration movement in reaction to official anti-Semitism and the growing neo-Slavophile xenophobia of the masses.

The dissident leaders were as diverse a group as the Jewish activists, and relations among them were often quarrelsome. Some of the Jewish activists dismissed the Russian dissidents as Narodniki, a reference to the nineteenth-century idealists who had the delusion that they could turn Russian peasants into socialists. Some of the dissident intellectuals were condescending toward someone like Shcharansky, "who has never written a book." But once they came to know him, that condescension was replaced by admiration for his intellect and for his fearlessness.

Anatoly's immediate enthusiasm for working with the Helsinki group was not shared by some other members of the Jewish movement. The invitation evoked profound apprehension not only among refuseniks but also among Israeli officials in Jerusalem. It was one thing to demand the right to emigrate; quite another to criticize the Soviet system. If the goal was to get Jews out, why complicate matters? Sharp warnings cautioning against involvement in the dissident movement reached Anatoly from abroad. He dismissed them. The struggle of Jews was another side of the human rights coin, he argued, and thus it was logical for Jews to participate in such a movement. Anatoly was his own man, and he was also an intellectual. There was tremendous sympathy for the dissident movement among the intelligentsia, Jewish and non-Jewish.

The struggle of the Jewish emigration movement was the struggle for a basic right of personal liberty—the right to emigrate. "Everyone has the right to leave any country, including his own, and to return to his country," the Helsinki accord said. This principle was also enshrined in international law, including Article 13 of the Universal Declaration of Human Rights and a multitude of other international agreements: the European and American conventions on human rights, the Racial Discrimination Convention, and the Covenant on Civil Rights and Political Rights. Since Soviet law included emigration as a basic human right, the watch group was trying not to change the system but to persuade the Soviets to honor their own laws. The guarantee of freedom to emigrate was clearly violated in the case of the Jews. How could Anatoly remain aloof from the Helsinki Watch Group? Refusing to join was unthinkable. Furthermore, he felt certain that in order to widen and deepen the scope of the Jewish struggle, it was necessary to link up with the human rights movement. (Anatoly's involvement in the Helsinki group proved important when the Soviet judicial machinery geared up against him, a fact that strengthened the convictions of those who opposed any mixing of the movements.)

His contribution to the group consisted of providing

information about the plight of Jewish refuseniks, of families who had been separated and were seeking reunification, of Jewish activists whose telephones had been disconnected and whose mail had been tampered with or confiscated. Some of the documents and reports produced by the group consisted of human rights offenses against Jews. But the watch group also issued a slew of documents on Ukrainian refugees, Lithuanian Catholic clerics, the dispersal of the Meskhetian tribe, as well as the use of psychiatric hospitals to punish dissidents. Anatoly felt honored to work with people like Orlov, Ginzburg, and Sakharov. His life took on a new and consuming dimension. But there was no relaxation of his rigorous activities for Jewish emigration: he simply added to his already punishing workload.

Anatoly and his refusenik comrades believed that, just as the issue of human rights was a universal cause, so too the Soviet-Jewish movement was not just a Jewish concern. In a message to Western supporters, they wrote, "There is no doubt that the renaissance of the Jewish nation in the USSR and the mass movement to return to Israel is not only the business of the Jews, but also of all those who cherish personal freedom, freedom of consciousness and conviction, of all those for whom man is the supreme value and not just material used for a government's purposes."

One of the reports Anatoly himself drew up for the watch group in 1976 was on "Punitive Conscription of Young Jews in the Soviet Union." The composition, which showed a definite journalistic bent, detailed the case of his friend Anatoly Malkin to illustrate the threat to all male Jewish university students who, if they applied to emigrate, were subject to expulsion and immediate conscription into the army. Malkin had been thrown out of university at age nineteen for "behavior unworthy of a Soviet student" when he announced his desire to live in Israel. After receiving an Israeli passport, he refused induction, was arrested, and was sentenced to three years in a labor camp. Anatoly pointed out that using conscription as a form of repression for those applying to emigrate was a clear violation of the Helsinki accords.

It was not an easy point to explain. The Soviet authorities could claim that the draft was a national obligation, which potentially affected every Soviet citizen. A number of activists tried to explain it in writing but were unable to express the complicated factors involved. Then Anatoly applied himself to the task and came up with a text that clarified all the fine points. The article, signed by many activists, was immediately published in the American Jewish press and picked up by political and public figures. It helped shape public opinion as people in the West suddenly realized that one-fifth of Soviet Jewry, families with sons, brothers, or husbands eligible for the draft, would be prevented from applying to leave for fear that their sons would be drafted. They would not be allowed to apply to emigrate until fifteen years after completion of service.

Another Helsinki Watch Group report dealing with the refuseniks gave the Slepaks, Shcharansky himself, and seventy-five others as examples of divided families. Vladimir Slepak's wife Masha had been refused an exit visa since March 1971. She was not allowed to join her seventy-year-old mother or her sister in Israel. The report, issued in June 1976, noted that for years the authorities had exposed the whole family, including the children, "to many different kinds of repression, i.e., numerous arrests, dismissals from work, blackmail, disconnection of telephones, complete cessation of mail service." The report was sent to the Soviet authorities, who never responded. Most of the information in the report was compiled by Beilina and transmitted up until 1975 to the West by Alexander Lunts. After that, Beilina herself compiled and transmitted the data. Robert Toth of the *Los Angeles Times* used it as the basis for an article a year later.

Foreign correspondents were captivated by Anatoly's personality and his abilities as a spokesman. David Shipler of the *New York Times* thought Anatoly was scrupulous with his facts and adept at giving busy reporters hard news. He avoided boring sessions where often insignificant open letters were read in a monologue. And he was good company. "In a country of political dogmatists, even among the dissidents, he had a refreshing air of open-mindedness, a kind of apolitical good-heartedness, and a certain faith in the ability of rational thought to emerge as the ultimate victor."

During this period, Anatoly was constantly on the go, dashing around Moscow in taxis, going from one meeting to another. He tried to be everywhere at the same time. At one moment, he might be at the home of Professor Lerner meeting with a group of foreign visitors. At the same time, he was supposed to be at Slepak's home to help a group of Jews who had traveled to Moscow from a remote town to receive advice on emigration procedures, or briefing foreign correspondents on some new development. When the price of cab fares doubled in 1976, Anatoly was devastated by the news, since he spent most of his money on taxis. On one occasion, when Anatoly hailed a cab, two of his KGB tails got in with him, while two Volgas cruised behind. Although he failed to persuade the agents to get out, he did manage to get them to pay half the fare.

THE JEWISH activists who opposed the Helsinki Watch Group position of Rubin, Slepak, and Shcharansky said that they based their opposition on a presentiment of danger. The watch group was an organization, and since the first meeting of Jewish movement leaders in 1969, formal organization had been anathema. Vladimir Lazaris, a coeditor of the underground publication *Jews in the USSR* until he emigrated to Israel in 1977, felt that the Jews did not need the dissidents, but that the dissidents needed the Jewish movement in order to gain access to its facilities: phone access to the West, a regular flow of Western tourists, the network of refuseniks and their *samizdat* publications. He held that Jews who fought for human rights "long ago lost their Jewishness. Such russification becomes the lot of all the Jews who enter the ranks of the dissidents." Professor Yermiahu Branover, who emigrated to Israel in 1972, advised Soviet Jews to dissociate themselves completely from the democratic movement. He claimed that Anatoly's close ties with the dissidents were what caused the KGB to fabricate its case against him. Vitaly Rubin, who emigrated to Israel in 1976, countered that the human rights and Jewish movements were indivisible and that it would be suicide for the Jews to split away. That would "fulfill the dearest dreams of the KGB, which devotes an enormous amount of its efforts to destroying the relations between the various groups fighting against Soviet totalitarianism." He felt it would also lead to a morally indefensible situation for Soviet Jews. While the Jews appealed for the support of world public opinion, they would be showing indifference to the destiny of the other victims of the system.

In the view of some of the Jewish activists, the debate about Shcharansky's participation in the Helsinki group was not as heated and divisive as another issue that emerged in 1976. The refuseniks were split over whether the Jewish movement should continue placing so much emphasis on emigration at the expense of Jewish education for those who would remain in the Soviet Union. The assimilation rate among Soviet Jews appeared to be so great that some members of the movement felt that resources should be thrown into preserving and building Jewish knowledge.

Anatoly's friend Lev Ulanovsky had a foot in both worlds as a Hebrew teacher in the emigration movement. But he continued to advocate with passion the cause of emigration, agreeing with Tolya that it should have top priority. They could study Hebrew, or Judaism, at the same time—as Anatoly was doing, attending weekly Torah study sessions given by one of the movement's religious mentors, refusenik Vladimir Shakhnovsky.

Dina Beilina, among others, vehemently opposed the group that emphasized promoting Jewish education. She believed that Jews could not be Jews in the Soviet Union: the only answer was emigration. Anatoly shared her strong sense that Jews in the Soviet Union were facing real and immediate danger; that the mass of Soviet Jewry had only begun to awaken, and that the overriding imperative was to get them out. Their view reflected that of another Russian Jew whom Anatoly's grandfather had greatly admired, Vladimir Jabotinsky. He said that the Jews of Russia should either become members of the Jewish nation in Palestine, or assimilate completely.

IN NOVEMBER 1975, Anatoly notified his friend Mark Nashpitz by telegram that he was flying from Moscow to visit him in his Siberian exile. He flew nine hours to the town of

Chita, then another five hours in a light plane before reaching Tupik.

"This is really Tupik," he wrote Avital of the aptly named village in the middle of nowhere.

The two friends greeted each other warmly. Anatoly found Nashpitz in terrible surroundings but in good spirits and living with a beautiful woman who later became his wife. He had met her there at the end of the earth, where she was spending a mandatory two years working at the two general stores in Tupik after having completed a state course in marketing. The KGB attempted to break up the affair by offering her a better job in a large town, but she had refused. The two men toasted the match.

"Now, tell me the news, my friend," said Nashpitz as they sat down at the table in the center of the room.

Anatoly reeled off a report on who had received visas and who had been refused. When he told of his joining the Helsinki monitoring group, Nashpitz's mien turned serious.

"I think this will put you into prison," he said abruptly.

The Soviets had distinguished between Jewish activists who wished to leave the country and dissidents who sought to persuade the Soviet authorities to fulfill their constitution's obligations. Of the two, the dissidents were far more threatening. By entering their ranks, Anatoly was endangering himself. "You're a very good candidate for arrest," Nashpitz argued. "The KGB prefers young men who are alone to older, family men. It makes for fewer problems."

"I'm not doing anything subversive," Anatoly said. "I'm just working for human rights."

Although they moved on to another subject, Nashpitz, immersed in the grim reality of his own situation, was left with an uneasy feeling about his friend's fate.

"Tell me about your situation, Mark," Anatoly said. "Is it very difficult?"

"What is difficult?" Nashpitz said wryly. "I'm stuck here, and that's it."

Anatoly wasted no time in calling his foreign correspondent contacts in Moscow on Nashpitz's telephone and giving them an impromptu news release about the Siberian exile of the Moscow dentist. The next day Nashpitz's telephone was cut off. It meant he would have to walk one mile to the post office if he wanted to use a telephone. In the Arctic cold, it would not be easy.

Anatoly stayed for five days, a great balm for Nashpitz. They spent the days talking of their plans, of their friends, of the future of the Jews. They walked a lot, but Nashpitz was forbidden to leave the boundaries of the village. His room had no running water, and in the mornings Tolya laughed when Nashpitz broke off a piece of ice outside and put it in a bucket on the stove. Impressed at how adept his friend had become at chopping wood, Anatoly tried his hand at it himself.

As he took leave on the final day, Anatoly asked Nashpitz what he could do for him back in Moscow.

"There's only one thing you can do—don't forget me. Write letters, call, visit again if you can."

"I'm not very good at writing," Anatoly said. "But I promise you, I'll call often."

"Sorry," said Nashpitz, "but I don't have a phone." Both men exploded in laughter.

In Chita, Anatoly stayed overnight in a hotel to await transportation to the village of Eniseisk, where Tsitlyonok was in exile. He also planned to visit Colonel Yefim Davidovich in Minsk on the other side of the USSR and Ilya

Glazer, another refusenik exiled in Boguchany. Anatoly caused a stir at the post office in Chita when he attempted to send a telegram to Avital in Hebrew transliteration congratulating her on her twenty-fifth birthday. In the end, he bowed to the bureaucracy and sent it in Russian.

Eniseisk turned out to be a horrid village. Yet Shcharansky found himself imagining, as he had at Tupik, what it would be like living in exile there with Avital. "How much fuller that life would be than life without you in Moscow," he wrote her. "Did we make a mistake? No, no, no. Destiny is letting us understand who we are and why we were given to each other."

WHILE ANATOLY was busy chopping wood, confounding postal workers, and shivering in the Siberian winter, Avital was walking through the sunlit streets of Jerusalem. Every day, she wrote to Anatoly and waited for his letters. But as he became more active, fewer letters got through the censor. When nothing came for days, Avital grew restless and walked around Jerusalem for hours, as if she could absorb comfort from the ancient city she and Anatoly had dreamed about. She felt that the beautiful city, surrounded by the terraced slopes of the Judean hills, was hers: from the very moment of her arrival in Israel, she had known it to be so.

Every face looked familiar; people seemed so unafraid and free, reminding her of Anatoly. In detailed letters to him, she described the land and its inhabitants lingering sometimes on the children: how beautiful they were, how gay and open. She longed to have children with Anatoly. She wrote often of how their life would be. Together, they would see their children off to school each morning with their schoolbags on their backs, Israeli-style, like hikers setting off on a journey. They would swim in the clear blue Mediterranean and picnic among the wildflowers of the Galilee; they would share their life with good friends and fill it with laughter and warmth.

Anatoly, moving from flat to flat in Moscow, seized these dreams and never let them go. "My dear Natulya," he wrote, "You offer me another life, and I avidly grasp it." He could not help mourning the time they were losing. "Each day here is another stolen from us together." But he found sustenance for both of them in the Bible. "Jacob worked for seven years for Rachel, but in his eyes they were like a few days because of his love for her." In an earlier letter, he recalled the Passover they had celebrated together in 1974. "Since then, you, Avital, have crossed through Sinai, received the Torah, and arrived in Jerusalem. . . . Although I am still in Egypt, we know that it's not for long."

Avital believed that, believed it so strongly that she postponed important decisions until his arrival: where to live, what to do. Her life seemed split in half. She took an intensive, five-month Hebrew course, and surprised Tolya with her progress during their infrequent phone conversations. She met people who knew him—Americans who had visited him in Moscow, Russians who had succeeded in getting out with his help—and others who knew of him. Anatoly was doing everything in his power to help Jews leave the Soviet Union, and people everywhere who were grateful for his efforts started to come to Avital to ask what they could do. Jerry and Jane Stern, the New York couple who had visited Anatoly in Moscow in 1974, came to Israel, met Avital, and kept in touch. During periods when Tolya's letters to Avital were intercepted, they corresponded through the Sterns and other American friends.

Some of these friends urged Avital to come to the United States and Canada to help organize a campaign on his behalf. "You can accomplish a great deal more for Anatoly in the United States than you can in Israel," they argued.

Avital was appalled at the idea of meeting strangers in order to beg for their support, and the thought of appearing on a public stage was terrifying. Gradually, however, she began to see the possibility of helping Tolya and to feel that she need not wait passively: it was in her power to change things. In December 1975, a year and a half after her own exit from Russia, she flew to North America for the first round of what was to become a dizzying, decade-long campaign to free her husband. Accompanying her was her brother, who had a good command of English, which she was slowly learning.

The brother and sister who had been raised in the depths of Siberia encountered in one big rush of experience the opulence, warmth, naïveté, and complexity of America. They traveled the length of the country, meeting with newsmen, public officials, and Jewish groups. Returning to New York at the end of the exhausting journey, they were urged by Jerry Stern to go down to Washington as well. The pivot of power was there. If the United States could in any way influence Soviet policy regarding the emigration of Jews, and of Anatoly in particular, it was the government officials and elected representatives in Washington who would be decisive.

Avital had entrée into this world via the congressmen and senators who had met Anatoly during visits to Moscow, where he had served as their translator and contact with the movement. She was warmly received by these men when she went to the capital. She felt that they were interested in Tolya's fate in human terms, not simply as a factor in interbloc rivalry. Her brother Misha, who had recently completed his Israeli army service as a tank commander, was a comforting presence and did much of the talking. Avital wept often as Misha described to the senators and congressmen how difficult life had become for Anatoly within the tightening KGB circle. Her sad eyes and unself-conscious beauty made a powerful impression on the congressmen; she personalized for them the struggle for human rights. At the same time, Avital was learning: she could sense the power in Washington and knew that as the campaign continued, this would be the fulcrum.

Back in Israel, she found it impossible to settle down into a regular pattern of life. She had worked part-time in an immigrant absorption center, where new arrivals live for up to a year in subsidized housing while they learn Hebrew. Then, continuing studies that had begun in Moscow, she went to Beersheba to take a course for art teachers, in order to have a profession. But she couldn't live a normal life when she felt that half her being was missing. She moved in with Ilana and Binyamin Ben-Josef in Jerusalem, friends from the Soviet Union who had adopted her as a member of their family since her arrival in Israel.

If Anatoly could not yet come to her, a possible interim solution was for her to visit him. After talking it over with Anatoly by telephone, Avital decided to apply for a visitor's visa to the Soviet Union. Perhaps her presence there might induce the Soviet authorities to let him accompany her back. She applied for the visa at the Finnish Embassy in Tel Aviv, which has represented Soviet interests in Israel since the Kremlin severed relations in the Six-day War. The application was forwarded to Moscow, but there was no reply.

When she informed her friends in America of her failed attempt to visit Anatoly, Jerry Stern raised forty thousand dollars and placed a full-page advertisement in the *New York Times* portraying Anatoly and Avital as tragically star-crossed lovers. Under a photograph of the two was the headline, "They Got Married Because They Were in Love. And Separated Because They Were Jewish." The text told how her "dreaded existence" without him had driven her to apply for a visa to return to the Soviet Union to visit her husband. "The toughest decision she's ever had to make. Between leaving the country she's grown to love in search of the man who is her whole life. And returning to the country that has ruined it." The ad was subsequently republished in the *Washington Post* on January 20, 1977, Anatoly's twenty-ninth birthday, and brought in thousands of dollars to the cause of Soviet Jewry. The Shcharanskys were becoming nationally known figures, their matyrdom providing recognizably human symbols to the movement. But Avital's hopes that the campaign would persuade the Soviets to rid themselves of Anatoly were dashed. The KGB had plans of its own.

3

The Turncoat

*E*very great political movement has in its annals a chapter on defection and betrayal: the stool pigeon is a universal phenomenon. But in a totalitarian system, the informer is an institution, and entrapment is often regarded as a legitimate tool. In Soviet society, the KGB agent, the school spy, and the worker who accuses his fellow of misdeeds are generally considered exemplary citizens. So it was in the betrayal of Anatoly Shcharansky; but the man who framed him was a complex villain, a Jew who apparently sold his soul to save his father's life.

Members of the Jewish emigration movement knew that they had been infiltrated by agents serving the KGB; but, feeling that they had no secrets to conceal, they were unafraid. Some even tried to present it as an advantage, arguing that once the KGB realized that their only object was emigration, not subversion, the authorities might stop persecuting them. This naïveté could not last long.

Dr. Alexander "Sanya" Lipavsky, a prematurely gray neurosurgeon in his early forties, was a kindly man with a Cheshire cat grin and twinkling brown eyes. He made his way into the movement in 1972 shortly after moving to Moscow. He came highly recommended as a fine doctor who could not yet apply to go to Israel because his father was in a prison camp for economic crimes and would suffer. All that the refuseniks knew about Lipavsky was what he told them. He had been born in Kiev in 1933, and spent most of the forties and fifties in Tashkent, the capital of Uzbekistan in central Asia. He had been chief neurosurgeon in the northern port of Murmansk in the Kola peninsula, but had lost his job because of anti-Semitism, he said. He volunteered to help the movement in any way possible.

He was a quiet, polite person, who was soon providing medical treatment for many refuseniks and dissidents. He called on Professor Lerner almost every day, treating the scientist's high blood pressure and giving him injections. Vitaly and Ina Rubin and Ida Nudel felt particularly close to the companionable, intelligent physician. Shcharansky and Vladimir Slepak also liked him. They knew little about him, but this was not unusual; people in the rapidly growing movement tended not to ask many personal questions. Lipavsky's elderly father was released in 1973, and a year later, the movement's "house doctor" applied to emigrate to Israel. He lived with his second wife, a nurse, and their seven-year-old son in a town some thirty-five miles from Moscow. A son by his first marriage was in the army, he said. His first wife was in Tashkent. Sanya drove an expensive black Volga sedan, which, he explained to his friends, he had bought with money his mother inherited from her brother, who died a wealthy man in America.

In Moscow, Lipavsky had been a chief surgeon in the largest Red Army medical facility, Buordenko Hospital, until he lost his post there, also "because of anti-Semitism." Afterward, he worked in the medical unit of the Intercity and International Automobile Transportation administration, a job that seemed to give him a great deal of free time. He never took part in the constant political arguments among the activists. He was neutral, quiet, with a perennial smile on his mustached, moon-shaped face.

Lipavsky seemed subtly but intensely interested in all the movement's activities. This was most evident during meetings with foreign visitors. Lipavsky often materialized on such occasions, invited or not. One night, for example, Shcharansky, the Slepaks, the Lerners, and the Beilins were invited to dinner at the home of U.S. Consul Ellen Nathanson. The activists met by arrangement in the street to go together to the restricted area where the consul lived. Just as they were about to set off for the apartment, Sanya arrived, bearing flowers. They assumed, incorrectly, that Nathanson had invited him, whereas she assumed that the others had brought him along, but was too polite to inquire.

On another occasion, Lipavsky and the Rubins had dinner at the home of *New York Times* correspondent David Shipler. The doctor made little impression on the journalist, except that he seemed too virulently anti-Soviet to be reliable as a source of information.

In the summer of 1975, Dr. Lipavsky approached an official of the U.S. Embassy, told him that he was opposed to the Soviet regime, and offered to provide classified information to the Americans. Despite the standing rules of the U.S. intelligence community not to recruit active members of the Soviet dissident or refusenik movements, the official accepted the offer. The CIA had fallen for a KGB trick. No one in the movement knew what Lipavsky had done—it would have been a shattering revelation. By successfully infiltrating the emigration movement, which was now about to link up with the dissident movement, and then offering to spy for the Americans, Lipavsky had set a trap. His superiors could bide their time, waiting for the right target and the best moment to inflict maximum damage to both the Jewish and dissident movements.

In his dealings with the activists Lipavsky was very accommodating, in matters large and small. He offered to drive the refuseniks anywhere they wanted to go. On one occasion, driving Anatoly and Dina Beilina through the beautiful Russian countryside on a brisk autumn day, Lipavsky mused that perhaps if they had a few more comforts, a little more money, life in the Soviet Union would not be so bad after all, and there would be no reason to want to leave. "What do you think, Tolya?" he said. Anatoly, lost in his own thoughts, seemed not to hear. It didn't occur to either passenger that Lipavsky might be on a fishing expedition.

In June 1976, Vitaly and Ina Rubin and Dr. Lunts were granted exit visas, raising Anatoly's own hopes. He wrote to Avital saying that people were telling him, "You're next," and that he would probably get permission very soon. "I try not to think about it and not to 'sit on the suitcases,' or else I could go crazy." Both of the movement's previous spokesmen had eventually been allowed to emigrate. Now perhaps his turn would come. He did not feel that he faced prison, believing that his increasingly high profile among Western correspondents and visiting dignitaries formed a protective mantle.

After Rubin emigrated to Israel, his place on the Helsinki committee was filled by Slepak, the bearded, bearlike Jeff to Shcharansky's Mutt. The two friends gave an interview to an English documentary team, who clandestinely filmed them in the backseat of a car. The Grenada Television interviewer asked them if they weren't afraid of being put on trial, and what the significance was of their partici-

pation in the Helsinki Watch Group. They answered that
they and the other refuseniks had only one aim. "We want
to leave this country," Slepak said. Anatoly explained that
he had not taken a stand *against* the government, but *for*
his right to emigrate. Asked if he regretted his stand, he responded: "I never regret . . . now I live in peace with myself—an inner peace, I mean. There is no constant irritation
because of the impossibility of saying what you think—and
to behave in the way you wish to do is very important." The
film was called *A Calculated Risk*.

Later in June, the two Jewish representatives on the
watch committee traveled with Sanya Lipavsky to the Ta-
lovski region in the Voronezski district, attempting to visit
Ilyinka village, a Jewish settlement of about one hundred
families in the heart of rural Russia. Anatoly had met several Ilyinka Jews at the Moscow synagogue and had learned
of the official pressure on the villagers to give up their Judaism. Half of the residents were refuseniks. The villagers
of Ilyinka were all Orthodox Jews, said to be descendants
of peasants who converted to Judaism in the nineteenth century. The residents of two neighboring Jewish villages reportedly succumbed to the pressure and assimilated. Two
generations earlier, most Russian Jews lived in rural areas.
But in the 1970 census, fewer than fifty thousand Jews were
located outside urban centers. The Jews of Ilyinka were a
disappearing breed.

In 1974, a few Ilyinka families had managed to leave
for Israel. But afterward, local authorities refused to allow
any more of the villagers to leave and denied that they were
Jewish. Anatoly and Slepak planned to write a report on the
village for the human rights group, because some had emigrated to Israel, leaving families divided. But the three visi-

tors from Moscow were seized a couple of miles outside the village, questioned for two days, and then thrown out of the area. In December 1976, the watch group issued a report on the treatment of the Jews of Ilyinka, declaring it another example of a "gross violation of the Helsinki agreement, namely the reunification of families, freedom of communication, and decent treatment of the rights of minorities."

After the excursion to Ilyinka, Lipavsky, more than ever, appeared to be just one of the boys, a member of the inner circle. As yet, he had aroused no suspicion—even after Dina Beilina caught him in a lie.

In September 1976, Beilina received information from two independent sources that a Jewish cemetery outside Moscow had been vandalized. About sixty headstones had been smashed and graves daubed with swastikas. Since Lipavsky's home was not far from the cemetery, she asked him to drive a photographer to the site so that the damage could be recorded. If this was the opening shot in a fresh campaign of official anti-Semitism, she wanted to transmit the evidence to the West. Lipavsky agreed to make all of the arrangements.

A week passed with no word from Lipavsky. When Beilina finally tracked him down, she learned, to her dismay, that the assignment had not been carried out. The photographer, Lipavsky said, was much too ill to travel to the cemetery.

On the following Saturday, when the activists gathered outside the Moscow synagogue for their regular meeting, Beilina was surprised to see the photographer. If he was well enough to come to the synagogue meeting, she asked, why hadn't he gone to photograph the desecrated cemetery? He didn't know what she was talking about.

By the time the photographer reached the cemetery—without Lipavsky's help—it had been cleaned up. The broken masonry had been removed, the swastikas painted over, and flowers adorned the restored graves. Still, Beilina did not yet suspect Sanya. He had been so very helpful in many other ways.

Dr. Lipavsky made what was thought to be a major contribution to the Jewish movement when he managed to solve the critical problem of communication with supporters abroad. The transmission of information was essential in focusing Western opinion on the plight of Soviet Jewry, issuing appeals to legislators, and engendering protests to Soviet embassies. The price of making a telephone call for such purposes was often the loss of telephone service, so activists used public call boxes at post offices. But the KGB tail often would have a word with the security officer in charge of the central telephone exchange, and the call would be mysteriously disconnected.

Dr. Lipavsky offered a remedy. He told the activists that several of his patients had moved, leaving behind connected telephones in empty apartments. When an activist wanted to make a sensitive call to England, Israel, or the United States, Lipavsky would take him or her to one of these empty flats.

It was Lipavsky who generally answered the phone when Michael Sherbourne called movement leaders. (A London high-school teacher fluent in Russian, Sherbourne had become the principal link between the movement and the outside world.) Before turning the phone over to others, he would read out to Sherbourne a list of ciphers indicating the date, time, and telephone number for the Englishman's next contact. Neither Sherbourne nor the refuseniks suspected that the KGB was making the arrangements. They believed Lipavsky when he assured them that since his patients had no connections to either the Jewish or dissident movements, the refuseniks could speak freely; and they were grateful for his help.

ANATOLY'S GYPSY existence, moving between friends' apartments, complicated his already frenetically busy life; so he was delighted when one of his colleagues on the Helsinki Watch Group offered him a temporary solution to his nagging housing problem.

Lydia Voronina, a philosophy graduate of Moscow University, was involved in both the human rights and the emigration movements. She and her Jewish husband, Anatoly Reznik, who was one of Shcharansky's closest friends, had applied for exit visas to Israel. When Reznik's was granted, he left the Soviet Union to await his wife's arrival in Israel. But Lydia Voronina's application was blocked by her mother, a senior official in the office of the chief state procurator who, like Avital's mother, was a bitter opponent of the Jewish movement. Voronina and her husband were in the same situation as the Shcharanskys, and Anatoly and Lydia became good friends. When she was hospitalized early in 1976, Anatoly brought Dr. Lipavsky to her bedside. The surgeon discovered that she was being given the wrong medicine, and with his help, she soon recovered from her ailment.

Voronina could not find work in her field because of her application to emigrate. Then, unexpectedly, a solution presented itself—a dissident couple in Moscow hired the young philosophy graduate as a live-in *au pair* to take care of their children, and she was no longer threatened by the charge of parasitism. The tiny room in a two-room apartment that she had been leasing from the Moscow municipal authorities was now vacant; Anatoly seized the opportunity to obtain a place of his own.

Apart from a good many books and his carton of letters from Avital in Israel, which now numbered over four hundred, Anatoly still had few possessions. But he craved privacy, and the room was ideal. It had a small sofa, a little table, and a radio. Most importantly, it was centrally located near a subway station and was equipped with a telephone. The room became his home for several months.

The room was searched only once, but the KGB agents confiscated his most precious possession—Avital's letters. Dina Beilina, who had seen Anatoly in any number of crises, had never seen him so upset and shocked. "You should have kept the letters at your parents' home," she told him. "It was bound to happen."

"I needed to read them," Anatoly said. "I couldn't part with them."

But he was too busy to stay depressed for long. In September 1976, Shcharansky organized a press conference to commemorate the thirty-fifth anniversary of the Babi Yar massacre and to assert the right of Soviet Jews to conduct traditional Jewish mourning services at the site.

For those who saw a potential physical threat to Jewish survival in the Soviet Union and felt that the sole priority must be to get Jews out—preferably to Israel, but elsewhere if necessary—Babi Yar offered the single most powerful symbol of Jewish vulnerability in the Soviet Union. On September 29 and 30, 1941, the Germans had murdered 33,771 Jewish men, women, and children in a ravine near Kiev. The local Ukrainian population scarcely knew that the Jews were being liquidated, but it was certain that they wouldn't have objected in any case. The Soviets never conceded that the victims at Babi Yar were Jews; officially, they were Russians or Ukrainians. In 1961, Yevgeni Yevtushenko's brief poem "Babi Yar" created a worldwide sensation for finally affirming the fact that the victims were Jews and that anti-Semitism was endemic in Russia. Ukrainian-born Nikita Krushchev lashed out at Yevtushenko for drawing attention to the doomed Jews whom no one would help, an accusation he considered an insult to the Soviet peoples.

When a memorial was finally built at the site, there was no reference to the fact that the victims had been Jews. Thus, Babi Yar came to represent not only the German extermination of two million Soviet Jews, but also the Russian cover-up of the Ukraine massacre: two sides of the continuing attempt to annihilate Jewish identity.

The KGB warned Shcharansky that anyone who tried to commemorate the anniversary of the massacre would be arrested. Nevertheless, Anatoly, Yosef Begun, Yosef Ahs, Genadi Khassin, and Yosef Beilin prepared to make the six-hundred-mile railroad journey from Moscow to Kiev. Their only luggage was a huge wreath of artificial flowers, which they were planning to lay during the ceremony. Just before they boarded the train, KGB agents plucked Anatoly out of the group and detained him. The others were allowed to travel on to Kiev before they, too, were picked up and detained at a local militia post in the city.

Still clutching their wreath, Beilin, Ahs, and Begun were forced to cool their heels in detention until the Babi Yar memorial ceremony was over. Only then were they permitted to return to Moscow, where they laid the wreath on graves at the Jewish cemetery. Anatoly was released with a warning.

In standard Soviet textbooks on ancient history, no word exists about the Jewish people or ancient Israel. It was in this spirit that the Jewishness of the Babi Yar victims was taken away from them. This practice of eradicating inconvenient bits of history was not confined to ancient events or even the relatively distant past. It is a general rule in the Soviet media never to mention Israel favorably in any context. So it was in describing the Entebbe raid of July 4, 1976, in which Air France passengers hijacked by PLO and German terrorists and surrounded by dictator Idi Amin's troops were freed by Israeli forces. Soviet news agencies termed it "a military operation by Israeli pirates against peaceful Uganda." The raiders "killed innocent bystanders and carried off, by force, the terrified passengers of a French airliner." Anatoly heard a different version on the Voice of America and the BBC. He wrote Avital four days after the raid, which took place on the second anniversary of their wedding, that "our boys' mission to Uganda" was a wonderful anniversary gift.

Soviet Jews have to rely on themselves to reconstruct their history and that of the Jewish people outside of Russia. Anatoly continued to be fascinated by details of the bold action at Entebbe. He gathered material from correspondent friends, who brought him articles, a quickie paperback on the rescue, transcripts of radio interviews, and other information about Entebbe. In October, three months after the "pirate raid," Anatoly delivered a memorable lecture on Entebbe to seventy refuseniks packed into the apartment of his friend, the writer Felix Kandel. The activists had been holding regular seminars for years, and Anatoly had lectured on a variety of topics—Jewish-American communities, an analysis of Saul Bellow's novels, the structure of the U.S. Senate, and now Entebbe.

It was hot and cramped in the book-lined room. Kandel's wife constantly refilled the samovar, as the professors and teenagers, scientists and artists sipped tea and listened to Tolya for almost four hours without interruption; the listeners were deeply moved. It was a unique moment for many of those in the movement, who had never heard anything like it. Tolya was not only brilliant, he was captivating. Anatoly himself could see how extraordinary it was to hold the audience's absolute attention for so long and to see the suspense on everyone's face, until the evening ended in wild applause. In a cassette he sent to Avital a few days later, Anatoly said it was the material itself that was so magical. "When I finished, such joy, as if everyone had relived it all." One of the refuseniks ran to kiss him, "acting as if I were the pilot." For the Soviet Jews, that's exactly what Anatoly Shcharansky was becoming.

A FEW DAYS after the talk on Entebbe, on October 19, 1976, a group of Moscow Jews were beaten by "Druzhinniki"—members of the "People's Guard." The KGB stepped up its pressure on Anatoly, with four agents dogging his footsteps, black Volgas driving behind him, and Druzhinniki with armbands waiting defiantly in front of his friends' apartments where he visited. The agents pushed him around and threatened him with reprisals. On October 26, just before the opening session of the Supreme Soviet, thirty Jewish activists, including Anatoly, were jailed in order to prevent demonstrations.

The Jewish activists never resisted arrest. Their movement, as well as the dissident movement, was totally nonviolent. They welcomed news of demonstrations abroad, which they believed would focus attention on their plight and win public sympathy. But they vehemently opposed actions that they considered counterproductive, like those of a small number of Western activists who, for example, physically disrupted foreign appearances of the Bolshoi Ballet. In early 1976, when a group believed to share the political beliefs of Rabbi Meir Kahane placed a bomb at the United Nations headquarters "on behalf of Soviet Jewry," the refuseniks in Moscow vigorously condemned "the attempted terrorist act." Shcharansky, Begun, Rubin, Slepak, Lunts, Shakhnovsky, and the Beilins said that similar actions would "only harm the cause of the Jewish people in their homeland and Jews everywhere else," including the USSR.

In November 1976, Anatoly and the other refusenik leaders organized a symposium on Jewish life and culture in the Soviet Union to be held in December, but they were constantly harassed. The topics that were to be discussed included "Bible and Talmud and their role in the spiritual enrichment of Soviet Jewry." Not surprisingly, Soviet authorities, who have described the Torah as "the blackest book created in the entire history of mankind," refused to allow several foreign religious leaders, including the chief rabbis of Ireland and Denmark, to attend. On the day of the symposium, none of the thirteen members of the organizing committee and only two of forty scheduled speakers showed up. They were either arrested, kept under house arrest, or otherwise prevented from attending. In Israel, Foreign Minister Yigal Al'on saluted the organizers of the symposium and said that the Soviet harassment was a violation of their own constitution. "The Jewish people and the State of Israel will not be reconciled to persecution of Jews by Soviet authorities," he said.

In January 1977, Lydia Voronina was unexpectedly granted an exit visa. This meant that Anatoly could no longer stay in her Moscow room and would have to move among the overcrowded apartments of his friends. His life was now so hectic that it was essential to have a permanent base, but he could not afford a room of his own.

At that critical moment he received a call from Sanya Lipavsky. The doctor told Anatoly that he wanted to do more for the movement. His problem was that living so far from Moscow limited his contribution; how could he attend late-night meetings, for example, if he still had to commute home? He had heard that Anatoly had a housing problem. He, too, needed a base in the city. Why not rent a flat together and share the costs? In fact, if Anatoly agreed, he had already located a suitable apartment. It was centrally located in Moscow, close to subway stations, and equipped with a telephone. It even had a separate entrance, and the heavy traffic of visitors would be less likely to anger the neighbors. It was being entirely refurbished and would be ready in a couple of months. Come in, come in, said the spider to the fly.

Anatoly gratefully accepted Lipavsky's offer. The stratagem was complete: Shcharansky, on the day of reckoning, would be thoroughly compromised, "living with a spy."

Lipavsky was still not arousing suspicion. But in early January 1977, four months after the cemetery incident, Dina Beilina caught him in a second lie. An emigration activist, Amner Zavurov, had been granted an exit visa, thereby losing his Soviet citizenship. But before he could use it, the exit visa was withdrawn. When Zavurov refused to take back his Soviet citizenship and his internal passport, he was charged with hooliganism. The trial was about to open in a small village near the remote Tadzhikistan city of Dushanbe.

His family had retained an excellent Moscow lawyer, but just before the hearing was to open, Beilina received a frantic telephone call from Zavurov's father. The trial was to be held not in Russian, as required by law, but in the Uzbek language, and no interpreter would be permitted. Their Russian-speaking lawyer would be unable to help.

Beilina remembered that Lipavsky had spent many years in Tashkent and would be able to understand the proceedings. He readily agreed to travel to Tadzhikistan for the trial. As an added precaution, Beilina asked another refusenik to fly to Dushanbe, obtain a copy of the judgment, and fly back again. She wanted to transmit the information immediately to Andrew Young, the U.S. ambassador to the United Nations, who had taken a special interest in the case, which contravened many aspects of Soviet law itself.

Three days later, Lipavsky came to Dina with the story of why he had failed to make it to Dushanbe. When he arrived at the main Moscow airport, he was so thoroughly searched by security officials in the departure lounge that he missed his flight. He immediately took a taxi to the second Moscow airport to get another flight, but there, too, he was prevented from boarding the plane. "This farce lasted for three days, as I shuttled back and forth between the airports," he said, "until it was too late."

Just as he finished telling his story, the other refusenik Dina had sent to collect material on the trial arrived at the apartment and handed her a copy of the judgment and sentence. He had taken the same plane that Lipavsky was to have boarded first, and could not have failed to witness Lipavsky being searched, if it had happened. Beilina looked inquiringly at Lipavsky, as the blood drained from his face. At that moment, she was sure that either he was working for the KGB, or that he was a coward, too frightened to carry out his mission. Suddenly, she recalled another suspicious incident.

Lipavsky had approached her months earlier with an urgent request: his son from his first marriage, who was in the army, had assaulted an officer who had called him "Yid," and he was in serious trouble. Lipavsky had negotiated a deal with the officer: in exchange for four thousand rubles, the army officer would withdraw the charges. But four thousand rubles was an unimaginable sum for the doctor—it would represent about two years' salary. Could Beilina help raise the money? Not from among the activists, of course, but possibly from a wealthy friend of the movement abroad?

Receiving money from abroad was strictly illegal, and it was an article of faith among the activists that they never, under any circumstances, accepted cash from visitors. They also had a rule against using the meager resources of the movement to help Jews accused of criminal activity. Finally, Beilina told him that she could not in good conscience ask other members of the group to contribute to winning a reprieve for his son while Lipavsky himself drove around in a made-for-export Volga, which must have cost at least twice the amount he was now seeking. If you want to save your son, she told him, you must sell your car. Beilina never heard about the problem again; and Lipavsky did not sell his car. Now, in retrospect, it seemed to her that the doctor had been trying to determine whether the movement had some secret source of financing. She believed that Sanya was a turncoat, not a coward.

Dina and her husband Yosef met with Professor Lerner, Slepak, and Shcharansky to confide her suspicion that Dr. Lipavsky was a KGB plant.

None of them believed her. Anatoly and Slepak both laughed. "You can't be suspicious of everyone," Slepak said. They thought Dina was being oversuspicious; they were convinced that as they had nothing to hide, they had nothing to fear. Beilina was not convinced, but she was quieted.

TIME WAS RAPIDLY running out for Anatoly. On January 4, 1977 Anatoly, accompanied by Lydia Voronina—who was just about to leave the USSR—paid a visit to the apartment of fellow Helsinki Watch Group member Lyudmilla Alekseeva. They stumbled upon a search being conducted by Investigator Smirnov of the Moscow Municipal Procurator's Office, whose man walked in and out of the apartment with bulging briefcases. Shcharansky and Voronina were detained on the spot and witnessed the illegal search. The next day, they wrote a full report on the incident for the watch group, noting that the most flagrant violation of rules was Smirnov's decision not to record most of the approximately two hundred items that were confiscated. The lawlessness of the search demonstrated the authorities' intention of falsifying the results and of continuing to persecute those who believed in the rule of law and in basic human rights. On January 7, the watch group issued a statement on the illegal searches being conducted by the KGB and other agents. Signed by Orlov, Ginzburg, Shcharansky, and seven others, the statement concluded that "in trying to apply archaic Stalinist methods of provocation and intimidation, the Soviet authorities *have lost their sense of reality*." It said that forced liquidation of circles promoting democratic change would be understandable if the authorities were preparing for war. Otherwise, "this is madness."

In fact, the authorities were gearing for a kind of war, preparing to smash the Helsinki Watch Group, the dissidents, and the Jewish emigration movement with one blow. On January 13, the day that Zavurov in Dushanbe was sentenced to three years imprisonment, Moscow Jews, including Anatoly and Dina, spoke on the telephone to senators and other American officials and reported the building pressure on the movement. Within a month, Alexander Ginzburg was arrested after foreign currency was planted in his apartment. The house of Yuri Orlov, leader of the watch group, was besieged. He was arrested on February 11, 1977 and three months later sentenced to seven years in prison. Members of the Ukrainian human rights group were also rounded up.

At the same time, the KGB pressure on Anatoly and his fellow Jewish activists intensified. On January 22, Soviet television broadcast nationwide and in prime time an anti-Semitic documentary, "Traders in Souls," in which Shcharansky, Begun, and other Jewish activists were shown and characterized as "soldiers of Zionism." The sixty-five-minute film asserted that Anatoly was a CIA contact engaged in anti-Soviet activity. It also portrayed a fat capitalist Western Jew distributing money to Jewish demonstrators in England, Soviet Jews in Israel living in squalor and misery, and Israeli soldiers killing innocent children. Moscow Jews were spying for the Israelis as well as for the CIA, according to the filmmakers, who invited reprisals against the "traders in souls" by not only naming several prominent Soviet-Jewish activists, including Anatoly, but also giving their exact addresses.

Anatoly attempted to sue Moscow Television for contravening the Civil Code. In his claim, he said that many people who saw the film now recognized him in the street as "an agent of world Zionism and Western secret services," that the allegedly illegal meeting with American congressmen referred to in the film took place not in some "secret apartment," as had been asserted, but in the Sovietskaya Hotel in the presence of the press. The suit was immediately rejected by the authorities.

Shcharansky, still waiting for Lipavsky's apartment to be "renovated," stayed with the Slepaks, then with his parents in Istra, and later in Beilina's apartment while she and her family were on vacation. At last Lipavsky's apartment was ready. The refurbishment had indeed been extensive: KGB technicians had transformed the flat into a veritable sound stage, with enough hidden cameras and bugs to record the occupants' every word and gesture. It was a massive effort, but largely wasted. For word had come down from on high that Shcharansky's gadfly career had lasted long enough; he was due to be swatted.

On March 1, 1977 Anatoly moved in. On March 4, while he was out, KGB men entered the apartment house. They told the terrified old landlady that the two men living in the flat were spies, and that they were authorized to conduct a search. The apartments of other refuseniks were searched that day, including those of Nudel, Slepak, Lerner, and the Beilins. In the afternoon, the mass daily newspaper *Izvestia* hit the stands. It was the eve of the anniversary of Stalin's death—a traditional date for the Soviet regime to signal a fresh crackdown. On the front page was splashed Dr. Sanya Lipavsky's "Open Letter to the Presidium of the Supreme Soviet of the USSR." It was a KGB parody of Zola's "J'Accuse," his thunderous letter accusing France of criminal anti-Semitism in the Dreyfus affair; and it shook the Jewish emigration movement to its foundations.

The letter was composed strictly along the lines of a timeworn KGB script. In it, Lipavsky "confessed" to having acted as an intelligence agent for the United States, describing his contacts and how he passed on information to his control agent in the embassy. He also "confessed" to collaborating with Zionist circles, which he described in terms of an elaborate American espionage network that included Professor Alexander Lerner, Anatoly Shcharansky, Alexander Lunts, Vladimir Slepak, Mark Azbel, and Vitaly Rubin.

"It was not easy for me to write this," Lipavsky's letter began, "but after long and painful thought, I arrived at the conclusion that I must do it. Perhaps this open letter will open the eyes of those who are still deluded, who are being deceived by Western propaganda that shouts from the rooftops about the persecution of 'dissidents' in the USSR and which inflates the so-called question of human rights." Lipavsky, claiming that he had been Rubin's secretary and "keeper of the archives," had come to understand that the Jewish movement, a tool of U.S. intelligence, was designed to damage the USSR's interests. The leadership, he said, worked hand in hand with two members of the U.S. Embassy staff, Melvin Levitsky and Joseph Pressel, as well as with American newsmen such as Peter Osnos of the *Washington Post*, Alfred Friendly of *Newsweek*, and others.

The Jewish activists, Lipavsky said, were unconcerned that many deceived Jewish families encountered privations and injustice in Israel, that many of them began to flee from the "promised land" and to spread throughout the world. All the activists cared about was provoking the Soviet authorities. The Jewish leaders, "alarmed by the prospect of declining interest in them by their foreign masters," decided to team up with the insidious Helsinki group. "Vitaly Rubin was introduced into the group and then Anatoly Shcharansky."

In order to "whip up tensions between the United States and the USSR, Lerner proposed to organize a secret collection of information about Soviet defense institutions and enterprises and under this pretext to persuade Western firms to stop supplying technical equipment to the USSR." Shcharansky, he alleged, was instructed by Lerner to collect the information and arrange its dispatch abroad, to assist CIA agents in support of "the notorious Jackson Amendment." Rubin and others had trapped Lipavsky into acting on behalf of U.S. intelligence, until he saw the light. "I also saw for myself that adventurers and money grabbers pose as champions of 'human rights.' " He added that Jews were dying now, as they had died at Nazi hands: "But this is happening not in the Soviet Union but in the deserts of the Middle East, as a result of Israeli aggression." The repentant Dr. Lipavsky would spare no effort "to expose the hostile activity of the renegades and traitors to the Motherland who have sold out to the CIA." He called on the U.S. Congress to investigate his erstwhile employer, the CIA, which engaged in "the foul cause of fanning hatred among nations" and which "relies on renegades, presenting them as heroes and martyrs." He ended on an altruistic note. "I would like to devote myself to the struggle for the ideals of peace, friendship of the peoples, for socialism. . . ." After delivering his friends to certain imprisonment, and possibly the death penalty, the secret agent vanished from sight.

On the following day, Saturday, Shcharansky and his

comrades telephoned a message to London, saying that Lipavsky's accusations were reminiscent of the notorious Doctors' Plot. They spelled out once again that all their activities were done openly within the framework of Soviet law, and to the sole end of obtaining the right to emigrate from the USSR to Israel. They knew that they were now facing "fresh anti-Jewish trials based on completely false evidence, or, in fact, on no evidence at all except lies."

Later, Anatoly went to the regular meeting in front of the synagogue. This time, the KGB tails no longer hung back at a discreet distance. All of the activists were under close surveillance, but Anatoly's tail was doubled. A "cage" of eight men pressed around him wherever he went. His friend Felix Kandel broke through the circle. "How are things, Tolya?" he asked. Anatoly, under his breath, said, "I'm ready for ten years."

The activists talked about Lipavsky's motives. Some conjectured that Sanya had been a KGB man for many years. It was said that when his father was tried in the sixties for economic crimes, he had been sentenced to death; and that Sanya had sold himself to the KGB in exchange for commutation of the death sentence. Anatoly felt in retrospect that it was strange that Sanya had spent so much time in Moscow away from his family, that he had found the apartment just when he did, and all the other little things. But, as he told a friend later, "I would like to think that Sanya was not an informant all along, that he became one recently—not last week, of course, but not very long ago."

Anatoly stayed on Arkhipova Street for several hours, savoring the warmth and camaraderie. He seemed to pull away with great reluctance. Kandel watched him head for the subway, a small figure surrounded by the platoon of KGB escorts.

EVEN AS ANATOLY faced the gallows, he tried to joke about it, boasting that he'd been promoted from hooligan and parasite to spy. But although he began a March 13 letter to Avital on a light note, in an attempt to reassure her, he was unable to conceal his profound feelings. "Thinking of it all, I regretted only one thing—so much that I could cry. I regretted that we didn't have children." Immediately, though, mindful of Avital's distress, he said that he was sure they would have them eventually.

Anatoly's mother was bearing up under the strain, but his father's heart condition worsened. Anatoly feared, rightly, that it would be too much for Boris. But his deepest sorrow was for Avital, and he didn't know how to comfort her, other than to say that everything would be all right in the end.

Avital had been celebrating Purim in her Jerusalem apartment when the news of Lipavsky's letter came. It was immediately evident to her that the implications were ominous. She sat for some time in shock, frozen, thinking that this had all happened before—the Dreyfus case, the Doctors' Plot—but now it was happening to Tolya and his friends. There was a knock at the door, and two friends came in laden with books. Zvi and Hannah were associated with the Mercaz Harav Institute in Jerusalem, to which Avital had turned to learn more about Judaism. The yeshiva had become the fountainhead of modern orthodoxy in Israel. It was not locked into other-worldliness, as were traditional talmudic academies, but was politically committed and intimately involved in settling the territories occupied after the 1967 war. Its students served in army combat units, unlike most yeshiva students, and its graduates spearheaded the wildcat settlements set up on the West Bank.

Avital's friends saw immediately that she was distraught. She told them what had happened. Something would have to be done, Zvi said, and they all studied and prayed together. Zvi and Hannah left at midnight and came back three hours later with a short, bearded man, whom they introduced as "Yankele, who knows how to do things."

Yankele questioned Avital for hours, pacing the floor. He left at dawn. The next day, Avital met with others in a modest apartment in the Kiryat Moshe neighborhood near the Mercaz Harav yeshiva. This apartment was to become the headquarters of Avital's campaign to free Anatoly. These efforts received the blessing and support of the institute's leader, the octogenarian Rabbi Zvi Yehuda Kook, who closed the yeshiva temporarily in order to free students and teachers to help the threatened Soviet-Jewish activists. "If your brother is in danger and you ask, 'How can I help?' you are like one who spills blood. Don't ask! Go and do!" the rabbi said.

Within days, the framework of the campaign had been established: news conferences held, statements issued simultaneously in Western capitals, and at the center of it all, the quiet young woman who must overcome her introverted nature to fight like a lioness.

In the wake of Lipavsky's betrayal, Anatoly had only one opportunity to call Avital in Israel. But when he got through, he was told that she had flown to Geneva to arouse public opinion over the plight of the activists. He was devastated. He didn't think he would get to talk to Avital again.

4

Show Trial

*I*n the hours after Sanya Lipavsky's bombshell appeared in *Izvestia*, Dina Beilina consulted with Sophia Kalistratova, a leading Moscow lawyer and member of the Helsinki Watch Group, who expressed fears for the future of the Jewish movement. Kalistratova knew the leading Jewish activists well. Referring to the refuseniks' unwritten rule of leaving the USSR immediately if granted a visa, she had told Anatoly a couple of weeks earlier, "We live in strange times. We're happy when friends depart." Now, she was certain that the *Izvestia* provocation was a prelude to the arrest of the movement's leading members. The threatened activists let it be known in advance that if they were arrested, they would refuse to participate in a show trial or a closed court.

For the next ten days, the lives of the refuseniks seemed to hang on an invisible thread. All the leading members of the group were closely followed by at least four KGB men; while Anatoly's eight-man "cage" continued to surround him wherever he went.

Beilina was not unused to this frightening world. She had become accustomed to being followed, to having KGB agents camped on her doorstep twenty-four hours a day. She was experienced, too, at coping with the sort of allegations that were now being hurled at many of the movement's leaders. In 1973, she had been accused of spying for

Israel, a charge that was later dropped. But the memory lingered on. Now, four years later, she handled the new crisis in her own way: she wrote a letter of complaint to the Soviet procurator-general about the intensive KGB surveillance. To her astonishment, she received a prompt reply. It was untrue that she was being followed, wrote an official from the procurator's office: she was obviously suffering from paranoia. If she had witnesses to this alleged harassment, she should produce them.

Even as the shadows lengthened, the activists maintained a semblance of normal life. They continued to attend their seminars and to study Hebrew. As the days passed, some thought that they might have overreacted. Perhaps no one would be arrested; for if arrests were in the offing, why did the KGB wait? Why give the prime targets time to think, to talk, to prepare themselves? Some activists decided that the *Izvestia* attack, the searches, and the continuing close surveillance were simply new, intensified forms of intimidation. They decided to fight back, to lodge an official complaint about the Lipavsky letter and an accompanying postscript by two *Izvestia* authors; but an experienced Moscow lawyer who was close to the group counseled against such action. Why complain about the open letter if it had produced no tangible consequences? Why invite trouble?

Anatoly Shcharansky was not so sanguine. On the day the *Izvestia* article was published, Anatoly moved in with the Slepaks. The Lipavsky apartment, where Anatoly had lived for four days, was taken apart by KGB agents, who tore out ceilings and walls to retrieve their equipment. Andrei Sakharov suggested to Slepak that it might be better if Shcharansky stayed with him. At that point, the Kremlin was reluctant to crack down on the Nobel Peace Prize winner and "Father of the Soviet Atom Bomb," and Sakharov still retained an illusory aura of immunity from the more flagrant forms of KGB harassment. But Anatoly declined.

On March 13, Lev Ulanovsky visited his friend at Slepak's apartment, where several activists were congregated. The mood was very bleak among those who had been accused by Lipavsky. All of them expected to be arrested; there was no reason to think that only one among them would be singled out. Anatoly, normally as funny and optimistic as he was bright, was more depressed than Ulanovsky had ever seen him. Tolya said he was afraid that he would be arrested very soon. Ulanovsky agreed, but tried to argue that perhaps the Soviet authorities would not act for fear of adverse public opinion in the West just as the Kremlin was seeking accord on strategic arms limitations.

Anatoly looked at him and said: "I still believe they will arrest me."

Ulanovsky nodded sadly. There was no point in offering false comfort. He said what he really believed, that the KGB's first priority would be to attempt to prove Anatoly was a spy. They would play up his role in the Helsinki Watch Group, depicting him as a dissident rather than as a Jewish activist, in the hope of reducing the level of protests from Jews in the West.

This was Anatoly's thinking, too. He emphasized to Ulanovsky, who, as assistant spokesman in the Jewish movement, might soon be *his* voice to the rest of the world: "Our friends abroad know very well that I am a Jewish activist, not a dissident." Turning to two journalists from the *Cleveland Plain Dealer* who had braved a swarm of KGB watchmen to get into Slepak's apartment, he said, "We have burned all the bridges behind us here, and we are like a bicycle rider on a tightrope. We can't go back, and we can't stop or we'll fall off. We must go ahead, because we want our children and our friends to be free." That same day, he wrote to Avital and compared the situation of the beleaguered circle of activists to Mikhail Bulgakov's *The Master and Margarita*, a riotously funny, visionary work in which Satan and his henchmen visit Moscow. The surrealistic book appealed greatly to Anatoly's sense of the absurd, evoking a period when the intelligentsia was under constant surveillance by the secret police.

The movement leaders knew it was a turning point in the history of Russian Jewry. A message was sent to Israel that day, via Sherbourne in London, saying that the recent dramatic events showed that the Soviet authorities would go to extreme lengths "to suppress the growing national renaissance of the Jews of Russia." The statement, from Shcharansky, Lerner, and Slepak, said that the current campaign recalled the trials of Beilis, Dreyfus, and the so-called doctor-prisoners of 1953. They felt they were in the hands of lawless terrorists, but said that they did not despair because of faith in Jewish solidarity and the belief that truth and justice would prevail.

The activists, feeling that they could not tarry on the tightrope, continued trying to conduct "business as usual." On March 15, 1977 several movement leaders assembled in Slepak's apartment for a press conference about imprisoned refusenik Dr. Mikhail Stern. Anatoly had promised Stern's wife that he would describe the prisoner of Zion's plight to the press. Stern had been incarcerated in a labor camp since 1974. The refusenik doctor had been accused of bribery, extortion, and poisoning his patients, and was sentenced to eight years in prison. Organizing the press conference under the present circumstances had entailed a great deal of work, but it was familiar turf for Anatoly and gave him a respite from his consuming anxiety. At the apartment with Slepak, Shcharansky, Dina Beilina, and Felix Kandel were Harold Piper of the *Baltimore Sun* and David Satter of the London *Financial Times*, who had arrived early for the press conference.

An hour before the other reporters were to assemble, Slepak's telephone rang. For once, there was good news: Stern had just been released. Dina Beilina, hardened realist though she was, suddenly felt that there would be no arrests, after all. For one happy moment, she thought the Kremlin was going to do the unthinkable and back down. But Anatoly told the newsmen: "I think they will arrest someone else instead of Stern." Someone opened the door to check whether the KGB tails had been called off. But they were still there. And then it occurred to them that the press conference suddenly was superfluous. The two correspondents got up to leave, but Anatoly said to wait, he would go down with them—he wanted to use a pay phone on Gorky Street to call the correspondents and cancel the conference. If he used Slepak's phone to talk to newsmen, it would almost certainly be cut off.

Before they left, the seven, including Slepak's wife, Maria, drank a toast to Stern's release. Slepak and Kandel walked Anatoly and the two journalists to the tiny elevator. Two of the KGB tails got in with Anatoly and the newsmen and descended eight floors to Gorky Street. Slepak and Kandel took the long way, racing the elevator down the stairs. They lost the race, but reached the ground floor just in time to see Anatoly Shcharansky being pushed into the backseat of a green Volga sedan by a posse of KGB agents. The door slammed shut, and the car pulled away into the midday traffic of central Moscow. Anatoly was gone.

The official Volga sped over the loose cobblestones on Energeticheskaya Ulitsa—Energy Street—past a row of cheerless dwellings. It swung into a narrow driveway running down the side of the white brick apartment building at Number 3, where a discreet sign on a wall pointed toward a building in the rear, 3A Energeticheskaya Ulitsa. This was Lefortovo Prison, the notorious KGB interrogation and detention center in Moscow.

The new prisoner was hustled through a glass booth and into a small, olive-drab reception hall, the entrance to the prison. Through a rectangular internal window, a KGB agent quickly identified the full-faced, balding young man; a door opened, and he passed into the heart of the building. Anatoly's worst fears were about to be realized.

Slepak rushed back to his apartment, his face chalky white. "I don't know what happened," he told Dina, "but Tolya has been arrested." Slepak called out to his wife: "Quick, get some toothbrushes and chocolate for all of us. We'll be next."

But when they opened the door again, the KGB tails had vanished. Beilina, aware that the KGB could hold suspects for up to ten days without giving a reason, nevertheless decided to call KGB headquarters. She spelled the name of the KGB's newest detainee and gave the license number of the Volga, which Slepak had managed to memorize. To her surprise, the reply to her question came without any hesitation. "Yes, yes," said the KGB official on the other end of the line, in a satisfied tone. "Shcharansky is with us now."

———

INSIDE LEFORTOVO, Anatoly was isolated in a cell for a few hours. That evening, a guard led him to the interrogation room, where a KGB officer sat unblinkingly. "You have been charged with treason under Article 64A of the criminal code," he said. "We want you to give us a complete account of your criminal activity." This was not another fifteen-day stretch in a lockup, like the previous four Anatoly had endured following or in anticipation of demonstrations. Now they were actually talking about killing him.

He'd been expecting it; but still, it was a shock. "I know nothing about treason," Anatoly said. "I know nothing about criminal activity. Everything I've done has been lawful, as you well know."

"If you don't tell us everything, every detail, you will face execution." The officer stood. "Go back to your cell. You have a long time to think about how you are going to save your life."

The isolation of prisoners is a crucial element in the KGB interrogation process. Imprisonment serves not only to deprive the captive of his familiar physical surroundings, but also to alter his perception of reality and thus make him more vulnerable before his interrogators. In these circumstances, the sole physical reality is the cell and the interrogation room. The only human contacts are with the interrogators by day and the cell mate by night—in Lefortovo, invariably a KGB informer. Thus, the prisoner loses his world of familiar faces and places and is enveloped by his new world; he is thoroughly disoriented; his resistance is eroded; his changed reality destabilizes his value system: and then he is "broken," a suitable case for interrogation.

The process can take hours, days, or weeks. Anatoly Shcharansky was held in Lefortovo Prison for sixteen months.

There were no visits, no letters from his family or friends; he was denied access to legal counsel. During this long stretch, he was permitted to see and talk with no one except his KGB interrogators.

Anatoly understood the process, and he quickly grasped the urgent need to devise an antidote. In order to maintain his own internal equilibrium, he needed to create his own reality and to reinforce his own set of values, independent of his physical surroundings. It was a matter of supreme importance not to forget for a moment the world outside, and never to accept the premise that any aspect of life in Lefortovo was normal. Shcharansky's strategy for survival involved an extraordinary emotional detachment from his predicament and a determined, conscious effort to live within his own framework of reality, underpinned by memories of family and friends, of Avital and their dream of being together in Israel.

The first imperative was for a period of intense introspection, a time not only for scrupulous examination of his values, but also for recollecting small details, particularly of Avital. This became the store of emotional and spiritual food that sustained him. He had a plentiful supply to draw on. Anatoly distilled the central issues of his life and forced himself to articulate them. These words became a mantra, and he made it an article of faith to repeat them—"like a prayer"—each day. He knew it would be a long, long haul, and it was essential to make this act of renewal a conscious, daily effort. Shortly after his trial he wrote to Avital of his belief that they would yet share a happy life together: "I repeat this hope every day in a prayer which I composed myself in my primitive Hebrew."

He repeated other things, too. His initiation into Lefortovo had been shocking and brutal. He had utterly failed to prepare himself for the first challenge he encountered: the prospect of his own possibly imminent death. With great effort, Anatoly forced himself to say aloud to himself the word *rasstrel*, Russian for "firing squad." *Rasstrel*. In the days ahead he pronounced it often in the process of toughening up his ear and his mind. Gradually, the word became engraved on his consciousness. Its meaning was absorbed, and he conquered the fear.

His own values were reinforced and set in concrete. Impervious to the threats and blandishments of his captors, he could dominate his environment. When, at an early stage of his interrogation, he was offered his freedom and the promise of an exit visa in exchange for a denunciation of the Jewish emigration movement, he rejected it out of hand. And when he was threatened with a charge of treason and execution if he did not cooperate, he continued the process of reconciling himself to the possibility that he might be shot.

When his interrogators insisted that he was not really married because his religious wedding ceremony was not recognized by Soviet law, he dismissed the suggestion contemptuously. And when they told him stories about his wife's activities in Israel, he drew encouragement from their crude tactics: it told him that Avital was not only campaigning hard for his release, but that her efforts were annoying the Soviet authorities.

Above all, his stubborn determination to hold fast to his own reality prevented him from embarking on the perilous course of attempting to make a deal with the KGB. He knew of others who had entered into "negotiations" with the KGB, but he had never encountered anyone who had succeeded. He would make no concessions, however innocent they might seem. The KGB interrogators, with their proved track record, were confident they would break him as they engaged in the psychological struggle to undermine his resolve. But Anatoly knew he could not make the slightest compromise. His life depended on it.

He was weaving a cocoon from his memories of the past and his hopes for the future; at its center was Avital. He was not parting from her. They were always together, everywhere. The psychological state he had induced now totally excluded Lefortovo and his interrogators.

He employed other intellectual exercises to help him through the sixteen months of interrogation. In late 1977, midway through his period in Lefortovo, Anatoly decided to resume his Hebrew studies—without, of course, the benefit of a teacher or textbooks, though he had a tiny book of Psalms that Avital had given him shortly before she left. Embarking on the exercise, he set himself the task of recalling every Hebrew word he had learned, and was surprised to find he had accumulated a vocabulary of two thousand words. Then he set about integrating the Hebrew words into his daily prison routine, translating from Russian into Hebrew everything he heard or read—not a word-by-word translation, but the general sense. Sometimes, he dragged out his conversations with the interrogators by answering them, deadpan, in Hebrew.

Anatoly endured a total of 110 sessions of interrogation, ranging from two to ten hours each. As the KGB inquisitors vented their fury, attempting to trap him in a contradiction or to extract a compromising statement, Anatoly would concentrate intently and translate what they were saying into Hebrew. Pitting his will against the will of a superpower, Shcharansky was confident that he would win.

They might easily squash him, but they would never conquer him.

IDA MILGROM, WHOSE SON had always kept her at arm's length from his emigration activities, attempted frantically to gain access to Tolya. But just as Anatoly had been hermetically sealed off from the world outside, so were those who waited for news of him denied any information. There was no word of his whereabouts, the charges being prepared against him, his condition, or whether he was in fact still alive.

Shortly after his arrest, his mother visited KGB headquarters in an attempt to gain some information, anything to reassure her that Anatoly was all right. She met a KGB colonel who had a nice voice and a kind smile. He told the elderly woman, in a regretful tone, that he knew nothing about her son, but he would certainly make inquiries. When Ida, relieved, reported the conversation to Dina Beilina, the activist was skeptical. The next time Ida went to KGB headquarters, Beilina accompanied her.

The KGB colonel came out to greet them, smiling affably. Dina froze. She knew the man. "He was my interrogator when I was charged with spying for Israel," she told Ida, staring daggers at the man. "Do you still lament the passing of Stalin? Do you still wish to knock my teeth out?"

"Did you really say such a thing to this woman?" Ida demanded, shocked.

The colonel's genial smile vanished. The women were dismissed. As they left the KGB headquarters, Beilina murmured to Ida, "That man is Anatoly's interrogator." She was only partially right. He was one of eighteen.

Ida Milgrom did not learn anything about her son's

condition and fate, but she did learn a valuable lesson about dealing with the KGB. After that initial encounter she would suspect everything they said and did.

The first priority for Anatoly's friends was to determine what charges were being prepared so that a lawyer could be retained. The next task was to inform emigration-movement supporters abroad about his plight.

For two weeks after his arrest, there was no word about Anatoly. No potential witnesses were summoned for interrogation. Then, on March 30, one of the officers conducting the investigation had some news for Ida Milgrom. Her son, the official told her, had committed "especially dangerous crimes against the state."

It was now clear to the activists that Anatoly was to be the sacrificial lamb in an attempt to crush the Jewish emigration movement. The plan was to break him and use his anticipated renunciation of the movement to pull in the other activist leaders. The arrest could also be used against the dissidents represented by the Helsinki Watch Group. According to Lipavsky's article, it was Professor Lerner who was the arch-villain and mastermind of a vast espionage network. But he hadn't been arrested, probably because he was an elderly man with a name recognized around the world. Lipavsky, his doctor, had last checked Lerner on the day before the article was published, and he knew that Lerner probably could not withstand the rigors of arrest, long interrogation, and trial. Shcharansky's name was little known in the West, yet he was connected with everybody the KGB wanted to reach, and they could do so without a storm of publicity. And in fact, the news of Shcharansky's arrest was buried in the inside pages of the *New York Times*. He was believed to be in the second rank of refuseniks. The KGB had badly miscalculated: Anatoly would not be broken, and they would not be able to assemble their case against the others.

A week after Anatoly's arrest, his mother and his ailing father were summoned to Moscow to be interrogated. They were not told what the charges were against Anatoly. Their apartment in Istra was searched while they were away.

Over a month later, on April 30, Ida Milgrom was presented with a clue as to what awaited her son. A note from Procurator Ilyukhin, who was supervising the KGB investigation of Shcharansky, informed her that Anatoly was to be charged under Article 64A of the Soviet Criminal Code. Soviet law obliged such notification to families of detainees facing court action. The precise nature of the charge was unclear. The article encompasses a grab-bag of offenses: attempting to leave the Soviet Union illegally, refusing to return to the Soviet Union, attempting to overthrow the government, giving aid to an enemy country, treason. It was clear that Anatoly faced a possible death sentence.

On May 10, the investigation went into high gear: Mark Azbel, a leading member of the emigration movement, was the first to be summoned to Lefortovo for interrogation. The following day, Dr. Victor Brailovsky was summoned, and the day after came the turn of physicist Benjamin Fain. To their surprise, the main line of questioning was not about Anatoly himself, but rather about the emigration movement; more specifically, about a formal, defined organization to which the KGB interrogators gave the name "Aliya" ("ascension," the Hebrew word for immigration to Israel). If they could establish the existence of a formal organization, all members of the organization would then be implicated in Shcharansky's "crimes." The three were thus being invited to be the instruments of an investigation that would condemn them all.

Of course, questions about Anatoly did come up: did he write this document, or translate that material? But they were peripheral to the main point the KGB was attempting to establish: that the Jewish emigration movement was, in fact, a formal, structured organization, with office holders and a membership. The three men—all eminent professors of science—were told that if they cooperated in the investigation, they would be permitted to emigrate to Israel; if not, they would be charged and jailed. All three were subjected to two days of intensive interrogation, and at the end of the ordeal, each independently refused to cooperate. All were let go.

On May 6, Sanya Lipavsky resurfaced briefly at an *Izvestia* press conference to reiterate the charges in his March open letter. Then, eleven days later, a second smear article by a "former refusenik" appeared in the Soviet press, this one by Leonid Tsypin, a twenty-six-year-old man with a serious drinking problem who had told the activists that he first applied for an exit visa in 1972. Unlike Lipavsky, however, Tsypin had aroused their suspicions. On one occasion in 1976, he drank too much vodka and boasted openly to a young woman that he was a KGB agent: contact between the movement and Tsypin ceased instantly. But there was clearly some mileage to be extracted from his former association with the movement. The Tsypin article, which appeared in a Moscow evening newspaper, accused the Jewish "provocateurs and adventurists" not only of being unscrupulous and lazy, but also of receiving large sums of money from the West. As for Shcharansky, he had been "paid by Zionist sources abroad" to distribute false information about anti-Semitism in the Soviet Union and had participated in "secret meetings" with U.S. senators and congressmen who visited Moscow.

That same day, some of Anatoly's friends—twenty-one of the leading Jewish activists—sent a message to the West saying that although the Soviet-Jewish problem stood apart and had its own specific aspects, it was inexorably linked to the dissident movement. "We cannot imagine these two movements to be absolutely separated." The leaders of the human rights movement also gave expression to their belief in the importance of the link between the Jewish activists and the dissidents. Sakharov, Elena Bonner, and their comrades called on people in the West to do everything possible for Anatoly, whom they described as a man "filled with benevolence and concern for others. . . . Anatoly gave all his strength and all of his ability to helping other people. He demanded not only the right of emigration—he insisted on the fundamental natural human rights. He helped all who are suffering, including the persecuted members of the religious communities of Baptists and Pentecostalists."

On June 11 Robert Toth, the *Los Angeles Times* correspondent in Moscow who had maintained a close relationship with Anatoly, was about to leave the Soviet Union at the end of his three-year tour when he received a call from Valery Petukhov, a parapsychologist and "dissident" he had met through refusenik and dissident circles. He had a paper about parapsychology that might interest Toth, Petukhov said; would the journalist care to see it? Toth agreed to a rendezvous.

They met in a Moscow street. As Petukhov handed over the papers, plainclothes policemen suddenly materialized all around them; they seized Toth and took him away.

The American embassy was advised that Toth was suspected of "engaging in activities incompatible with the status of foreign journalists in the USSR, that is, collection of
secret information of a political and military character."
Therefore, he would be subjected to questioning by security
agencies and "his departure from Moscow was not desired."
This last ominous reference meant that Toth's exit visa was
canceled; he would not be permitted to leave. This was a
form of arrest, and the entire statement sounded like a pre-
cursor to a charge of espionage.

Toth was summoned three times for questioning at Lefortovo, on June 11, 14, and 15. His KGB interrogator
warned him that under Soviet law, he was required to answer all questions put to him. The interrogator displayed
intense interest in Toth's association with Moscow scientists, writers, dissidents, activists, and refuseniks. In particular, they wanted to establish Shcharansky's role in setting
up meetings with such people. At the end of each interrogation, Toth was presented with a protocol—the record of
the investigation—and ordered to sign it. Twice, the protocol was in Russian, which Toth did not understand. The
journalist objected, but the KGB major in charge of his interrogation told him that refusal to sign would be seen as a
denial of the truth of his own statements, which was tanta-
mount to perjury. Under Soviet law, the major said, he had
no right to refuse. Toth understood that unless he signed he
would not be allowed to leave the USSR. He signed—adding
to each protocol a statement that he did so under duress.
Within days, he and his family were allowed to leave the
Soviet Union. Petukhov, who had entrapped him, was
awarded a medal for exemplary work shortly afterward.

Meanwhile, Ida Milgrom was trying anxiously to engage a lawyer for Anatoly's defense. She asked to see her son in order to discuss the matter with him, but was refused. On June 15, she approached a Moscow lawyer, Dina Kaminskaya, and asked her to take the case. Kaminskaya, who had heard of Anatoly but never met him, agreed. But there was a problem: she did not possess a *dopusk*. This clearance, issued by the Presidium of the Collegium of Advocates through the KGB, was the essential prerequisite for any lawyer representing a client charged with security-related matters. Seven years earlier, Kaminskaya had undertaken the defense of a dissident in Tashkent. Because she asserted her client's innocence, the judge had recommended that she be disbarred and prevented from practicing on political grounds. The Moscow collegium did not take away her license, but they did cancel her *dopusk*, thus removing her from the list of "approved" lawyers.

Ida Milgrom wrote to the Moscow Collegium of Advocates requesting clearance to hire Kaminskaya. This was turned down two days later, and Kaminskaya was required to hand over all her cases. On June 28, less than two weeks after she had agreed to take the case, the Presidium of the Collegium of Advocates announced that she had been expelled from the collegium and barred from practicing law. It was the end of a thirty-seven-year career for Kaminskaya. But her problems were not over yet: on November 6, she and her husband, neither of whom had ever contemplated emigration, were forced to leave the Soviet Union.

The search for a defense counsel went on. Armed with a list of the best candidates, which she had obtained from Sofia Kalistratova and others, Ida, her son Leonid, and Dina Beilina started knocking on doors. Of the thirty lawyers they approached, most had learned of the Kaminskaya affair and refused to touch the case. Not one was prepared to argue his innocence. One lawyer said quite openly that because *Izvestia* had already pronounced Shcharansky guilty, "to defend him would imply that I share the same political opinions, and I will lose my job." Other lawyers refused to participate in a show trial, to lend "an illusion of justice" to the proceedings.

Despairing of finding a Soviet lawyer, Anatoly's family and friends decided to look abroad. There was no shortage of eminent jurists in the West who were prepared to travel to Moscow to attempt to persuade the collegium to allow them to appear: Irwin Kotler from Canada, Isadore Fish from England, Baruch Caine from Philadelphia, Herbert Kronish from New York, Roland Rappaport and Maitre Jacoby from France were among the volunteers. All were rejected by the Soviet authorities.

The bitter irony was now becoming fully apparent: Anatoly's only real possibility of counsel was for the court to ask the collegium to provide a lawyer; and the collegium would only appoint a lawyer on the recommendation of the KGB. Thus, the KGB would provide not only counsel for the prosecution but also counsel for the defense. It was like a convoluted scene out of Kafka's *The Trial*, with devious lawyers offering to "help" the defendant. "Someone must have been telling lies about Joseph K., for without his having done anything wrong, he was arrested one fine morning."

The KGB investigation went into high gear. Potential witnesses were being pulled into Lefortovo every day. Early in the morning of July 4, Lev Ulanovsky was hustled out of his apartment and into a black Volga for the drive to KGB headquarters, where he was subjected to a rigorous interrogation in which he was pushed around. It seemed odd to him that the KGB should feel the need to resort to strong-arm tactics—simply being in Lefortovo itself was frightening enough. But he had prepared himself long before for just this moment and was well versed on his legal rights as a witness. He refused to answer questions relating to his friend on the ground that they would not provide details of the charges against Anatoly.

By the end of his second day of interrogation, Ulanovsky had had enough. He demanded his legal right to use an interpreter from Russian into his "native language—Hebrew." He was not summoned for further interrogations.

Refusenik Leonid Shabashov, among many others, was told by one of the Shcharansky interrogators, "Your departure for Israel depends on your cooperation with this investigation." Dina Beilina, Galina Kremen, and others were informed by their interrogator that Anatoly was to blame for the Jackson-Vanik Amendment linking U.S. trade to the emigration of Soviet Jews. Abe Stolyar, who was stopped on his way to the airport and deprived of his emigration visa, was interrogated and threatened. Ilya Tsitovsky refused to testify because he had no information about the case. Vladimir Lazaris was told: "Today you are a witness, but soon you'll be a defendant."

The investigation had spread to twenty cities and towns throughout the Soviet Union. Potential witnesses were being summoned to their local KGB headquarters in Dushanbe, Saratov, Kaliningrad, and Krasnodar; in Minsk, Vinnitsa, Kharkov, Odessa, and Vilnius; in Riga, Leningrad, Kiev, and Tula. In Kaunus, Lithuania the two isolated refuseniks who were pulled in for interrogation had never met Anatoly.

In distant Siberia, dentist Mark Nashpitz was roused

from the dull routine of his exile to travel under KGB guard to the regional town of Chita. There, he was questioned for five days about Anatoly.

"We know he's your best friend," said the interrogator. "He spent more than ten hours on planes flying out to see you—only the closest of friends would do that." The KGB official wanted testimony about Anatoly's contacts with Westerners.

When Nashpitz persisted in denying knowledge about any illegal activities, they called him a liar and threatened him with punishment. "Excuse me," said Nashpitz. "I'm already under sentence. What more are you going to do to me?"

The questions were generally the same: Do you know Shcharansky? Who introduced you, where, and when? What are his financial resources? Did he receive postal orders, money orders, gifts, currency? What is the nature of his friendships? What is the state of his mental health? What do you know of his criminal activities? What foreigners did he meet? Did he introduce you to foreigners, "useful" people?

There were questions about the Helsinki Watch Group and Shcharansky's role as one of the representatives of the Jewish movement, about how information was transmitted from various Soviet cities to Moscow and then abroad, about meetings with American politicians in Moscow, about collective letters and statements, about press conferences and demonstrations. The refuseniks recognized it as a gigantic fishing expedition. The KGB believed that with the sort of rewards and punishments they had to offer, compliant witnesses would fall into their hands like ripe fruit. They were wrong. Over two hundred refuseniks were interrogated by the KGB, but not one agreed to give false evidence against

Anatoly. Nor, indeed, were they able to provide material that could be used: there simply was nothing that would substantiate the KGB's charges.

Even though Shcharansky was less well known in the West than Lerner, Slepak, or others, his detention, once the charges were made public, created an uproar. Demonstrations were held throughout the free world: in the United States and Canada, in Europe, Israel, and Australia. On June 13, 1977 President Jimmy Carter broke with the longstanding United States tradition of silence in cases involving espionage. He said that he had inquired deeply within the State Department and the Central Intelligence Agency "as to whether or not Mr. Shcharansky had any known relationship . . . with the CIA. The answer is no." In making this unprecedented declaration, Carter was committing the reputation of the presidency.

From Philadelphia, Dean Peter J. Liacouras of the Temple University School of Law sent President Leonid Brezhnev a resolution signed by the deans of over seventy law schools in the United States and by more than a hundred other U.S. law professors and administrators, deploring the action against Shcharansky.

In the Soviet Union, too, voices of indignation continued to be heard: in June 1977, twelve alumni of the Moscow Institute of Physics and Technology, including Lev Ulanovsky, signed a letter to "professors, lecturers, and students throughout the world" calling on them to "use your connections and influence in order to prevent the repetition in our times of the nightmare of the Dreyfus case." They saw a direct parallel between what was being done to Anatoly and the framing of another Jew by anti-Semitic army and government officials in France at the turn of the century. Dreyfus, innocent of the charge that he was a spy for the Germans, spent years on Devil's Island. His retrial, as Anatoly noted later at his own trial, was the catalyst for the modern Zionist movement.

In July, eighteen refuseniks from Minsk wrote to President Brezhnev expressing alarm at the persecution of Shcharansky. In Jewish history, they wrote, there were other examples of such trials: the Dreyfus affair, the Beilis case, the Doctors' Plot. In each instance, the truth ultimately emerged; but not before an upsurge in anti-Semitism had been provoked.

On November 22, Anatoly's brother addressed "A Complaint" to Soviet Procurator-general R. Rudenko. Only a few months earlier, Leonid had told a foreign correspondent that his father, Boris, "lived within the system" and that since Anatoly's arrest, he was afraid. Now he was writing the procurator-general to report that Boris Shcharansky would refuse on principle to appear for interrogation, as he regarded the case against his son as "biased and fabricated." Leonid himself had been summoned to an interrogation at Lefortovo Prison the previous day. He, too, had told the investigator that he would not be a witness, as he knew his brother to be innocent and the investigation biased. Nevertheless, he said, the investigator persisted "by deceit" to extract testimony from him. It was "intolerable and immoral" to attempt to set brother against brother, he told the procurator-general, and even worse to try to "falsify his testimony."

On December 15, 1977 Anatoly's mother was informed by the director of investigations at Lefortovo that her son's detention was being extended for a further six months. Again, she was refused permission to see her son.

In one strand of a whole web of lies, the chairman of the Moscow Collegium of Advocates informed American attorneys that Ida Milgrom did indeed visit her son and that they had agreed to the appointment of a lawyer by the collegium. Shortly thereafter, it was announced that the collegium had appointed Sylva Dubrovskaya to represent Anatoly. She was rejected by him at the start of the trial.

One year after Anatoly's incarceration, on March 16, 1978, his mother, for the first time since his arrest, received evidence that he was still alive. The authorities permitted her to read part of a statement he had made three months earlier. "Dear Mother!" he wrote. "I told the investigation authorities and I repeat here as well that the choice of my lawyer has been delegated by me to you and Natasha [Avital]. I rejected the lawyer appointed by the collegium. If you do not succeed in finding a lawyer according to your choice, I shall conduct my own defense." Again, Ida Milgrom petitioned the KGB to be allowed to consult with her son about his legal counsel; again she met with a contemptuous refusal.

That same month, Dina Beilina, Ida's guide and supporter, was summoned for interrogation. Beilina did not refuse to testify; she *insisted* on testifying, in order to demolish the KGB's fabricated case. She told the interrogators that if she was denied the opportunity of testifying in court, she would stand outside and give her testimony to the waiting reporters. Within weeks Beilina, her husband Yosef, and their daughter were on a plane to Israel. Seven years of waiting for a visa had ended, but their joy at being allowed to leave was clouded by the perilous situation of their young friend, for whom Israel was now a distant dream. In June 1978, just before the Soviets planned to try Shcharansky, two other leading activists and close friends of Anatoly were also re-moved from the scene. Vladimir Slepak and Ida Nudel were charged with "hooliganism," given five-year and four-year terms, respectively, and exiled to Siberia.

On July 7, 1978 the Soviet authorities abruptly an-nounced that the trial of Anatoly Shcharansky, on charges of "high treason in the form of espionage" and anti-Soviet agitation and propaganda, would open in Moscow in three days, on Monday, July 10. At the same time, it was an-nounced that the trial of Alexander Ginzburg, another founding member of the Helsinki Watch Group, would open on the same day in the town of Kaluga, 125 miles south of Moscow. Ginzburg was charged with anti-Soviet agitation and propaganda. Two months earlier, Soviet justice had al-ready dealt with the chairman of the Helsinki Watch Group, Professor Yuri Orlov: he had been sentenced to a total of twelve years in prison and exile. Slepak, who had been the second Jewish representative of the watch group, was al-ready in Siberia. Both the Jewish and the human rights movements had suffered terrible blows.

But only Anatoly was charged with a capital offense. If, as seems likely, the KGB chose Anatoly as the scapegoat because they believed that he would break easily and in-criminate others and that his arrest would not provoke the sort of outcry abroad as that of better-known refuseniks, then they had made a disastrous miscalculation.

In the West, the Shcharansky and Ginzburg cases, in the wake of Orlov's sentence, were being hailed as the most important dissident trials of the post-Stalin era. New strains were reported in relations between Washington and Mos-cow. For the next week, the Shcharansky trial was a top news item in the Western media.

When the trial opened it was immediately evident that it would be "open" only in the most limited sense of the word. The paint was still fresh on the new, six-foot-high fence surrounding the front of the courthouse. Barricades had been set up along all of the side streets, manned by police and militiamen wearing red armbands. Among all of Anatoly's relatives and friends, only his brother, Leonid, was permitted into the court. Attendance was by invitation only. No foreign observers, diplomats, or journalists were allowed to enter the courtroom. Not even Ida Milgrom was given a glimpse of her son. Although she had refused to give evidence at the trial, the KGB insisted it would call her as a prosecution witness. And according to Soviet court rules she could not, as a future witness, attend sessions of the trial before being called to the stand. Only one concession was made to the world media: the Soviet authorities arranged for a twice-daily briefing on the progress of the trial. In fact, though, the job of informing the world about the trial of Anatoly Shcharansky fell to his older brother, since the official briefers felt no compunction about fabricating testimony.

WHEN ANATOLY walked into Moscow's People's Court at 10:00 A.M. on Monday, July 10, his eye quickly found his brother Leonid. It was the first familiar face he had seen in sixteen months. He smiled and called out: "You've put on weight." Leonid shouted back: "Shalom from Avital." Then Tolya held up a small picture of Avital that he had kept with him throughout his detention. It was his salute of victory and defiance.

Leonid Shcharansky exerted all his powers of concentration to memorize his brother's words and relate them later to his mother and the estimated 150 people waiting outside. He was not allowed to take notes. All the other spectators in the court were government approved and brought in especially for the occasion.

Outside in the sultry midsummer heat an odd assortment of activists, dissidents, friends, sympathizers, journalists, and KGB agents waited. The air was thick with tension and excitement, mingled with the stench of rotten vegetables wafting over the crowd from a former church that had been converted into a grocery warehouse and the smell of resin from the newly built wooden fence. But the disquiet abated suddenly when a truck with a portrait of Stalin on the windshield lumbered past. The irony was not lost, and laughter spread through the crowd—today, it was pure theater both inside and outside the People's Court. A Russian nationalist who used a pseudonym borrowed from the head of Ivan the Terrible's secret police, was among the crowd. He told *New York Times* correspondent David Shipler, "We support the emigration movement. We think all Jews should leave Russia."

In the courtroom, the main charge against Anatoly was read out. He was accused of "having betrayed his motherland and deliberately engaged in activities detrimental to the state's independence and the military might of the USSR." It was alleged that between 1974 and 1977 he maintained regular contacts with representatives of foreign intelligence agencies, supplying them with information about the location and security systems of a number of defense enterprises. Specifically, said the prosecutor, he passed information to Western diplomats and to the "agent of a foreign military intelligence service"—a reference to Robert Toth of the *Los Angeles Times*. Another charge related to the assembling and disseminating of "slanderous" Helsinki Watch Group documents, which had formed the basis "for broadcasts by hostile radio stations" such as the Voice of America, Radio Free Europe/Radio Liberty, and the BBC. Among specific documents cited were Anatoly's reports on the Jews of Ilyinka village and on the use of conscription as a weapon to curb emigration.

Shcharansky was also accused of encouraging various organizations and governments to pressure the Soviet Union to change its domestic and foreign policies. It was alleged that the information he supplied was used against the Soviet Union by "reactionary circles of capitalist states." In particular, he was charged with endorsing Washington's decision to link its trade policy with the Soviet Union to Jewish emigration. He was also charged with holding "secret meetings" with an American history professor, Richard Pipes, at the Sovietskaya Hotel in Moscow, where he allegedly received instructions on how to carry out his propaganda and anti-Soviet activities. (In fact, the only time Anatoly met Pipes was at the July 1975 social gathering at Vitaly Rubin's apartment, when their brief conversation was monitored by KGB undercover agent Riabsky. As Pipes said later, "Out of this, Riabsky at the trial said that I had lunch with Shcharansky at a hotel and gave him information about how to subvert the Soviet system. It shows you what the whole thing rests on." Anatoly's meeting at the Sovietskaya Hotel was an open session with American congressmen, with the participation of many newspaper correspondents.)

At the outset, he rejected the court-appointed defense attorney, Sylva Dubrovskaya, and she was dismissed. Anatoly was greatly relieved. Only at this moment, when he was not compelled to have a lawyer and could speak for himself, did he know for sure that he wouldn't be executed. According to Soviet judicial law, the death sentence cannot be applied to anyone who has not been defended by a lawyer.

Shcharansky pleaded innocent to all the charges filed against him under Articles 64A and 70 of the Soviet Criminal Code, ranging from espionage to hostile activity to slander, and told the court he regarded the accusations as "absurd."

Anatoly submitted a forty-page list containing evidence he wished to introduce and witnesses he wanted to call. Judge P. P. Lukanov dismissed all but six of his applications, which made a mockery of Anatoly's right to defend himself. But though he knew the outcome of the trial was a foregone conclusion, Anatoly felt an inner strength, drawing inspiration from Jewish history. "The fact that there is a history of resistance always helps," he said later.

The second session, on Tuesday, July 11, was devoted mainly to Anatoly's relationship with Toth. Upon his return to the United States, Toth had denied in a series of sworn affidavits that he had ever worked as an intelligence agent; but these affidavits were not accepted by the court. According to the prosecution, Shcharansky had "repeatedly assisted him . . . in establishing on a conspiratorial basis contacts with bearers of secrets from among Soviet scientists and experts in various fields of knowledge."

The official account of the trial—issued to the foreign correspondents—said that Shcharansky helped arrange interviews for Toth while the latter was "worming out information that is not subject to publication in the open press." It mentioned specifically the Soviet space research program and classified information in the field of sociological research and parapsychology. Reference was also made to an article by Toth in which the journalist had used a list of refuseniks to show that the Soviets unjustly barred people who worked at ordinary jobs on the grounds that they knew state secrets. This article was, in fact, the focus of the Soviet charges of espionage. It had appeared in the *Los Angeles Times* on November 12, 1976 under the headline "Russ Indirectly Reveal 'State Secrets'; Clues in Denial of Jewish Visas." Some neutral observers felt that the headline was provocative and not reflective of the article Toth had written. Toth defended the original piece in an article that appeared in his newspaper on the second day of the trial in Moscow. He wrote that the "state secrets" article had been written from material collected over a period of at least a month. "Shcharansky and other Jewish activists provided the data—the names and former work places of some Jews refused exit visas on grounds that they possessed 'state secrets' as a result of their jobs."

Shcharansky had been among those named in the article, along with a group of refuseniks who had been denied visas on the grounds they possessed state secrets and who had attempted to show this was absurd. "There was nothing secret about any of it. . . . It had occurred to me after two years in Moscow that Jews from a strikingly wide range of vocations were being denied exit on secrecy grounds, from soccer players to scientists, from waiters to engineers . . . the capricious use of the 'state secrets' excuse to refuse an exit visa to a former worker in the Soviet Milk and Meat Institute, for example, seemed worth a story. Further, Shcharansky and others already had compiled long lists of refuseniks and had transmitted them to their supporters in the United States and Britain to elicit public support for their cause. The lists, which were compiled both inside the USSR and abroad by various Jewish organizations and which were well known to the KGB and showed that some of the same work places at which the refuseniks supposedly had received 'secret information' were officially classified as 'open,' or nonsecret, by Soviet officials. The Soviets labeled these institutions as open when they wanted to buy advanced technology equipment such as computers from West Europe and the United States."

Toth attested once again that Anatoly had not provided him with any secret information, "and even under Soviet rules of what is secret information—traffic statistics, salaries of athletes, or all information not officially released—there is no basis in my experience with him to support conviction for treason."

At the third session on Wednesday, a number of witnesses were paraded through the court, including one particularly bewildered man, identified only as Platanov from Leningrad, who, it transpired, was at the wrong address: he was to have given evidence at the Ginzburg trial in Kaluga. Then came the young alcoholic KGB-paid informer, Tsypin, who reaffirmed that Shcharansky was a "hooligan." He referred to U.S. Embassy officials Melvin Levitsky and Joseph Pressel as CIA agents who, he said, met with Anatoly in a café on Kutuzovsky Prospekt. Anatoly also read forbidden books, including provocative books in English.

Tsypin had never made much of an impression on anybody. But the next witness had a special presence. The "reformed" refusenik and American spy, Dr. Sanya Lipavsky, had surfaced for the first time in fourteen months, since his *Izvestia* press conference. Following the trial, he vanished again.

Lipavsky testified scornfully about how Anatoly had tried to sue the producers of the anti-Semitic TV documentary "Traders in Souls" because he "feared that the crowd would start to lynch Jews on the streets of Moscow since their faces [the Jewish movement leaders] were now familiar to Soviet citizens." His slander suit was itself a slander, Lipavsky said, and he had been justly charged under Article 70 for his attempt to bring the producers to court. Then the surgeon, looking Tolya straight in the eye, asked him: "How can we Soviet Jews who do not want to leave the USSR live here after what you have done?" The accused, he continued, was also involved in writing subversive, libelous letters to Jewish communities abroad. And of course, he had signed letters regarding the Jackson-Vanik Amendment. Anatoly was a spoiler: because of him the Americans had denied most-favored-nation trade status to the USSR, and the Soviet economy had been weakened.

Shcharansky: "Did you ever see me writing or signing these letters?"

Lipavsky: "No."

Shcharansky: "Then how can you testify about my connection with these documents?"

The judge disallowed the question. Anatoly later reminded the court that the Jackson-Vanik Amendment to the Soviet trade act was introduced in 1972, long before he had become involved in the Jewish movement or had applied to emigrate to Israel.

Lipavsky also alleged that Shcharansky's aim was to change the Soviet system and that Vitaly Rubin had given him espionage assignments. The doctor then threw in the names of two foreign correspondents who had been based in Moscow: George Krimsky of the Associated Press and

Peter Osnos of the *Washington Post*—Osnos and Alfred Friendly had been mentioned in Lipavsky's "J'Accuse" letter—intimating that they too were spies. He also testified at great length about the attempt to visit Ilyinka village and said that Toth had intended to join Anatoly, Slepak, and himself.

At the fourth session, on Wednesday, July 13, the prosecutor asked for a stiff term of fifteen years: three in prison and twelve in a special regime prison camp. Shcharansky, he said, deserved the harshest possible sentence, execution, but the prosecution was taking into account the fact that he was, at thirty, a young man. The espionage and hostile activity charges based on Article 64, and the anti-Soviet activity and slander charges based on Article 70, were recapitulated, after which Anatoly was permitted to address the court.

"I understand that to defend myself in a semiclosed trial like this is a hopeless case from the very beginning," he said, "all the more so since I was declared guilty by *Izvestia* a full year and a half before the trial took place, and even before the case was opened and the investigation begun.

"My social activities were transformed by the editors of this newspaper and by my accusers to antisocial deeds and antistate activities. My open efforts to produce information of a nonsecret character, available to all, were transformed into espionage. I have no doubt that this court will carry out the instructions given to it, and support the request of the prosecutor in the sentencing."

Then he described the birth of Zionism, portraying, in counterpoint to his own trial, that other infamous affair centered on an innocent Jew: "At the end of the last century, the world witnessed the disgraceful Dreyfus trial in France.

A spectator at that trial—which can better be described as a civil execution—was the assimilated Jew Theodor Herzl. After this, political Zionism was born." Implied in his reference to Dreyfus was an intimation that the "Shcharansky affair" could have a similar groundshaking effect on the Jews of the USSR.

"The history of the Jewish nation is distinguished by the fact that for two thousand years it has remained scattered, and therefore it is not surprising that it has been partly assimilated. . . . What is surprising is something else—that Jews have maintained themselves as a nation. In the 1960s, an emigration movement arose again. Seven or eight years have passed, and 150,000 people have left. What is that? A provocation by American special services? It is a natural, historical process. Now Jews are seeking not the path of assimilation, but of Judaization. That is the ground over which my activities passed at the end."

After describing the historic oppression of Jews in Russia and explaining their newfound affinity for the Jewish homeland, Anatoly concluded: "Our reborn state of Israel, in which we take such pride, will continue to flourish and be an example to the other nations of this earth. I am proud to be part of this movement of renaissance." He defended the Helsinki Watch Group documents that he had signed and which had been introduced as alleged evidence of his crimes. One of those public statements had condemned the Soviet use of psychiatric hospitals to persecute people for their political convictions. He related the case of one dissident, of whom it was written: "He suffers from the mania of reformism, requires further treatment." A refusenik was said to "suffer the mania of emigration, needs further treatment." Anatoly also addressed the court about his sources of information about conditions in Soviet prison camps: he had learned about the prison system from friends, relatives, and now, through personal experience.

The prosecutor had plunged into Jewish religious law to "prove" that the marriage of Anatoly and Avital was invalid. He introduced a document from Rabbi Yakov Fishman of Moscow's Great Synagogue, which cast doubt on whether Avital had performed the prenuptial ritual immersion in a *mikva* bath. Anatoly commented that "all this discussion is theater of the absurd, and I don't intend to participate in it."

On Friday, July 14, 1978, the last day of the trial, the defendant gave his final speech before the court pronounced its sentence. Anatoly had had sixteen months to prepare himself for the moment, and he'd had access to the rich library at Lefortovo, which is filled with rare volumes confiscated from intellectuals killed under Stalin. He had found inspiration for his speech in the Greek classics, from the speech by Socrates to the court that sentenced him to death. It was also important to him to emphasize the necessity for solidarity between the dissident and Jewish movements. He himself had seen that it was possible to fight for justice in general and for the Jewish people in particular.

"Five years ago, I requested permission to leave for Israel. Now I am farther from my dream than ever before. One would think that I must regret what has happened, but that is not so. I am happy that I lived honestly, at peace with my soul, never having violated my conscience, even when I was threatened with death. I am happy that I helped people. And I am proud that I knew and worked with such honest, brave, and courageous people as Sakharov, Orlov, and

Ginzburg, who are accused of carrying on the traditions of the Russian intelligentsia.

"I am fortunate to have witnessed the process of liberation of the Jews from the Soviet Union. I hope that the absurd accusation against me and against the entire Jewish emigration movement will not hinder the liberation of my people. My near ones and friends know how much I wanted to exchange my activity in the emigration movement for a life with my wife, Avital, in Israel.

"For more than two thousand years, the Jewish people, my people, have been dispersed. But wherever they are, wherever Jews are found, each year they have repeated, 'Next Year in Jerusalem.' Now, when I am further than ever from my people, from Avital, facing many arduous years of imprisonment, I say, turning to my people and my Avital: 'Next Year in Jerusalem!' And I turn to you, the court that is required to confirm my predetermined sentence—to you, I have nothing to say."

By the time the trial ended, Leonid felt drained, exhausted, "like a squeezed lemon." Outside the courthouse he repeated to the highly charged group the sentence of the court: three years in prison, ten years in a strict regime labor camp. It was five years more than the term given to Ginzburg, who had been sentenced the previous day. The spectators in the courtroom had applauded, Leonid said. Some shouted, "They've given him too little." Above the noise, Leonid had yelled to his brother, "The whole world is with you!" Anatoly raised his head as if to respond but was dragged away by uniformed guards.

Now, Leonid's voice broke as he repeated his brother's final address. His wife, Raya, steadied him. Dan Fisher, who had replaced Robert Toth as the *Los Angeles Times* correspondent in Moscow, felt that "a sense of history" accompanied Leonid that bleak day when he recited Anatoly's speech. It was clear to him that the eloquent address would be engraved forever in people's memories. Those who had been waiting outside did not need a cue: as a heavy summer rain beat down on the raised umbrellas, the strains of "Hatikvah"—The Hope—Israel's national anthem, filtered into the court.

Ida Milgrom was beside herself. She still had not been permitted to see her son. In a trembling voice, she read an open letter to President Carter: "All the difficult days of the trial, I have been standing in front of the iron barriers, in front of a thick wall of KGB men and militiamen, hoping to see my child, at least from far away. All these days, I have heard your sincere, authoritative voice in defense of innocent men. Would you accept, Mr. President, our deep, heartfelt gratitude?" Comforted by Andrei Sakharov, she watched as the olive green police van drove out of the compound, carrying her son to prison. "Shame on you, shame on you," she cried helplessly at the Soviet guards who barred her way. "Why wouldn't you let me see him?" She wept on the shoulder of the man who had contributed so much to making the Soviet Union a great power, and had won the Nobel Peace Prize for his pursuit of human rights. Sakharov held Tolya's old mother tightly, and screamed at the guards: "You are not people. Fascists. Fascists!" The crowd shouted, "Tolya! Tolya!"

Even before his arrest, Anatoly Shcharansky had been branded in the Soviet media as a traitor to the motherland, an enemy of the people, a hooligan, and a parasite. He was denied choice of legal counsel, the right to defend himself properly, call witnesses or submit documents in his own defense. He was an innocent man, victim of the controlled frenzy of an authoritarian state. His only crime, as Lydia Voronina told a U.S. congressional hearing in Washington shortly before the mock trial opened, was "to tell the truth—and to tell it in English."

AT THE MOMENT that sentence was passed on Anatoly, Avital was en route to the United States for a speaking tour arranged by the American Committee of Scientists for Shcharansky. She knew that by the time she landed, the show trial would be over and his fate sealed. Although his guilt was predetermined, she prayed for a miracle.

In choosing Anatoly as their scapegoat, the KGB had discounted his young wife. That was their miscalculation; but how could they have known? Every blow to Anatoly made Avital stronger; every separation brought them closer. When she closed her eyes, she felt that Tolya was beside her. They were, in a sense, on the same plane; and she was determined to accept the news that awaited her with the calmness and dignity that Anatoly himself would display.

Simcha Dinitz, the Israeli ambassador to the United States, was waiting to collect her at Dulles International Airport in Washington. In the car, he broke the news. "Anatoly spoke brilliantly," he said, trying to comfort her. "He really is a hero."

Before entering the room where a news conference had been called, Avital phoned her brother. Michael repeated Anatoly's final words and reaffirmed that the sentence was thirteen years. "We knew this was coming," he said.

"But in thirteen years I'll be too old to have children!" Avital cried.

"Calm yourself," Michael said. "This is not the end. Nothing will stop us until Tolya is free."

She had to steel herself, as she knew her husband had done. A few minutes later, Avital entered the packed room to face the press. Dry-eyed and composed, she stepped up to the podium, and began to speak. Michael was right. It was not the end. It was the beginning of a new, unrelenting struggle.

5

On Captivity
and Freedom

When the czars built the massive prison of Vladimir one hundred miles east of Moscow along the Volga River, the windows were four times wider than they came to be under the Communists, who also added metal shutters that cut off almost all the natural light. Vladimir Ilyich Lenin had been imprisoned at Vladimir in cell 193, on the fifth floor. Following the revolution and the death of the Bolshevik leader, his cell was preserved as a relic. Now, in contrast to the gloomy rusted shields on all the other windows, the light of day flashes from the unoccupied cell's squeaky-clean panes.

A few months after Hillel Butman was transferred from a labor camp in the Urals back to Vladimir—the "Mansion," as it is called in the prison circuit—the half-starved prisoner was sitting on his bed thinking about food when he heard a voice call, "Butman, Butman. Get up to the window."

The cry came from outside, apparently from the occupant of the cell directly above his, calling through his shuttered window. The muffled shout was intended to be heard by Butman but not by the guards prowling the corridors. Butman made no move. By chance, he believed he was the only political prisoner and probably the only Jew in the bloc at that time, and he had no wish to strike up an acquaintance with any of the criminal convicts. He had come to know them all too well at the labor camp where he had spent most of the previous eight years, after being sentenced in the 1970 Leningrad trial of would-be airplane hijackers. There was nothing romantic about the criminals. They were a loutish, bestial lot for the most part, and he was thankful that the prison regime had at last separated him completely from their presence.

"Butman. Do you hear me? Get up to the window."

The high window could be reached by standing on the bed, as the convict upstairs undoubtedly was doing. If the guard opened the peephole and saw him, he'd be thrown into the punishment cell. But the criminals were always looking for some excitement, such as forbidden contacts, to pass the time, even at the risk of severe punishment.

This was Butman's second stint in Vladimir, which, like Lefortovo in Moscow, is run by the KGB. Although Vladimir was still the main prison in the country for political prisoners, many of its current inhabitants were criminals.

Butman had been sent back to Vladimir from Camp Thirty-five in the Urals as punishment for participating in strikes against the labor camp's administration, which was notorious for the inhuman and illegal way inmates were treated. A second remand to Vladimir meant a harsher regimen than that accorded the rest of the prison's inmates. Butman was fed only fourteen ounces of bread and three ounces of herring at breakfast, a bowl of watery soup for lunch and thin gruel in the evening. Altogether, this came to 1,400 calories a day, compared to 2,200 for prisoners on an ordinary regimen.

Until a few days before, Butman had had a cell mate, an Armenian from the central Asian Soviet republic of Azerbaijan. The man had been given a six-year term for writing a letter to Communist leader Leonid Brezhnev in which he

compared the wages and conditions of Soviet workers un-
favorably to those of workers in the West. He had admitted
showing the letter to his sister, which made him guilty of
"conducting anti-Soviet propaganda." The Armenian was a
good soul, and when his punishment was eased with a slight
increase in food allowance, he shared part of his bounty
with a grateful Butman. But then they transferred him to
another cell, and the Zionist activist was temporarily alone.

"Butman, answer me. Shcharansky is here and wants
to communicate with you."

Butman was transfixed. In the labor camp, where new
arrivals regularly kept the inmates up to date on what was
happening outside, he had heard much about the courageous young man from Moscow, and he had read Dr. Sanya
Lipavsky's article in an issue of *Izvestia* snatched from the
cigarette smokers, who used newspapers to roll their tobacco. To have a kindred spirit in the same prison bloc was
to be restored to the human community.

Butman leaped on his bed and reached through the bars
to open the window as much as possible. Beyond the first
set of bars was another, and the iron shutter through which
only the sky could be seen. Nothing of the city of Vladimir
was visible.

"This is Butman," he shouted. "Where is Shcharansky?"

"Just a minute."

As Butman stared outward, an object cut across the
slashes of sky visible through the shutter and hung there.
The convict upstairs had dangled a weighted object on a
string. Butman would have to grasp for it and reel it in,
hoping that he himself would not be reeled in by the guard
fishing for erring prisoners at the peepholes.

Hopping off the bed, he took a page from the newspaper on the table in the center of the room and folded it thinly, bending back one end for a hook. He was able to push the paper rod through a broad slat in the shutter and haul in the line. Attached to the weight at the end was a note indicating the position of Shcharansky's cell—one flight up, two cells over.

In the thick-walled fortress of Vladimir the guiding principle of the authorities was to prevent prisoners from meeting outside their cell. Elaborate arrangements were made to keep prisoners from even seeing one another. They were allowed outside to exercise each day for thirty minutes to an hour, in tiny yards no bigger than the cells, though unroofed. Only the occupants of a single cell could share an exercise yard at any particular time. There was no common dining hall where prisoners might see each other; all inmates were fed in their cells. If they were led out into the corridor to the shower room or the primitive clinic, care was taken that no two prisoners were out at the same time. Prisoners lived out their sentence at Vladimir for years without ever seeing another prisoner except for their cell mate.

Nevertheless, in the world within walls, methods of surreptitious contact have been developed over the centuries. Ingenious means of communication were devised by prisoners for whom there was no more pressing need than to affirm their own humanity.

AFTER HIS SIXTEEN months of detention in Lefortovo Prison and the tension of his trial, Anatoly could regard his arrival at Vladimir with a measure of relief. The threat of death that the KGB had held up before him was now removed. It had not been easy for the ebullient Tolya to adjust to the prospect of imminent death, the idea that he would never again see his family and friends or reach the shores of the promised land. But confronted by the deep hatred in the eyes of his interrogators, he had forced himself to accept the possibility that the authorities might indeed execute him in order to frighten the others. His thirteen-year sentence meant the eradication of his most fruitful years, but at least it left life and hope. The clock was now running on his prison term, and with luck—and changes in the international climate—there was a chance of getting out before the time fixed by the court.

His cell mate was a young Ukrainian nationalist, a devout member of the Russian Orthodox faith who had been handed back by the Finnish authorites after escaping the country. Despite the deep-rooted anti-Semitism among many Ukrainians, the pair soon established a warm and trusting relationship. The Ukrainian was impressed by the diminutive Jew's cheerful disposition, so out of keeping with the gloom of their environment. Anatoly would hum Hebrew songs to himself; much of his time was spent writing letters and working out chess moves. At Vladimir, he could assume that the tiresome game of planting informers in the cell in order to gain evidence against prisoners was no longer considered worth the effort: he could accept the Ukrainian for what he said he was.

Anatoly was thrilled when he heard that a Zionist prisoner named Butman was in the bloc. He knew Butman's name well as one of the participants in the desperate Leningrad incident, which had been a turning point in the movement. For the first time since his arrest sixteen months earlier, he was close to another Zionist prisoner. The grapevine informed him that Butman was on the floor below. Given prison ingenuity, it might be possible to make contact and cheat the authorities of the spiritual isolation they meant to impose on him. It already eased his heart to know that a kindred spirit who shared his background and his aspirations was so near, only one floor away.

They were sharing one of the six buildings that made up the prison complex, the oldest of which dated to the eighteenth-century reign of Catherine the Great. In the years following the Bolshevik revolution, the buildings had been modernized with the installation of toilets in most of the cells. Some even had sinks. The cells accommodated between two and ten prisoners, but two to a cell was the norm. The rough cement walls were damp and did not encourage graffiti. The heating system was totally inadequate, and the prison officials used cold as a punishment, with the heat often being turned off entirely at the whim of the warders. Even in summer it was cold in some cells. The cells were lit glaringly throughout the night, as in all Soviet prisons, and the inmates were forbidden to cover their faces when they slept.

As Anatoly sat in his cell one day, there was a familiar clatter and a small section in the middle of the door fell inward to form a shelf. "Let's have your bowls," said a disembodied voice outside. The food distributor, a criminal convict, was making his thrice-daily rounds. Accompanying him was the guard whose task it was to ensure that nothing but food passed through the door. Anatoly took his metal bowl off the cell table and held it out. His hand touched that of the convict, and Anatoly felt something being slipped up his sleeve. When the trap door had been pulled shut again, he turned his back to the peephole and slowly eased the object out. To his amazement and delight, it was a note in Hebrew. Anatoly laughed as he read greetings from Butman, welcoming him to his new home and asking for news from the outside.

A prison veteran, Butman had mastered the system of survival and communication within the walls. He had long since earned the grudging respect of the food distributor by rigging a scale—from a pencil, an empty toothpaste tube, and string—in order to weigh the bread and herring he was receiving. Until then, the trustee had been shorting him in order to give more rations to his friends in the criminal cells, and also shortchanging him on soup, ladling only a watery substance off the top. Since Butman had made an honest man out of him with his implicit threat of going to the prison authorities with "documented" proof of being given less than the regulations called for, the convict was dipping the ladle to the bottom of his pot where the potatoes were. The vegetables were usually dark castoffs from army bases, but at least they provided nourishment.

To obtain the distributor's services as a mailman, Butman paid with a three-dimensional postcard. A number of such cards had been sent him by his wife, who had already reached Israel, in the knowledge that they served as a common currency inside the prison. By peering through the opening, Butman could see that the guard was standing a few yards away, not paying close attention. He slipped the note to Shcharansky up the food distributor's sleeve and whispered its forwarding address. The convict responded with an almost imperceptible nod.

He wrote in Hebrew both as a measure of identification and in the admittedly thin hope of avoiding KGB monitoring. One assumed that functionaries like the food distributor played a double game, accepting payoffs from prisoners for illicit services while reporting to the KGB as well. In such cases, a KGB man would probably peruse the note being passed and let it go in the hope of finding something more incriminating later on. On the top of his note, Butman had written the day and hour so that Anatoly could check it against the time received. The prison authorities would have to obtain the services of a translator, but they could make a copy of the note and let it pass while awaiting its translation. It was, in short, wise to assume that big brother was watching and to write nothing incriminating.

Although Anatoly was new to the game, he understood the rules immediately. In informing Butman of what was happening in the movement, he wrote nothing that wasn't generally known, since he was aware that the note would probably pass through a KGB filter. His first note to Butman, also in Hebrew, responded warmly to his greeting and offered a list of subjects he was ready to expound on, depending on Butman's interests. This included an updated Who's Who of the Zionist movement in Moscow and elsewhere in the Soviet Union and an account of the various international organizations that had begun to work on behalf of Soviet Jewry since Butman's internment eight years before.

Butman smiled at the multiple-choice list and recognized that he was dealing with a rich and orderly mind. In the ensuing correspondence, Anatoly informed Butman about the activists of the emigration movement, the demonstrations and sit-in strikes, the publicity in the Western press and the contact with the outside world provided by numerous concerned visitors. They were now at the center of world interest, and Butman could see how the Jews of Moscow had put them there. Anatoly told of the price as well: the tightening grip of the KGB, the numerous fifteen-day deten-

The Moscow Synagogue on Arkhipova Street, where it all began.
David Frishberg, Jerusalem Post

Anatoly Shcharansky in 1976, flanked by refuseniks
Vladimir Slepak on left, Yosef Beilin on right. *Enid Wurtman*

Anatoly with Elena Bonner and Andrei Sakharov. *Enid Wurtman*

Moscow refuseniks celebrate Israel's Independence Day. Anatoly dancing in right foreground. The celebrants were surrounded by 150 KGB men, who arrested and later released several participants. *Rabbi Joseph Weinstein*

First day of hunger strike by seven refusenik scientists in June 1973. FROM LEFT, BACK: Dan Roginsky, Alexander Voronel, Mark Azbel, Victor Brailovsky. FROM LEFT, FRONT: Alexander Lunts, Anatoly Libgober, Moshe Gitterman. *Alexander Lunts*

FROM LEFT: Yosef Beilin, Sanya Lipavsky, Anatoly Shcharansky. *Union of Councils for Soviet Jews*

Dr. Sanya Lipavsky.

Avital Shcharansky.

Avital with Joan Baez at a rally at the University of California in Berkeley, July 1978. *UPI/Bettmann Newsphotos*

A gathering of friends. BACK ROW, FROM LEFT: Vladimir Slepak,
Lev Ovsischev, Alexander Druk, Yosef Beilin, Dina Beilina,
Dr. Alexander Lerner. FRONT ROW, FROM LEFT: Dr. Vitaly
Rubin, Anatoly, Ida Nudel. *Union of Councils for Soviet Jews*

Anatoly in his role as spokesman, with Ida Nudel and
Dina Beilina, May 1976. *Union of Councils for Soviet Jews*

Ida Milgrom, Anatoly's mother. *Union of Councils for Soviet Jews*

Opposite the Soviet Embassy in Washington, Avital celebrates
Anatoly's 30th birthday. To her right is Irene Manekofsky, to
her left are Representatives Newton Steers (R-MD) and
Millicent Fenwick (R-NJ). Cake is black bread and
potatoes. *Union of Councils for Soviet Jews*

Father Robert Drinan, Chairman of
the International Committee for the
Release of Anatoly Shcharansky.
Union of Councils for Soviet Jews

Avital in press conference in Dulles International
Airport, minutes after learning of Anatoly's
sentence. *UPI/Bettmann Newsphotos*

Children's protest in Washington, D.C., on behalf of Soviet
refuseniks. *Union of Councils for Soviet Jews*

Avital speaks to the press.
Union of Councils for Soviet Jews

Storefront in England sponsored by the Women's
Campaign for Soviet Jewry.
Union of Councils for Soviet Jews

Avital, after her religious renaissance. *Union of Councils for Soviet Jews*

Avital's last vigil at the Soviet Embassy in Washington in November 1985. To her right is Representative Ben Gilman. *Union of Councils for Soviet Jews*

Avital gestures as she speaks to West German Foreign Minister Hans-Deitrich Genscher prior to a session of the EEC Foreign Ministers meeting. *UPI/Bettmann Newsphotos*

President Reagan and Vice President Bush receive Avital and Yosef Mendelevich in the Oval Office, May 28, 1981. *UPI/Bettmann Newsphotos*

A few small steps: Anatoly, accompanied by U.S. Ambassador Richard Burt, crosses the Glienicke Bridge to freedom. Jerusalem Post

Holding hands, Anatoly and Avital step off the jet that brought them home to Israel. At right is Israeli Prime Minister Shimon Peres. *Reuters/Bettmann Newsphotos*

Anatoly and Avital at airport reception. *André Bruttman*

Anatoly and Avital at Jerusalem Hilton press conference.
AFP/Sven Nackstrand

Rabbi Weiss embraces Anatoly upon his arrival in New York.
New York Daily News

Mayor Ed Koch welcomes Anatoly during Solidarity Sunday
Rally before a crowd of 300,000. *UPI/Bettmann Newsphotos*

A warm welcome from President Reagan in the White House.
Official White House photo

Flashbacks . . .

1978: Avital thanks actor Charlton Heston
prior to "Free Shcharansky" rally. Present are
Los Angeles mayor Tom Bradley and former
California governor Jerry Brown.
UPI/Bettmann Newsphotos

1985: Hearing of the House Foreign Affairs Committee. LEFT
TO RIGHT: Rep. Jack Kemp (R-NY), Avital, Rep. Steny Hoyer
(D-MD), and Rep. Wyche Fowler (D-GA).
Union of Councils for Soviet Jews

tions, the five-year exile in Siberia of Nashpitz and Tsitlyonok.

For the first time Butman learned of the organizations
created in the West to help them, such as the Union of
Councils for Soviet Jewry and the National Conference for
Soviet Jewry. Anatoly explained the differences between them
and who their leaders were. The notes coming out of the
sleeve of the food distributor as the days passed were long
and detailed, as Anatoly's didactic and analytical talents,
dormant for so many months, were at last given scope for
expression before an audience hungry for information—even
an audience of one.

The audience doubled in size after a few weeks when
Butman was joined by Yosef Mendelevich, an Orthodox Jew
who had also participated in the Leningrad trial. Mendelevich had been sent to Vladimir from labor camp as punishment for his insistence on observing the Sabbath and Jewish
holidays. Also joining them in the cell was an Armenian nationalist who had burned a portrait of Lenin adorning a
building in the main square of Yerevan, the capital of Soviet
Armenia. This affront to "our dear Vladimir Ilyich," as Lenin
was commonly referred to, cost the Armenian seven years
imprisonment. Butman and Mendelevich accepted him as
one of the family.

In September 1978, communications were severed when,
for reasons never made clear to them, Butman and his two
cell mates were transferred to another building in Vladimir.
Anatoly found himself alone except for his Ukrainian cell
mate, the food trustee proffering nothing more from then
on than dark bread and thin gruel. Two months later, however, all political prisoners in Vladimir were suddenly notified that they would be moving to another prison. Even

though the Moscow Olympics were over eighteen months away, the authorities were already taking precautions. They expected numerous journalists to come many months ahead of the event to write travelogues and other articles and did not want to risk their being brought to Vladimir by relatives of prisoners seeking publicity. The city was close to Moscow, and foreign visitors required no special travel permit. Even without seeing the prisoners, the journalists could describe the town and its prison. The Soviet Union was not seeking that kind of travel article. It would be better if the politicals, embarrassing symbols of dissent, were shifted out of reach and, it was hoped, out of mind long before the Olympics.

The men were taken out to the prison train by cell groupings and placed in cages. Here at last the long and painstaking efforts of the prison authorities to keep the inmates from seeing one another gave way. Although the cages were walled on the sides, their fronts consisted of bars and wire mesh. Shouting "Shcharansky!" through the bars, Butman and Mendelevich heard a response down the corridor. They estimated that he was five or six cages away from them. Regulations required that the prisoners be taken at least once a day to the toilet, which was located at the front of the car. Since Butman, Mendelevich, and the Armenian were in a cage at the front, they would be able to see all the prisoners as they passed.

The parade of dissidents and nationalists went on throughout the day, but none responded with more than a curious look to the hissed calls of "Shcharansky?" Anatoly had in fact been taken out the rear of the car to the toilet in the guards' car. The authorities were determined that his stubborn spirit should not be encouraged by any contact with fellow Zionists.

When the train halted on the second day, the prisoners found a convoy of familiar police vans, Black Marias, awaiting them. They were hustled aboard and driven for seven hours across the vast Tatar steppes. At one point, the vehicles were driven onto rafts to cross the Kama River, a tributary of the Volga. When the convoy finally halted, the men found themselves inside the walls of a low, fortresslike structure. "Welcome to Chistopol," said a guard.

When the czars built the Chistopol prison in the eighteenth century following the Pugachev army uprising, it was a solitary building in the midst of the desert, five hundred miles east of Moscow. A small town that had grown up around it did little to mitigate the prison's isolation in the Tatar Republic.

The train ride had given Butman and Mendelevich the chance to learn that only twenty of the political prisoners, including themselves and Shcharansky, shared the same regimen. Regulations stated that only prisoners with the same regimen could share a cell; they also forbade leaving a prisoner alone in a cell for more than a few days unless he was undergoing special punishment in solitary. It occurred to Butman and Mendelevich that if the other prisoners refused to share a cell with Anatoly, the prison authorities might have to put him in with them.

The idea was passed on to the others in the wing of Chistopol in which they were concentrated, and all agreed. Anatoly's Ukrainian cell mate started a noisy mock fight with him; when guards burst into the cell to separate them, the Ukrainian insisted on having a different cell from the "dirty

Jew." When he refused to relent in his demands, the prison authorities decided not to return him to Shcharansky's cell for fear that one might be injured, to the displeasure of Moscow authorities. The Ukrainian was thrown into a punishment cell for fifteen days for his obduracy. Upon his release he was placed in the cell with the two other Jews. The prison authorities undoubtedly viewed this as an appropriate punishment for the crime; the Ukrainian, however, was delighted with his new cell mates, and they with him.

For the first time, Butman and Mendelevich learned from him that Anatoly was a very short person and balding. The description totally surprised them. The Ukrainian also said that Shcharansky was not at all depressed by his circumstances, that he believed he had been true to himself. "He feels that he's done what he had to do and is now simply paying the tax." Shcharansky did not have two personalities—a normal "outside" personality and a closed-up prison personality. He was whole with himself, said the Ukrainian. He was also good company, with a lively sense of humor.

The other political prisoners refused to be put in with Anatoly even though some were placed in punishment cells as a result—an expression of the solidarity existing among the politicals despite their championship of widely dissimilar causes. Anatoly waited hopefully in his cell for the appearance of the two other Jews. The KGB authorities, however, were intent on preventing this from happening. Determined that Anatoly remain isolated from contacts with fellow Zionists, they instructed that a prisoner with a different punishment regimen—someone not involved in the plot—be put in with him, even though this violated standing prison regulations.

But Anatoly soon discovered that his cell was next door to the one occupied by Butman and Mendelevich. In the context of prison life, this was almost like sharing a common hearth. By banging on the wall, they would alert each other to the initiation of communications. The "receiver" would place the mouth of a cup against the section of the wall where the banging had been heard and put his ear to the base. The "broadcaster" would press the base of his cup against the wall on the other side and shout into the mouth. The resultant sound was extremely faint but could generally be made out.

Later, they discovered other means of communication. Once every ten days, the prisoners were taken to the shower room. Anatoly began exchanging messages with his two compatriots by inserting notes in bars of soap affixed to the bottom of the shower-room bench. After a few weeks, however, the guards discovered one of Anatoly's notes, and he was thrown into solitary for several days.

But oppression breeds ingenuity; and a much more sophisticated communication system was soon devised. Each cell contained a toilet that was linked horizontally to a vertical collection pipe. The pipe ran through the thick connecting wall on its way from the top floor of the prison to the basement. The water in the toilet bowl could be removed by absorbing it with a rag, which was wrung out into a pail, until the bowl was dry. When this was done in the adjoining cells, there was a direct air link between them. On their first try, Anatoly and the others were astonished at how well they could hear one another.

Thereafter whenever anyone wished to communicate, he would rap on the wall and ask the person on the other side via the tin cup system to prepare for "telephone" contact. After the drying out process, the communicators had to put their heads almost inside the bowl to hear and be heard. During this time, one person in each cell stood before the peephole to block the view of the roving guard. The periods when the guard was being changed were relatively safe, since their minds were elsewhere and buzzers were being sounded in the corridors.

Butman would call Anatoly on the latrine whenever he received mail from his wife in Israel and would pass on her descriptions of the country. Anatoly awaited these letters almost as eagerly as Butman did. Since his arrest he had heard nothing at all from Avital. Her daily letters to him had all been confiscated.

He was not allowed to write to Avital, but could refer to her in his letters to his parents. He kept her picture before him. In September 1979, he wrote to congratulate his parents on their golden wedding anniversary. He wished them long life, a seventy-fifth wedding anniversary, and fantasized them playing with his and Avital's children: "In the next twenty-five years, you'll have plenty of time for educating Natulya's children and maybe grandchildren."

PRISON LIFE after the move to Chistopol had settled down into a routine. Anatoly was happy to have access once again to newspapers, even though most of the news had to be read between the lines. By working in their cells on netting material, the prisoners could earn up to three rubles a month, enough to pay for about four pounds of sugar from the prison store. They placed their orders with a trustee who made the rounds once a month. Anatoly kept in shape doing gymnastics and breathing exercises, reading, and simulating chess games. He likened his life to that of a likable robot in a book called *Artificial Intelligence*. The robot moves on his own by commands given in simple language, and his whole outer world consists of a series of rooms, doors, boxes, windows, and sources of light. But Anatoly constantly reaffirmed his existential belief that freedom can neither be given nor taken away, because man *is* freedom.

During the daily exercise period, Anatoly and his two Jewish neighbors were sometimes in adjoining courtyards. They exchanged shouts over the top of the wall. Once Butman stood on Mendelevich's shoulders in an attempt to see into the other courtyard, but the barbed-wire fence on top prevented this.

On Friday evenings, Butman and Mendelevich held improvised Sabbath services. They made candles from strings taken from sacking material and dipped in oil purchased from the prison store, lighting them to usher in the Sabbath. When they informed Anatoly of this during one of their telephone conversations, he said he believed the candles were not kosher since they were made from several different kinds of material. Jewish law forbids mixing certain textile materials for clothing. "You've got to find a sack made of flax," said Anatoly. The question of whether the candles were kosher had not occurred even to Mendelevich, who had had Orthodox training. Anatoly's observation—even though it was not correct in this fine point of Jewish religious law— was not an expression of pedantic religiosity but of his intellectual approach to Judaism. It was also an indication of the broad range of material on the Jewish religion he had begun to absorb since determining to emigrate to Israel.

On February 20, 1979 Butman and Mendelevich summoned Anatoly to his toilet bowl to wish him a happy birthday.

"Thanks very much for your kind wishes, my friends,"
shouted Anatoly. "But you're a month late."

Although his good spirits remained intact, his health
began to deteriorate. The difficult living conditions and
meager diet afflicted normally healthy inmates with a variety of ailments, from stomach ulcers to vascular diseases.
Early in 1979, Anatoly complained in a letter to his mother
of constant pain in his eyes and head. "If you know of some
techniques to reduce the pain—perhaps massage or yoga—
please let me know." Although he was permitted to write
one twenty-page letter a month, this letter was only five pages
long because of the difficulty he had in focusing. He has-
tened to reassure his mother that his spirits were intact. "My
optimism and my conviction that I did what I had to do
remain the same." He did eye exercises and took to wearing
dark glasses to protect his eyes from the bright artificial light
flooding his cell—but this was permitted only after a long
struggle with the authorities.

Anatoly's two fellow prisoners of Zion were convinced
that, because of pressure from the West, he would be released before them, despite his long sentence. Butman even
drafted a public message which he transmitted to Anatoly
with a request that he release it when he reached Israel.
Shcharansky would not be able to carry the message in writing, because of the thorough search he would undergo before release, but his exceptional memory would permit him
to repeat it verbatim.

However, it was Butman who was released first. One
evening in April 1979 he was placed overnight in an empty

cell; the next day he was led down the corridor on his way to the front gate. As he neared his old cell, he shouted out "Shalom." He could hear both Mendelevich and Anatoly call out, "Where are they taking you, Hillel?"

"I don't know," shouted Butman.

From the adjoining cells came farewells and good wishes. A few weeks later, Butman was on a plane heading for Tel Aviv as part of an East-West prisoner exchange.

In August 1979, Ida Milgrom was permitted to visit her son for the first time since he left Lefortovo the year before. Both she and Leonid were shocked at his emaciated appearance. She told him that Edward Kuznetsov and Mark Dymshits, the ringleaders in the Leningrad plot, had been traded for Soviet spies. The news heartened Mendelevich when he heard it.

On Anatoly's thirty-second birthday, January 20, 1980, his father Boris died of a heart attack on a Moscow bus. He was on his way to the apartment of Zionist activist Alexander Lerner to attend a gathering to celebrate Anatoly's birthday. Father and son had not seen each other since Anatoly's arrest three years earlier. His father's health had been a source of constant concern to Anatoly, who was haunted by the fear that he would never see him again.

"The last three years have given me enough time to realize how much I received from our family," wrote Anatoly to his mother upon receiving the news of his father's death. "There was a constant atmosphere of goodwill, of optimism, of concern for other people, of interest in everyday events and readiness for new experiences. . . . Right from my childhood, which was so full of Father, I remember those wonderful winter days, my birthdays. Life twists events into such painful symbols! . . . Father died on January 20, and

I dream of being able to tell our children, with Avital, what Father bequeathed to his sons."

In the letter from Chistopol, Anatoly noted that his parents had always feared they would not live long enough to raise and educate their two sons, who had been born to them at an advanced age. Therefore, they had taken out an insurance policy for that eventuality. "You succeeded in bringing us up and in giving us what no insurance could provide. You were afraid you would not be able to educate us, but you did that too. You felt you would not see your grandchildren—in his last letter, Father told me what a wonderful boy Sashka is [Leonid's son]." Anatoly attempted not only to console his mother but also to fortify her. "I ask you to learn this, Mother, before it is too late. Don't forget that you are 'the captain of the family ship,' as Father used to say. A captain must be more than wise and strong—a captain must be quiet and serene. The fortunes and the spirit of the entire crew depend on it.

"The day after I received your telegram telling me of Papa's death, I decided, in his memory, to read and study all hundred and fifty Psalms of David. This is what I do from morning till evening . . . as I read these verses, my thoughts return to Papa, to you, to Avital, to the past and the future. . . . Gradually, my feeling of great loss and sorrow changes to one of bright hopes. I am denied the right to visit Papa's grave, but when, in the future, I hear these wonderful verses, these lines that encompass the lives of all the Jews . . . I shall remember Papa. It will be as if I had erected a memorial stone to him in my heart, and he will be with me all the days of my life."

Among Anatoly's favorite passages in the small book with the tiny Hebrew print was Psalm 27: "The Lord is my light and my salvation; whom shall I fear? . . . Though a host should encamp against me, my heart shall not fear. . . ."

Each day, he copied out a psalm in Hebrew and translated it, making lists of the words he did not understand. Working slowly, he recited the unfamiliar lines again and again until they were firm in his mind. The work was exhausting, but it left him little time for black thoughts and enriched his knowledge of Hebrew. It also created an aura of spirituality in which the images of his parents and Avital appeared as objects not of longing but of closeness and warmth.

Anatoly remained in Chistopol for a year after Butman's departure, continuing to converse with Mendelevich two or three times a week via the telephone. Once, when the guards made a mistake in timing, the two men passed each other in the corridor. Although they had never met, they instantly recognized each other and, ignoring the guards, embraced briefly.

In April 1980, Anatoly was transferred 150 miles eastward to Labor Camp Thirty-five. He had completed the three years in prison his sentence called for. All that remained now was ten years of "reeducation" in labor camps. The Soviet penal system does not make automatic allowances for good behavior. Unless political pressure was applied successfully, he could expect to be forty-two years old when he boarded a train again for Moscow in the middle of 1990.

CAMP THIRTY-FIVE WAS ONE of three labor camps for political prisoners in the Perm district in the foothills of the Urals, the mountain range dividing European and Asian Russia. Anatoly found it a vast improvement over the prisons he had left. The biggest difference was that the prisoners were not locked in cells with one or two others but were housed in large barracks with some fifty men in each room. The politicals included dissidents who wanted democratic reforms and nationalists who wanted autonomy and national renaissance for their people. They were cynically placed together with some elderly men serving terms for collaboration with the Nazis. About 10 percent of the prisoners were criminals. Other prisoners were aware that the Nazi sympathizers and many of the criminals collaborated with the camp administration. Because of the danger from informers, prisoners who were like-minded usually talked politics as they strolled outside rather than while sitting around the barracks stove. Although it was against regulations to visit other rooms, this was generally ignored.

Guard towers and a high wooden fence topped by barbed wire limited views of the rolling countryside. The guards, mostly young central Asians, were often accompanied by police dogs. Rows of razor-sharp concertina wire emphasized the prohibition on prisoners approaching the wall itself. Every morning during the long winter months, guards on skis patrolled a strip of land between the rows to check for footprints indicating that someone had attempted to reach the fence during the night. A would-be escapee was unlikely to get very far even if he somehow got through the fence and the numerous other barriers. The only community near the camp was the village of Vsevyatskaya three miles away, which was founded in the eighteenth century by members of a dissident Russian Orthodox sect seeking to avoid persecution by isolating themselves in this remote region. The crest of the Urals, with peaks rising no more than 5,400 feet, was about fifty miles to the east. Beyond that lay Asia.

Prisoners could receive visits by relatives once a year

for up to three days. Married prisoners were given a private room to share with their wives during such visits. Since these rooms were known to be bugged in order to pick up political indiscretions passed during moments of intimacy, the prisoners controlled their conversations accordingly. The second daughter of Hillel Butman and his wife was conceived on such a visit. Mrs. Butman received an exit visa a few months later, and the child, born in Israel, was named Geula—redemption.

Food in the camp was much more plentiful than in the prisons, and new arrivals entering the communal dining room were astonished to find bread on the table, free for the taking. It was of poor quality, but it stilled the hunger pangs. There was a prison library heavy with the writings of Marx and Lenin, but a wide range of other reading material could be ordered from a literary mailing house in Moscow, paid for from the maximum pay of five rubles monthly for prison labor. Anatoly read books on ethnogenesis and phenomenology, computer technology and Islam, and works by Rilke, Joyce, Cervantes, Rabelais, Homer, Vergil, and Dante; but he couldn't obtain books by his favorite writers, Dostoyevsky, Bulgakov, Chekhov, and most Western novelists. If the authorities deemed the books unacceptable, they got lost in the mail. The prisoners worked eight hours a day and officially had Sundays off, though the camp administration sometimes used the men on this day for cleaning the grounds or other maintenance work.

Each prisoner was issued baggy gray trousers and a padded jacket tagged with his name and the number of the team to which he was assigned. His head was shaved when he arrived, and he was instructed to remain clean-shaven. He marched in formation to and from work and the dining hall several times a day after responding to a roll call. A siren woke him in the morning, and at the sound of the signal at night, lights were dimmed. When relatives came to visit, they would be completely stripped to ensure that they would not pass illicit items to the prisoners. Sometimes, to punish a prisoner, the relatives would be sent back after their long journey without being permitted to see their loved one.

Prisoners enjoyed some privileges, such as receiving one parcel a year weighing up to eleven pounds and purchasing up to five rubles' worth of "luxuries" from the camp store every month. However, every privilege was also a potential punishment in that it could easily be revoked. Camp officials had to be respectfully addressed—"Good morning, citizen chief"—or the prisoner would face punishment, including incarceration in a punishment cell. If enough punishment points were accumulated, he could be sent back to Vladimir or Chistopol. As unpleasant as the labor-camp regimen may have been, no one wanted to go back to prison.

Anatoly, who unlike Leonid had always been inept with his hands, was assigned to be a lathe operator working on metals. He found the work difficult in his impaired physical state. Half a year after his arrival, he collapsed at his job with back pains and stomach cramps. On October 18, 1980, the camp authorities decided to crack down on Anatoly. They assigned him to repair the barbed-wire fences around the camp, but, predictably, he refused because he considered it immoral to contribute to his own imprisonment. He was sentenced to two weeks in the punishment cells; later, he spent two more such periods of punitive confinement. He was released from the punishment cells in December weighing 105 pounds, 30 pounds less than he weighed upon his arrest. His mother had been scheduled to visit him the following month, but permission was withdrawn without explanation.

His moral health concerned Anatoly as much as his physical condition. In the perennial war that the penal authorities waged against the inmates to keep them divided and under control, ethnic differences were useful: one group was pitted against another. When KGB officers indicated that it would be worth his while to let them know what the Ukrainian politicals were discussing ("They're all anti-Semites anyway," the KGB authorities said), Anatoly refused to go along. "I consider you a criminal organization," he told them, "and I want no contacts with you."

Despite warnings that prisoners were forbidden to write collective letters of protest, Anatoly joined in protests against the lack of necessary medical attention for certain prisoners and other violations of the regulations. "Look, your letters don't help," said a camp official, trying to dissuade him. Anatoly understood that the official had logic on his side. But, as he would say later, "There exists another, inner logic. The prisoner who writes such a letter may not save his neighbor in the next cell, but he saves his soul." Anatoly had determined that the secret of his moral survival was to remain true to himself without any of the compromises that would have made his prison life so much more bearable; such compromises would have cost him the only thing his persecutors had been unable to take away—the key to his independent spirit. When the prison authorities offered him the prodigious favor of more mail in exchange for a more cooperative attitude, Anatoly refused. Little compromises inevitably led to bigger ones. If he were to sustain his integrity, there must be no compromise with the KGB, ever.

Long experience with human nature under pressure had

given the KGB a well-seasoned formula for bringing around recalcitrant prisoners. Defiant spirits could not be allowed sway. They not only challenged the authorities' own self-confidence, but their defiance was also contagious. Someone as popular among the prisoners as Anatoly was perceived as being particularly dangerous. The small, outspoken Jew with the sparkling sense of humor had become a well-known figure in the camp. More important, his continued refusal to "confess" to cooperation with the CIA undermined the KGB's campaign to discredit the Zionist movement.

Since Stalin's time, when far more serious confessions were routinely extracted from men who had been among the most powerful in the land, conventional torture had rarely been used; but there was no real need for it, considering the numerous other forms of pressure available. Threats of solitary confinement, reduced food allocation, subjection to the cold, or suspension of mail privileges were usually sufficient deterrents; if necessary, they could be combined with the promise of increased privileges. Anatoly, however, seemed impervious to this natural law. He remained defiant in action and demeanor, regardless of what the camp authorities promised, did, or threatened to do.

In December 1980, a year after his arrival in Camp Thirty-five, the authorities, seeking to find his weak point, confiscated the book of Psalms Avital had given him. "Religion is a bad influence," they told him. "We'll save you from it." Anatoly immediately declared a strike and refused to leave his barracks in the morning for work. In demanding his book back, he cited the fact that there was no Soviet law against possessing a prayer book. He was sentenced to solitary confinement in the camp's closed prison section. Guards led him out to the patrol path between the concertina wire and took him to the other end of the camp, where the prison was located. There he was placed in a punishment cell.

Regulations limit prisoners' stays in punishment cells to a maximum of 15 days. In the coming few months, Anatoly spent 185 days in these cells, 75 consecutively: the guards took him out of the cell for an hour after 15 days in order to honor the regulation, and then put him back inside.

There is no heating in a punishment cell, and the prisoner entering it for the first time, wearing thin clothing in the Russian winter, does not believe he will survive an hour. But death rarely provides such an easy way out. Somehow, the body adjusts. The prisoner survives, though he must keep in virtually constant motion to provide body heat. A wooden sleeping platform folded back against a wall of the otherwise bare cell is let down by the guard each night at the designated sleeping hour. But there are no blankets, and the need to keep moving makes sleep impossible, until exhaustion finally becomes too powerful. The oversize clothing given the diminutive Shcharansky, normally a flapping nuisance, provided a bit of extra material to be folded back, a few additional calories of warmth. But it is hunger, not cold, that is uppermost in the mind of a prisoner in a punishment cell.

Warm food of abysmal quality is provided every other day in a quantity barely enough to keep a man alive—once fifteen hundred calories, the next time nine hundred calories. On the alternate days, a chunk of dark bread and water is all there is. Constant hunger grips the body and mind. In these conditions of continuous cold and hunger, even healthy men contract illnesses that remain with them for the rest of their lives.

The prisoner is permitted to take nothing with him into

the punishment cell—no book, no pencil or paper. He cannot send letters, and although prison regulations entitle even punishment-cell prisoners to be shown letters upon their receipt, this is generally not done. The object is to break the prisoner by severing him from any connection with the outside world and from his routines, by reducing him to a state of utter helplessness in which he accepts the norms of his tormentors.

Anatoly was determined that this would not happen to him. They could control his body, but he would not let them insinuate themselves into his mind. He had enough resources to fill it himself. The guards in the corridor were startled to hear loud singing coming through the door of the punishment cell shortly after Anatoly was put inside. Every day he sang all the Hebrew songs he knew, uninhibited in his solitude about singing as loudly as he wished despite his off-key voice. Singing is a balm for the soul in any circumstances; in solitary confinement it can tilt the balance toward sanity.

Falling back on a favorite pastime, Anatoly began playing mental chess—moving both the white and black pieces in his head and analyzing the game as he went along. He ran through the two thousand words of his Hebrew vocabulary and rethought computer problems. He systematically set out every day to remember the things in life that pleased him. "You must choose the things that are most important to you," he said later, "and repeat them to yourself every day like a prayer—not to forget what the world is like."

The object of most of his thoughts was Avital. He slowly ran through the hours of their life together, savoring every moment and wondering at its resonance. It was a memory reel he never tired of running, one that gained new dimensions over time. He thought of his friends, his happy childhood, his experiences as an activist.

Anatoly was sustained, too, by an awareness that his resistance would serve as a symbol. The authorities were using him and the other refuseniks to intimidate the rest of Soviet Jewry into silence. It was a well-tried tactic that had proved itself during centuries of authoritarian rule in Russia. In the prison camps, just a handful of punishment cells was enough to keep hundreds of men in line, and if this were true in the "security zones" it was just as true in "the big zone," as the prisoners sardonically referred to the country as a whole. Anatoly believed the reverse was also true: "When many people are silent because they are afraid, and then people appear who are not afraid to speak, they see it is possible to live in these conditions, to survive in honor and dignity. Such an example can have a snowball effect."

He himself had been sustained in his terrible isolation at the trial by the behavior of others who had passed through this fire without giving in. He had been inspired too by Jewish history, particularly the story of Judah Maccabee, who, 2,100 years ago, rebelled against Syrian Hellenistic rule and restored an independent Jewish state.

Anatoly was initially sentenced to half a year in the labor-camp prison, but within the span of eighteen months he spent nine months in solitary confinement, both in punishment cells and in regular prison cells. "For a long time, my only contact with living beings has been with a bird on my windowsill and the insects in my cell," he wrote to his mother, in one of the few letters he was permitted to send during this period. In addition, his privileges had been sharply reduced. Instead of being permitted to receive two letters a month, he could now receive only one every two months. Avital was writing every day, but none of her letters reached him. Regulations permitted family visits twice a year, but his mother and brother were informed that Anatoly would be permitted no visits at all in 1981 as punishment. In March, he wrote to Soviet leader Brezhnev, reminding him that the Twenty-sixth Communist Party Congress a month earlier had lifted curbs on religion. Anatoly said he wanted his book of Psalms back. It is unlikely that Brezhnev ever saw the letter; nevertheless, the KGB relented. In his letters, Anatoly quoted extensively from the book. The Psalms gave him solace, and he felt they brought him closer to God.

Anatoly's spirit survived his extended stay in punishment cells intact, but his body collapsed. He suffered occasional loss of consciousness and an irregular heartbeat in addition to other ailments. One day late in the summer of 1981, he fainted. But when he was revived, prison officials refused to give him any nourishment because it was a non-food day for him. Several days later, the officials had second thoughts and brought him to the camp hospital, where doctors confirmed that he had developed a heart ailment and was suffering from malnutrition. He was kept in the hospital for thirty-three days on a better diet, but when he returned to the camp prison, the previous starvation diet was reimposed.

In October 1981, the still defiant Shcharansky was brought to a room where he found himself in the presence of a People's Court judge from the region, two people's assessors, and a prosecutor. He was being tried for violation of camp regulations. There was no defense attorney. It took only five minutes for the court to find him guilty of a continued refusal to confess to the original 1978 charges and of exerting a bad influence on other prisoners. The judge accepted the camp administration's proposal to send him back to Chistopol Prison for three years. Although the court, at that time, had no power to extend his term beyond what the court in Moscow had fixed, it could convert up to three years of his labor-camp term into prison time. In November 1981, twenty months after he left Chistopol for Camp Thirty-five he set out again for the grim prison in the Tatar Republic.

AVITAL SHCHARANSKY's metamorphosis had become noticeable by 1980. Her short-cropped hair, prematurely shot with gray, was regularly covered with a head scarf. She wore dresses and skirts with hems below the knee, never slacks or sleeveless tops. On the Sabbath, she no longer rode in a car, lit a match, or lifted a telephone.

The young woman who had arrived in Israel six years before virtually ignorant of Judaism had found religion. Her speech was laced with "God willing" and "with God's help," and her permanently mournful look had taken on an aspect of devoutness.

The transition was gradual; it began in the customary way, with study. Throughout her unhappy childhood, Avital's parents had sought to deny their Jewishness. They had eschewed the symbols and ceremonies of Judaism, repudiated its laws, rejected their ties to the land of their forefathers. Avital's first introduction to Judaism came through Anatoly; when she was free to do so, she sought to strengthen that cord which bound her to her husband, their people, and their homeland.

Her friends at the Mercaz Harav yeshiva were patient, thorough teachers; but in addition to lessons in Jewish law, culture, and history, they also provided Avital with invaluable practical assistance. They supplied the logistical support necessary to launch her campaign on her husband's behalf. At the behest of Rabbi Zvi Yehuda Kook, headquarters were set up in a Jerusalem apartment by the institution's students and teachers, who organized Avital's trips abroad and dispatched men to Europe to handle the day-to-day arrangements for her travels and meetings. She was surrounded by supporters throughout the world, but in the vacuum created by Anatoly's absence, Avital was increasingly drawn to these warm-hearted friends and to the deep faith which permitted them to build for themselves the tranquil, integrated family and communal lives so alien to her cold parental home.

She needed faith to sustain her in her own torment— not only the torment of her husband's prolonged imprisonment, but also the maddening realization that her biological clock was running faster than Anatoly's sentence. He too had been plagued by the absence of children and, in moments of weakness, had been hounded by "what ifs." If instead of urging her to go abroad he had kept her in Russia, they would at least have had children by now, and these years of their lives would not have been a waste.

In Avital's new social milieu, to have six or more children in a family was common. In the streets of the Kiryat Moshe neighborhood around the yeshiva, young women of her age were generally surrounded by clutching little hands as they pushed a baby carriage. Her friends sensed how painful it must be for her to see them in maternity clothes, and some even sought to avoid her during their pregnancies. But in the women's section of the yeshiva synagogue, where Avital prayed on the Sabbath and holidays, she chose not to sit in the fixed seats overlooking the prayer hall below. Instead she normally found a place in the adjacent room, where mothers sat with babies and young children so that their cries would not disturb the proceedings. She found a poignant pleasure, when she looked up from her prayer book, in watching the young mothers rock their babies and feed them, and seeing the small children play among the benches. For some of the mothers watching her, it was heartbreaking.

Twice, Avital applied to go to the Soviet Union for conjugal visits with Anatoly in prison, but there was no reply. In view of the fact that the Soviets refused to recognize her as his wife, there was no alternative but to await his release, even though she could not be certain about his state of health when he came out, nor even his feelings for her. But his messages to her left little room for doubt. "I can no longer say anything about myself without including you," he had written in September 1978. "Everything becomes so intertwined and blended that our separate lives simply do not exist any longer. I used to live through memories but now I have the sensation that we are living together." Anatoly knew of and delighted in her growing religiosity, even though he himself "kept the Sabbath inside," not observing the ritual aspects of the religion. "At least I'll be exempt from doing any work in the kitchen when I get to Israel," he joked. "I'd only mix up the meat and milk dishes."

Avital had become a vegetarian and slept only fitfully. When friends told her she was becoming painfully thin, she replied, "How can I eat or drink when at the same moment Anatoly could be dying of hunger?" Although she took additional teaching courses, she could not muster the peace of mind to teach and lived on a small government stipend. If Anatoly felt that he was living in freedom in some inviolable inner world, Avital felt in the same way that she was sharing his imprisonment. Her face with its high cheekbones, lovely olive skin, and doe eyes took on a dark and haunted beauty over the years; and even among close friends, she was rarely seen to smile.

The one thing that animated her was the campaign. Tirelessly she continued her forays to Europe and the United States, pushing herself to the limits of her endurance to keep the embers burning. Funding, support, and contacts came from Israel and abroad. Overcoming her shyness, she met with national leaders, dressed in prison uniform to stage street-corner demonstrations, addressed rallies, and submitted to countless media interviews. She kept in telephone and mail contact with Anatoly's mother and brother and relayed their information about him to the press.

Her fantasy of being able to establish similarly intimate relations with her own parents had long since been shattered. At one point, Avital's mother publicly denied that her daughter was Jewish or that she was indeed married to Anatoly. Her parents apparently were told by the KGB that Anatoly would never leave prison alive, but that if they cooperated in the case against him, they would be given an opportunity to see their daughter again, perhaps in Europe or even in Israel. A few months before Anatoly's sentencing, Avital, at her brother's urging, phoned them from the home of a friend in Washington. She had not seen them in four years or spoken to them in one year. When she got through to Moscow, they asked for her number and said they would call back. She waited for a long time and told her hostess that her parents probably were consulting with the KGB about what to say; and when they did call back, it was only to confirm her darkest expectations. "You married a traitor," they said, "and what you have done is even worse because of what this government did for you. They educated you and gave you everything you needed. Then you turned around and got involved with a traitor. We disown him and we disown you." Avital ran weeping to her room and did not emerge the rest of the evening. She felt that her parents were not unfeeling villains, but prisoners themselves—of their past and of the Soviet mind-set. It seemed now that the power of love would not prevail over the system that so estranged parents from their children. "It was a tragedy," said a friend, "a typical Soviet tragedy."

Wherever Avital was on her travels, she refrained from any public activity on the Sabbath. On one Friday night in the elegant suburban Washington house of friends, Avital excused herself to go to her room to light candles. When she did not return, her hostess went up to see if she was all right. She peered into Avital's room, and saw her sitting and praying at a table on which Anatoly's picture had been placed between the two lit Sabbath candles.

Avital's repeated visits to the seats of Western power, particularly Washington, could not sustain the initial impact of her campaign, and came to be regarded by some as a growing nuisance. "She's a pain," said an official in the Reagan administration some time after she succeeded in meeting with the president. "She wants to see the secretary of state every two or three months. She wants to see the national security adviser every two or three months. The whole idea is to make it look like she is close to the president. She is always pressuring and is not well liked. She's a very difficult personality to deal with. No matter what you do, it isn't enough."

Nevertheless, her lobbying was successful in keeping Anatoly's name in the public consciousness. Another White

House figure termed her presentations among the most compelling he had ever heard. "I dare say that without her constant lobbying, two administrations would not have devoted so much time and attention to Shcharansky, important though he might have been. She is a very vibrant, almost saintly woman who personifies the very nature of the administration's overall human rights policy."

A leader of an American organization dealing with Soviet Jewry termed Avital "a possessed person" who made great demands on the resources and time of her American contacts. "You can't expect that she would always be welcomed with glee," he said. "But I can only say that if I was locked in a Soviet prison, I would want a wife like Avital."

THE VISITORS' ROOM in Chistopol Prison was so cold that Ida Milgrom and Leonid Shcharansky had to keep their coats on. A prison official sat to the side listening to every word. If the conversation strayed off personal matters, it would be terminated. Otherwise they would have two hours in this, their second visit in three years. When Anatoly was led in, he was as pale and thin as starvation, and his wan smile could not hide what he had endured for the past year and a half.

He, too, was shocked. How old his mother looked! He was seized with deep sadness over what she must be enduring. For a woman in her mid-seventies, the trip to Chistopol was a terrible strain. Leonid attempted to smile and offer encouragement, but Anatoly could see the emotion his older brother was fighting to control.

"How is Avital?" asked Anatoly.

His mother and brother told of the worldwide campaign she was waging on his behalf, and of her life in Jerusalem as she described it in a constant stream of letters and telephone calls. They spoke of his numerous friends in Moscow and elsewhere in the Soviet Union. Many had emigrated to Israel. A record number of 50,343 Jews had emigrated in 1979, two years after Anatoly's arrest. This was ample evidence that the public struggle had not harmed emigration, as some had maintained. But the number of emigrants had been drastically cut to 20,319 in 1980. Some of his friends were still being refused exit visas, others were in prison or exile. Precisely two hours after Anatoly was let in, the official auditing the conversation rose and announced the meeting over.

It was many months before Anatoly's family heard from him again. The prison authorities accused him of transmitting secret messages about prison life by using code words in his letters, and refused to let his mail go out. On Yom Kippur of 1982—September 26—he declared a hunger strike. Anatoly's mother, who had not had a letter from him since her visit to Chistopol nine months before, was informed by authorities in Moscow that he would be force-fed.

The force-feeding began on the twenty-fifth day of his strike. Handcuffed by prison guards, Anatoly was held still, a pipe was inserted down his throat, and liquid nutrients were pumped through. It was a highly unpleasant experience. When the pipe was extracted and the guards' grip relaxed, he would come up gasping for air, his heart racing wildly. His stomach swelled up after these treatments, until it felt as if a needle prick would make it burst. Against regulations, he was force-fed every third day, but strength from these infusions faded rapidly, and most of the time he was only half conscious. Once again, as at Lefortovo during his interrogation, Anatoly came to terms with the very real possibility that he would die.

His family was frantic. Ida had made the five-hundred-mile trip to Chistopol twice since her visit in January 1982 and had been turned away both times. Now she traveled again in November with Leonid. It was the fifty-fifth day of Anatoly's strike. Once again, the officials refused her appeal to visit her son. The journey involved a thirty-six-hour train ride followed by a drive of several hours in whatever transportation she could hire on the spot to take her across the Kama River to the prison. On one occasion in the dead of winter, the old woman had been unable to find transportation on the railway side of the river. She crossed the treacherous ice of the frozen Volga tributary on foot, walking four miles.

Meanwhile, world support was being mustered by Avital and others. British Prime Minister Margaret Thatcher publicly called upon the Soviets to release Shcharansky. Responding to a plea from Avital, she wrote, "Your husband's case has caught the imagination of people of many faiths and nationalities, symbolizing as it does the right of every citizen to the basic freedom of movement and non-violent dissent." In Paris, Avital met with French government officials. United Nations Secretary-general Javier Perez de Cuellar, meeting with Israeli President Yitzhak Navon in New York, agreed to ask the Soviets to permit Anatoly's family to visit him. The Canadian Parliament unanimously urged Moscow to free Shcharansky, whose incarceration was termed "a fundamental denial" of human rights.

Ida went daily to Communist Party headquarters in Moscow to await a reply to her request to visit her son.

Finally, she succumbed to the continuing strain and was bedridden with nervous exhaustion.

After 110 days it was the system that surrendered, not Anatoly. Discomfited by the wide publicity his strike was receiving, the authorities informed his mother that she could enter the prison to send a note to her son and receive one from him, to confirm that he was still alive. She would not, however, be permitted to see him. She arrived at Chistopol on January 14, 1983 and submitted her letter in the prison office. It was rejected by the KGB officer in charge because it mentioned the world efforts on his behalf. Her second note said only that she and Avital were concerned about his health. The officer accepted it and asked her to wait. Two hours later he returned with a nineteen-line reply in Anatoly's handwriting. Five of the lines had been crossed out. In the part that remained, he had written that he urgently needed hospitalization.

The Kremlin was manifestly concerned about the pro-Shcharansky campaign in the West. Soviet leader Yuri Andropov, who was head of the KGB when Anatoly was framed, personally involved himself in the issue when he responded to a query from French Communist leader Georges Marchais. Andropov asserted that Ida Milgrom had "recently visited her son" and that Anatoly had stopped his hunger strike. "His state of health is satisfactory and nothing endangers his life," said the new Soviet leader. To the press Ida vigorously denied having visited her son, and fired off a telegram to Andropov asking for permission to make such a visit.

On February 22 the official Soviet news agency, Tass, hinted at parole for Shcharansky if the campaign on his behalf were called off. "Soviet legislation, like the laws of many other countries, does not exclude the possibility that prison terms may be commuted in response to pleas for pardon. But the only grounds for pardon is the conduct of the prisoner and by no means noisy propaganda campaigns and attempts to put pressure from outside." The pressure was obviously having an effect. Just as plainly, the Soviets did not intend to surrender Shcharansky in a way that would make them lose face. Some experts viewed the hint of pardon in exchange for silence as a KGB trap designed only to score propaganda points in the West.

It was not until a month after her visit to the prison that Ida Milgrom received confirmation in a letter from her son that he had ended his fast on the day she sent him the note. His fourteen-page letter, the first she had received from him in more than a year, suggested serious medical problems. He was receiving vitamins and injections since his fast had ended, he wrote, but had not been hospitalized despite worrying heart pains. He felt the pains strongly when he walked, though not when he lay down. When he had halted his strike, he had been down to fifty-five pounds, half his normal weight. He was too weak to walk in the prison courtyard.

Ida and Leonid were finally permitted to see Anatoly through a window in July 1983, half a year after he had resumed eating. He had regained about forty pounds but still looked emaciated. When they informed him that there were reports in the West about a pending exchange that would free him, he said that prison authorities had given no hint of it. In a subsequent letter to his mother, Anatoly wrote that he had worn a hole through one of the shirts she had sent him by rubbing his heart to gain relief from the pain.

An electrocardiogram performed in the prison hospital had shown no problem. However, he knew the pain was real. Anatoly was also experiencing allergic reactions to medication. Two of Israel's top cardiologists, Dr. Zvi Schlesinger and Dr. Henry Neufeld, diagnosed the problem from Ida Milgrom's description as angina pectoris, a particularly painful disease usually associated with organic change in the heart or aorta. In an interview with Western correspondents, Ida said that her son would not survive the second half of his prison term without hospital treatment.

In January 1984, Avital received the first letter from Anatoly the prison authorities had permitted him to send her since his imprisonment seven years earlier. In the same month, his mother visited Chistopol and saw Anatoly for the first time since she had talked to him through a glass partition the previous July. The deterioration in his condition was so great that she did not immediately recognize him. His face was pale and drawn, his eyes lined by dark rings. For a moment, Ida was speechless. She spoke to herself: *What have they done to you, my son?*

Behind those sunken eyes, however, the spark of defiance was undimmed. Anatoly and five fellow prisoners undertook a week-long hunger strike to protest the treatment of psychiatrist Anatoly Koryagin. Anatoly did it again when his mail privileges were once more curtailed. The attachment to the broader issues of human rights that had motivated him to join the Helsinki Watch Group had not eroded. Anatoly learned that the prison authorities were attempting to persuade a Jew and a Ukrainian in a neighboring cell to inform on each other by sowing ethnic discord between them. He drafted a long letter to the general prosecutor of the Soviet Union complaining about the KGB's attempt to drive wedges between the Soviet peoples. As expected, he received no answer; but the practice stopped for several months.

As the long years passed within the walls, Anatoly's sense of his Jewish identity grew stronger. His suffering made sense only in the context of a tale as old as the Bible, the story of a particular people searching for its way. His grasp of Hebrew improved, despite his years of isolation from other Hebrew speakers.

In the autumn of 1984, as Shcharansky's three years at Chistopol were nearing an end, Ida Milgrom, now seventy-six, set off once again for the prison despite the onset of winter weather. She wanted to ensure that her son would be taken from the prison upon completion of his time and to find out which camp he would be sent to.

Anatoly was shipped back to Camp Thirty-five, lugging with difficulty in his weakened state ten books he had accumulated. It was during such transits that he had contact with other prisoners, including criminals. He found none of the anti-Semitism that other Jewish prisoners had experienced in such circumstances and enjoyed what he would call "a good international atmosphere."

Almost immediately upon his arrival in the camp, Anatoly was placed in hospital—which had been denied him in Chistopol—and subjected to a bewilderingly "royal" treatment. He not only received vitamins and injections to strengthen him, but was plied with rich and abundant food such as he had not thought existed in the Gulag, including meat, butter, and milk. The treatment lasted for two months, and it seemed clear that he was being fattened for some special purpose. In January 1985, he was taken from the hospital to another building. There he found his mother and brother waiting for what would be their first private meeting with him in five years.

Upon his family's departure, Anatoly's royal status gave way immediately to the familiar labor-camp regimen. Twice during the coming year his mail privileges were suspended. Anatoly retaliated with renewed hunger strikes. The authorities in turn sentenced him to 110 days in the camp prison, half that time in solitary. He was to spend a total of 400 days in solitary confinement. The ailments that had receded with the hospital treatment reappeared as his weight fell, this time in a more virulent form. The prison-camp authorities refused him medical treatment. When he remained defiant after returning to the main camp in the autumn, he was sentenced to another four months in the camp prison. As 1985 was nearing its end, Anatoly had more than four years of his sentence ahead of him. It was clear that the battle for control of his will had not ended.

6

The Winding Road
to Freedom

*I*srael might not have come into being when it did without the support in 1947 and 1948 of the two world powers, the United States and the Soviet Union. But because of traditional Russian anti-Semitism, most Zionists were always wary of Soviet support (which was not only diplomatic but military, through the Kremlin's Czech surrogates), and indeed, it proved short-lived. By the time the Soviets finally cut diplomatic ties with Israel in 1967, all trace of that initial goodwill had long since faded. On the other hand, despite many fluctuations since the state of Israel was founded, its relationship with the United States has proved to be enduring and, in the view of many, mutually beneficial. In matters concerning the repatriation of Jews to Israel from countries of oppression, the United States has taken in recent years an active role—in big ways, as with the Soviet Jews, and in smaller but highly dramatic ways, such as the 1984–1985 rescue of some eight thousand Ethiopian Jews from the pestilential refugee camps of Sudan.

The Soviet-Jewish movement, involving hundreds of thousands of people, has received consistent bipartisan support in the United States. Anatoly Shcharansky's road to freedom ran through Washington, interwoven with the politics of détente.

Israel, which has no diplomatic relations with the USSR, played no direct role in the struggle to release Shcharansky.

Some officials took a critical view of his linkage of the Jewish and human rights movements, maintaining that it damaged prospects for a mass exodus from the Soviet Union. American Jewish groups were sharply divided over the philosophical issue that the Shcharansky affair was coming to represent: a broad universalistic approach versus a particularistic focus on the Jews.

The administration of President Jimmy Carter placed unprecedented emphasis on human rights issues; it was in keeping with the spirit of his administration that the Shcharansky affair became a major factor in relations between the superpowers. At a meeting with Soviet Foreign Minister Andrei Gromyko at the White House on September 22, 1977, the president raised the issue of human rights in the Soviet Union and cited the Shcharansky case in particular. Gromyko replied that Shcharansky was "a microscopic dot who is of no consequence to anyone." Carter insisted that the persecution and trial of activists like Shcharansky was assuming great symbolic importance in shaping American opinion about the Soviet system of government; therefore, it was a major factor in determining the degree of friendship and trust that could be built between the two superpowers. But despite this and other disputes, both agreed not to link the SALT II arms-control talks to any other issue.

On several occasions after Anatoly Shcharansky's arrest, Carter reaffirmed that the Soviet allegations of a CIA connection to Shcharansky were untrue. He wrote to a distant relative of Anatoly's in the United States, saying that his administration would keep the issue alive in its diplomatic contacts and negotiations with the Soviets. Although Carter himself never met with Avital, his administration responded quickly and helpfully to her appeals. Dr. Joyce Starr, a White House liaison to the Jewish community, got very much involved in the struggle to free Shcharansky, spurred on by Irene Manekofsky, head of the Union of Councils for Soviet Jewry.

Manekofsky had kept in close touch with Anatoly from her first meeting with him in Moscow in December 1974 until his arrest in 1977. She had led a personal crusade to get him an exit permit and later to free him from prison. New York businessman Jerry Stern and his wife Jane had been among the first to help Avital meet important officials. But during the Carter administration, Manekofsky became the prime mover in arranging Avital's meetings with congressmen and leading administration officials like Starr. In addition, at Anatoly's request she disseminated up-to-date information on both the Jewish and the dissident movements. This got her into trouble from an unexpected direction. She came under intense fire from certain influential circles in Israel and the "establishment" National Conference for Soviet Jewry. The Israelis insisted that the dissident movement in Russia should be kept completely separate from the emigration movement. It was important, they argued, to show that the emigration movement had nothing to do with attempts to "change the system." But they had no control over Shcharansky or the many other refusenik leaders who believed the two movements had to be interlinked. Manekofsky was summoned to the Israeli Embassy and told in no uncertain terms that she should cease her efforts on behalf of the dissident movement. She understood the logic of their position, but felt that Israel itself was not doing enough to help Anatoly.

According to Manekofsky and others, Israeli officials had warned Avital that nobody would help her if Anatoly were arrested because of his work with the dissidents. Nehamia Levanon, the chief Israeli official involved in Soviet Jewry, "wanted everything to be kept quiet—nobody should make any noise," Manekofsky said. "This was why the Union of Councils always had so much trouble with him, because he never wanted us to do anything that he did not have control of." American activists alleged that the Israelis and the "establishment" sought to downplay the Shcharansky case in favor of refuseniks like Yosef Begun and Ida Nudel, who were considered to be "more Jewish."

From the point of view of one activist leader, Glenn Richter of the Student Struggle for Soviet Jewry, "What came through from Jerusalem was an attitude, which was that when Shcharansky was arrested, he got what was coming to him" because he had not heeded Israeli warnings against linking the Jewish emigration movement with the Helsinki Watch Group. Levanon's foreign ministry office—sometimes called "the office with no name," "the Lishka" (the bureau), or, pejoratively, "the black foreign ministry"—had grown out of the Mossad secret service in the early 1960s. "Their whole style to this day remains very secretive," Richter said. The Israelis told the activists that if they pursued an independent course, they would be cut off from access to all of the Israeli information related to Soviet Jewry—including the most complete lists of refuseniks and prisoners of Zion. The covert Israeli style was fundamentally different from the grass-roots movement among the American Jews. At a 1978 Soviet Jewry conference in Israel, Richter said, he was told by Levanon's top aide, Zvi Netzer, "The problem with you is that you don't follow orders."

Alan Dershowitz, a Harvard University law professor, found that the Israelis tried to discourage advocacy of Anatoly's case by withholding important information. Dershowitz, together with Canadian jurist Irwin Cotler, served as Anatoly's main advocate. When the Israelis cut the activists off, however, the Americans were able to get the information they needed through their own contacts with refuseniks in the Soviet Union, as well as through American authorities and other sources.

Jerry Goodman, executive director of the National Conference for Soviet Jewry, encountered no Israeli pressure to downplay Shcharansky, although the Israelis did express opposition to linking the dissident and Jewish struggles, saying that it could have dangerous consequences. But there was "a nagging sense of concern that perhaps we were allowing Anatoly's strong personality and charisma" to eclipse the larger movement. That was why the establishment groups pushed for more effort on behalf of people like Begun and Nudel. "They did not have an Avital fighting for them in the West."

Another leader of a mainstream American Jewish organization, Abraham Bayer of the National Jewish Community Relations Coordinating Council (NJCRAC) also said that Levanon "only expressed a viewpoint, one held by many of the refuseniks in Moscow, that they ought to stay within the Jewish sphere. People were warning Anatoly that it was a dangerous path. The Jewish business is risky enough without getting involved in a cause that threatens the Soviet order, and which they will never accept."

One key figure in establishing official Israeli policy on Soviet Jewry bluntly criticized the American activists who focused on Shcharansky, whom he felt had inadvertently harmed the Jewish emigration movement. It was a mistake, he said, to concentrate on the Shcharansky case as though it were the only one. He maintained that from a Jewish perspective, there were other cases that were more important—Begun and Nudel—and that Shcharansky was "a borderline case" because he was interested in both Jewish and dissident activities. Begun, in contrast, was severely punished in his Hebrew teaching, and was interested only in Jewish activities. "But we certainly did not abandon Anatoly Shcharansky, or urge others to do so." The official Israeli position was that any connection between the two movements was ill-advised. The refuseniks who wanted to leave the country were treated by the Soviets as a nuisance, whereas the dissidents were seen as a real menace. There were enough people to worry about human rights around the world, went the argument; Israel's role was to worry about Jews, whether in Russia, South Africa, or Argentina.

Dershowitz refuted the charges that Anatoly's American supporters neglected other prisoners of Zion, noting that he had served as counsel for such prominent refuseniks as Mark Dymshits and Edward Kuznetsov and had signed legal briefs for Ida Nudel, Vladimir Slepak, and others. What attracted activists like himself to the Shcharansky affair was that they considered Anatoly to be a bridge case, someone who was working on behalf of all oppressed people. It was precisely because he was more than a refusenik that his case had such broad appeal among many Jewish liberals in the West. "Anatoly's courageous stand for human rights triggered the involvement of the scientific and legal communities in the fight for his freedom and that of the other Soviet Jews, as well as the involvement of the White House and congressmen. He transformed the struggle from a parochial one to a battle that inspired people everywhere."

The issue of Soviet Jewry was too important to be left

to the Israeli government, Dershowitz said, since Israel's interests do not necessarily coincide with those of Soviet Jews: for that reason, there must be grass-roots Soviet-Jewry groups independent of Israeli leadership.

While some of the establishment American Jewish organizations may have thought it unwise of Shcharansky to link up with groups fighting for the rights of Crimean Tatars or Seventh Day Adventists, they clearly did not abandon him to his fate. He was too powerful and compelling a figure. But the refuseniks in Moscow, hearing of the differences of opinion among Western Jewish organizations in the weeks following Anatoly's arrest in 1977, sent a sharply worded appeal on his behalf. The message, signed by Mark Azbel, Ida Nudel, Alexander Lerner, Victor Brailovsky, Vladimir Slepak, and Ilya Essas, said that Anatoly had been arrested because of his Jewish activism; and that although the Jewish problem in the USSR stood very much apart, it was essential for the Jewish and human rights movements to work together.

DESPITE THE ISRAELI threat to withhold information, American activists kept the focus on Shcharansky. Irene Manekofsky continued to communicate with Soviet Jews through Michael Sherbourne, the Russian-speaking Jewish activist in London who called refuseniks in the Soviet Union almost every day.

Sherbourne, who coined the word *refusenik,* had made five thousand calls to Jews throughout the Soviet Union over a twenty-year period, his huge phone bill paid by a Jewish philanthropist. He taped his conversations, typed up reports, and released the information to the press and to organizations in Europe and the United States. He kept

Manekofsky, in her key post in Washington, regularly up to date. She passed the information on to the State Department, Capitol Hill, and the press in Washington. Glenn Richter released the material to the Jewish and general press in New York.

Sherbourne was aware that the KGB monitored his calls. He sometimes heard the voices of KGB eavesdroppers informing colleagues about the identity of callers. He was not unduly concerned. Nothing secret was being said; in fact, the idea was to provide as much publicity as possible on the subjects being discussed.

The KGB even facilitated the calls, as evidenced by the efforts of Dr. Lipavsky to find "open" phones for his friends. The phones of many of the dissidents and Jewish refuseniks had been cut off by the KGB, yet Lipavsky's facility in solving the communications problem never aroused suspicion. Even in retrospect, the refuseniks and their supporters in the West dismissed the argument that perhaps the KGB actually wanted to promote the link between the Jewish and human rights movements in order to tar them with the same brush. Was the Israeli and Jewish establishment correct after all in insisting that the Jewish emigration movement keep its distance from the democratic dissidents, lest the Jews be accused of that cardinal sin in a Communist country, trying to reform the system? Was the KGB manipulating and exploiting the humanist bent of naive people like Shcharansky, Rubin, Slepak, the other leading refuseniks, and their Jewish helpers in America and England?

Many of the most thoughtful and dynamic refuseniks and former prisoners of Zion believed then and believe now that it was the other way around. Edward Kuznetsov, who spent a total of sixteen years in Soviet jails, argued that the

KGB feared a union of the Jewish and human rights movements, that the struggle was inseparable. "Whoever believes that the two struggles can be separated as a principle is stupid." He said that it is Soviet propaganda that Jewish emigration will be helped if the Jews distance themselves from the general human rights movement, and that Israel, by subscribing to this belief, is harming the movement. Jews should get involved in "Russian issues," in his view, just as "there are also Russians who get involved in the Jewish issue." The effort to free Shcharansky "is not just a struggle for the freedom of one more political prisoner. . . . Primarily, it is a struggle to have the very concept of political prisoners eliminated forever." There was every reason to tie this principle to such substantive matters as détente, disarmament, and trade.

THE CHAIN OF communication went straight from the refuseniks and dissidents and the "open telephones" of Moscow to the activists in the West and up to the White House. Through the efforts of Manekofsky and Joyce Starr, Carter aide Patricia Derian—the State Department's assistant secretary for human rights and humanitarian affairs—became very much involved in the Shcharansky case, as did other administration officials. When Vice President Mondale met with Avital at the White House in June 1978, he told her that Americans were impressed by Anatoly's courage and dignity in the face of the injustice visited upon him. He added that Shcharansky's trial was in clear violation of the Helsinki talks. Mondale met with Ambassador Dobrynin for half an hour, telling him that "this issue is not going to go away. It's going to get worse. You ought to let the man go."

The vice president pushed hard for a vocal, tough response to the Soviets. If the matter were left to quiet diplomacy, he believed, no one would ever hear of Shcharansky again.

On July 14, 1978, the day Anatoly was found guilty and sentenced, Carter met informally with the press at the U.S. Chancellery in Bonn, where he had been holding talks with Western leaders. Asked about the Shcharansky verdict and the trial of dissident Alexander Ginzburg, Carter said that these "courageous dissidents" were tried and punished because they had sought to uphold the basic freedoms that were guaranteed by the signatories of the Helsinki agreement, including the Soviet Union itself.

He expressed sympathy and support for Shcharansky, Ginzburg, Orlov, and others. Obviously, he said, the United States had no desire to interfere in any way in the internal affairs of the Soviet Union, but he felt it incumbent upon him, as president, to arouse public condemnation around the world for the violation of basic principles of human freedom.

In June 1979, at Carter's summit talks with Soviet leader Leonid Brezhnev, the president once again raised questions about the Shcharansky affair. He reminded Brezhnev that human rights issues were very important in shaping American attitudes toward the USSR, and that since the USSR voluntarily signed the Helsinki accords, this issue was a proper item for state-to-state discussions. The United States, he said, was gratified at the more liberal emigration policies Brezhnev had established (1979 proved the high mark of Soviet-Jewish emigration, with over fifty thousand allowed out). "Now you need to continue this policy and release Mr. Shcharansky and other dissidents," Carter said.

Brezhnev countered that Shcharansky had been tried

and convicted in the Soviet court of law for espionage, and that as the leader of the nation, Brezhnev was bound to support the laws of his country. Carter reminded him again of the importance of the issue and insisted that the United States would continue to press for progress. But it didn't seem to have any effect on the Kremlin's intransigent stand. And to America's NATO allies, Carter's approach appeared to complicate foreign policy matters.

The Carter administration's criticism of Soviet and Eastern European human rights abuses and the controversy surrounding the Shcharansky case made many European leaders nervous. The affair was also becoming entangled with a wholly separate debate in the administration over the continued sale of high-technology computers and other equipment to the Soviet Union. The bureaucratic fight was brought to a head by the Soviet decision to arrest Shcharansky and Ginzburg. This move provoked widespread public outrage, and Carter's top domestic advisers—Stuart Eizenstat, Robert Lipshutz, Jody Powell, Hamilton Jordan, Jerry Rafshoon—all became greatly aroused and urged the president personally to take the lead in responding. But others in the administration, including Secretary of State Cyrus Vance, did not want to link high-tech trade to the human rights issue.

Eventually, Carter decided to deny the Soviets a Sperry Univac computer for use during the 1980 Olympics and to impose other trade restrictions. The cumulative effect of these steps meant that America's permissive attitude toward technology transfer to the Soviet Union was now being reversed. There was widespread support in Congress for the decision.

Even before Anatoly's trial, efforts were being made to arrange a prisoner swap that would bring him to the West.

But the Soviets would not consider it. In May 1978, after the FBI arrested two Soviet United Nations employees allegedly engaged in spying activities, Soviet Ambassador Dobrynin asked for a meeting with Carter's national security adviser, Zbigniew Brzezinski, in order to raise the possibility of a prisoner swap. When Brzezinski suggested that the exchange should include Shcharansky and Ginzburg, Dobrynin offered him two convicted hijackers, which was unacceptable to Brzezinski. He continued to press for Shcharansky and Ginzburg, though he knew that he would probably fail at this stage.

Finding no mobility on the Soviet side, he switched the focus to other Soviet dissidents. The White House officials encountered a palpable and singular hatred for Shcharansky. When Carter met with Gromyko, the Soviet foreign minister went out of his way to mock Shcharansky, even pretending that he did not know the name. Gromyko ostentatiously turned to one of his aides—Carter and Brzezinski were sitting across the table from him in the Cabinet room—and asked, "What's the name of that man?" And then Gromyko mimicked the name as his aides sneered.

The Kremlin's decision to single out Shcharansky was not just an accident of the Soviet system of repression, Brzezinski felt. Rather, it was a deliberate effort to come down hard on someone who seemed to have attracted American attention and who was very much the focal point of the dialogue about human rights. In Brzezinski's view, the American government could not ignore that fact or pretend that the incident had not transpired. A simple protest over the Shcharansky affair would not have been enough. The Soviets would have laughed that off. Thus he proposed a strong American reaction, including the holding back of high-technology transfers. It was a matter on which the Soviets were as sensitive as the Carter administration was on human rights issues.

Brzezinski, like Mondale, also met with Avital at the White House. She struck him as a serious, dedicated person, carrying a torch not just for her husband but for others who were suffering as he was.

It was very much in character for Carter to come personally to Shcharansky's defense and to deny that the spokesman for the Jewish and human rights movements had any association with the CIA. It was harder for the bureaucratic echelons to say so, since the policy was neither to deny nor to confirm such charges. And some people in the government were uncomfortable with Carter's position, concerned that a precedent might have been established. But Carter had no doubt; and Brzezinski supported the president's decision to speak out.

It was the Soviets who elevated the Shcharansky affair to international headlines, not the United States. The Americans did not create the Shcharansky case, nor did they identify him with the administration's human rights position. The Soviets did that: by charging that Shcharansky was a CIA agent, the Kremlin acted in a manner that could only be perceived in Washington as deliberately provocative. What might have passed as an internal matter was thus propelled into the international arena.

AMERICAN JEWS in general, and thousands of non-Jews, appeared to be much more active on behalf of Soviet Jews than were Israelis, with a handful of exceptions. This ostensible lack of enthusiasm has been attributed to a variety of social, economic, and political factors: the Israeli public is too busy struggling for financial survival in a society where men serve in the reserves forty-five days a year until age fifty; Israelis of Asian and African origin, who now comprise a majority of the population, appear somewhat less concerned with the fate of Ashkenazi Jews; and even most of the tens of thousands of Soviet-Jewish repatriates seemed to lose interest once they became absorbed into Israeli society. Some segments of the Israeli religious population, mostly from the right wing of the observant community, did become involved, while people on the left appeared to be more concerned with human rights problems closer to home—treatment of the Arab minority and the Palestinians in the territories. Mass rallies for Soviet Jewry were mostly a Diaspora phenomenon. Israeli political leaders often seemed to pay little more than lip service to the cause, though there are indications that on the covert level Israel acted much more vigorously and constantly than appeared on the surface.

On May 21, 1978 White House Counsel Robert Lipshutz spoke at a 'Soviet Jewry Solidarity Day' rally in New York's Battery Park that drew a crowd estimated at over a quarter of a million. "When I saw the Statue of Liberty in the background as I walked through Battery Park today," he said, "I recalled that all four of my grandparents sailed into this harbor almost ninety years ago as refugees from the oppression of another Russian government. It is my hope that through the efforts of all of us as demonstrated by this Solidarity Day, many, many others will be able to do so in the future." Lipshutz was taking a realistic view—the promised land was still America for most of the Jews wishing to leave Russia. But this was because the Jewish movement had grown so fast and had actually separated into two movements: those who had acquired Jewish national, religious, or ethnic identity and were basically Israel-oriented, and those who were only vaguely aware of their Jewishness but harbored fears of anti-Semitism. In his speech, Lipshutz lashed out at the Soviet government for persecuting Shcharansky and other dissidents and noted the intensity of America's concern for Anatoly's fate.

Throughout this period, a growing number of prominent Americans were becoming involved. Philip Handler, president of the National Academy of Sciences, wrote to Brezhnev and warned that U.S.–Soviet scientific cooperation might be undermined by Soviet handling of the Shcharansky affair. The involvement of the scientists came about, it was said, specifically because of Shcharansky's participation in the broader human rights movement.

On July 8, 1978 Secretary of State Vance added his voice to the condemnations of Soviet actions against the dissidents, saying that the upcoming trials violated fundamental principles of justice. Because of Soviet abuses of human rights, two American delegations scheduled to visit the USSR would stay at home, Vance said.

However, he also said that the United States would persist in the attempt to negotiate a sound SALT II arms-control agreement with the Russians. "It is in the national interest and in the interest of world peace to do so," he said. Senator Henry Jackson urged Vance not to go to a scheduled meeting with Gromyko in Geneva in order to register American disapproval over the Shcharansky affair and related issues; but Carter supported Vance's position against any delay in the arms-control talks. Vance said the talks had a "special quality" because they dealt with the possibility of "mutual annihilation."

But the arrest and trial of Shcharansky and other Soviet

violations of human rights seriously complicated the Carter administration's efforts to reach a new SALT agreement with the Soviets. This was especially evident at the meeting in Geneva, where Vance vigorously protested against the Soviet actions, and Gromyko showed his irritation over the Shcharansky issue.

On Capitol Hill, Democratic Representative Robert Drinan of Massachusetts, a Catholic priest, had emerged as Shcharansky's chief supporter. He was enlisted in the campaign by Manekofsky, who stalked the corridors of Congress looking for someone to chair the International Committee for the Release of Anatoly Shcharansky. Everyone turned her down until she got to Drinan's office. Drinan, speaking for himself and his aide, Doug Cahn, said: "Absolutely, we'll take it." Drinan, who had met Anatoly during a visit to the USSR in 1975, proved to be a dynamic crusader, persuading many people on the Hill to get involved in the committee. Drinan had found Shcharansky to be "enormously committed to his belief in the letter of the Helsinki Final Act, and extremely effective in mobilizing the Moscow Helsinki group from its inception."

Avital had become a well-known figure in Washington, working closely with Drinan and Manekofsky. She remained the driving force in keeping the issue of her husband alive. Her brother Michael, who accompanied her on many trips, appeared to be critical of the American Jewish establishment's cautious position. But Avital tried to bridge the differences between the organizations. In July 1978, however, she went public with her disenchantment over the bitter squabbling between the establishment and activist groups. In an interview with the *San Francisco Jewish Bulletin*, Avital termed the infighting "horrible," saying that it sapped energy from the movement and "hurt the people who are the most involved." Manekofsky, her closest ally in Washington, rebuked her friend in a letter to the Jewish newspaper, saying that Avital did not understand the diversity of a democracy."

On July 10, 1978 Congressman Drinan introduced a House resolution in support of Shcharansky. The resolution, which passed easily, warned that a conviction "can only adversely affect relations between the United States and the Soviet Union." It urged the Soviets to release Shcharansky immediately and to allow him to emigrate to Israel. That week, as Anatoly was sentenced to thirteen years in prison, his picture appeared on the covers of *Newsweek* and *Time,* with the latter showing a crumbled word, détente. But the Kremlin was not impressed; it was widely believed that Shcharansky would have to serve at least half his sentence before any deal for his release could be worked out.

Nevertheless, a year later reports started to surface that the United States was trying to arrange a prisoner exchange with the Soviets. Drinan wrote to Brzezinski, asking that Shcharansky be included if at all possible. By then, Anatoly was reported to be in poor health. The authorities would not allow his mother or Leonid to visit him. "Clearly," Drinan added, "swift action must be taken in order to prevent the Soviet Union from continuing its deliberate degradation of Anatoly Shcharansky."

Drinan continued to introduce more resolutions, make speeches, and write letters on Shcharansky's behalf. Among the congressional colleagues he recruited was Republican Representative Ben Gilman, who later played a minor behind-the-scenes role in efforts to obtain Anatoly's release.

Republican Congressman Jack Kemp of New York, like

many of his colleagues, also wrote personally to Leonid Brezhnev, saying that Anatoly was simply a Jew who wished to make his home in his historic homeland with his wife. Another letter, dated October 26, 1979 and signed by sixty-eight congressmen, was sent to Ambassador Dobrynin. It urged the USSR to allow an American neurologist to examine Shcharansky. From the Soviet point of view, such a request was outrageous, and they turned it down.

Détente was collapsing in 1979 and 1980, as evidenced by the Soviet invasion of Afghanistan, the U.S. boycott of the Moscow Olympics, and the failure of SALT II. The Kremlin leadership seemed less likely than ever to make any major concessions on releasing Shcharansky. Irwin Cotler, the McGill University law professor who produced an eight-hundred-page brief on Shcharansky's behalf, found out just how adamant the Soviets were on the subject when he arrived in Moscow in the autumn of 1979 with a Canadian delegation of jurists. Cotler was on the way to visit Anatoly's parents in Istra, accompanied by Leonid Shcharansky and Professor Lerner, when he was stopped and interrogated by Soviet militia. They tried to force him to sign what amounted to a confession of wrongdoing. His legal briefs were seized and he was expelled from the Soviet Union.

SOON AFTER RONALD REAGAN was sworn in as president on January 20, 1981—Anatoly Shcharansky's thirty-third birthday—Avital issued a statement in Jerusalem thanking Jimmy Carter for all his attempts to secure the release of her husband and all other innocent political prisoners. She expressed the hope that Reagan would continue to use all means possible to help. "If we continue to pressure the Russians, one day they will surely release my husband and all prisoners of conscience. People all over the world should know that you cannot keep innocent people locked up behind barbed wire like animals in a cage—innocent people whose only wish is to live peacefully in their rightful land."

President Reagan responded positively to a request for a meeting with Avital. It came on May 28, 1981, a few hours after Avital was received by Secretary of State Alexander Haig, who had also met with her earlier that month. She was accompanied to the White House by Yosef Mendelevich, who had been released by the Soviets three months earlier after serving eleven years in prison for his role in the Leningrad hijack affair. Reagan, joined by Vice President George Bush and top White House aides, expressed deep sympathy for the persecuted Jewish and other religious communities in the USSR as well as for the plight of Anatoly Shcharansky. He promised to do all in his power to alleviate the situation. The White House spokesman later told reporters that although American officials would continue to raise the Shcharansky case with the Russians, "This is a time for quiet diplomacy."

Reagan himself told Avital that he believed in "quiet diplomacy," according to Professor Richard Pipes, whose 1975 conversation with Anatoly in Moscow had been listed among Anatoly's "crimes." Pipes was now Reagan's adviser on Soviet affairs. The president was against publicly preaching to the Russians to release Shcharansky. He felt that pushing the Russians against the wall would be counterproductive.

It was about this time that the media started to report on renewed efforts to arrange a prisoner swap that would involve Anatoly. "Top-Secret Deal May Free Soviet Dissident," a *New York Post* headline blared. It reported that

Rabbi Ronald Greenwald of Monsey, New York, had won the "quiet and unprecedented" help of the Reagan administration to explore an exchange. Greenwald had just returned from South Africa, fueling speculation that a Soviet spy jailed in Johannesburg might be involved. Greenwald was also in contact with East German lawyer Wolfgang Vogel, whom he had befriended during complicated negotiations involving an Israeli citizen held in Maputo, Mozambique and an American student arrested in East Germany. But these reports were premature by several years, and Greenwald and others like him were only on the periphery of events. There had been many similar reports in the media over the years, stemming from sources who were "directly involved" in negotiations over Shcharansky.

Even before Avital's meeting with Reagan, the Soviets, whose sensitivity over the issue was mounting, intensified their attacks on the "Free Shcharansky" campaign. Thus, on May 15, 1981 Tass criticized the fact that Secretary of State Haig had met with "a certain Madam Shcharanskaya." The official Soviet news agency dispatch, in a peculiar syntax that dripped venom, declared: "What 'Madam Shcharanskaya' is, is an open secret. It is well-known that this person is not Shcharanskaya but a certain Shtiglits, a crook, who in 1973 [sic] left the USSR for Israel. She has never been officially married to Shcharansky, which back in the past was officially reaffirmed by the Chief Rabbi of the Moscow Synagogue, Yakov Fishman."

The news agency said that "the self-proclaimed wife" was specializing in "anti-Soviet slander" and was a tool of Zionist plotters. That, it said, was no surprise. "What is surprising is why and for what purpose such a high-ranking official as Alexander Haig should be hobnobbing with a patent swindler."

Three days later, Tass protested against another "provocative" congressional resolution calling for Shcharansky's release. "Certain circles in the United States are making another attempt (this time through the Senate) to come to the rescue of their agent who was caught and sentenced in another country." This "unseemly action" attempted to portray Anatoly as an innocent victim, "although it is no secret that he was sentenced for a concrete and very grave crime—high treason in the form of espionage and assistance to a foreign state in conducting hostile activities against the Soviet Union." It called the congressional resolutions interference in the USSR's internal affairs. "And this, to put it straight, does not in the least help improve Soviet-American relations, and, by the way, does not benefit Shcharansky himself." That last statement was interpreted by American analysts as a hint that improved American-Soviet relations might have a positive effect in freeing Shcharansky.

Reagan's meeting with Avital set off a fresh barrage of attacks from Soviet commentators, who accused the president of a "sordid" and "astonishing" act that further damaged American-Soviet relations. American newspapers praised Reagan for meeting with Avital. The *Los Angeles Times* called it "a decent and sensitive thing for the President to do" and advised the Soviets that the only way to alleviate their embarrassment and chagrin was to "release Shcharansky and all the other innocents."

The most dramatic expression of appreciation to Reagan came in the form of a letter from fifteen leading refuseniks and Anatoly's mother Ida Milgrom. The letter was forwarded to Reagan by an American Jewish organization leader, Theodore Mann, who brought it back from Moscow. "We are very grateful to you for the attention which you showed to the cause of the Jewish emigration movement hero A. Shcharansky by receiving his wife Avital and discussing with her the possibilities of gaining the freedom of our beloved Anatoly," the letter said. "We count on the fact that you personally, and your associates, will do your utmost to assist us in our struggle for the right to emigrate, in the great tradition of your freedom-loving country."

Reagan personally phoned Mann to assure him that the fate of Soviet Jews would continue to be a top priority in negotiations with the USSR. He added that he had already communicated this fact to Brezhnev in a personal note. The president told Mann that he was "working on the issue" but believed it was sometimes wiser to deal not through the press, but in a more direct manner.

THE WHITE HOUSE did not understand that Anatoly Shcharansky—despite his ill health, his suffering in the Gulag, his longing to be reunited with Avital—had priorities higher than his personal freedom. That he was not willing to compromise to obtain his liberty became evident during an amazing development in 1983, which stunned top officials in the Reagan administration.

The intense diplomatic efforts to arrange some kind of deal with the Soviets continued throughout Reagan's first term. In early 1983, the U.S. representative to the Helsinki accords meeting in Madrid, Washington lawyer Max Kampelman, came within a hair's breadth of nailing down an agreement with the Russians that would have resulted in Shcharansky's release that year. But it was scuttled at the last moment. Some former White House officials privately blamed Avital for killing the deal, but they were mistaken: the decision to stay in prison was made entirely by Anatoly.

Kampelman, long active in Democratic politics and Jewish affairs, had received Reagan's blessing to do whatever he could to try to win Shcharansky's release. The Madrid talks were crucial to what remained of the U.S.–Soviet dialogue in the "post-détente" era, and it was the most appropriate—as well as convenient—forum for discussing the Shcharansky case.

Under the deal worked out in Madrid, Anatoly would be released if he would write a one-sentence letter to Kremlin leader Yuri Andropov, saying, "I hereby request release on the grounds of poor health." There was no reference to a pardon or clemency, nothing that could reasonably be interpreted as an admission of guilt. Shcharansky, the Soviets promised, would then be released. According to American officials, the letter was a Soviet idea. The Soviets' original condition had been that Shcharansky should admit some form of guilt by seeking a pardon. But Kampelman managed to get the Soviets to change their stance, and the final terms did not, in the American view, include any negative implications. But Anatoly felt otherwise.

During the many months of negotiations and under Kampelman's continuous prodding, the Soviets permitted Ida Milgrom, who had not been allowed to see her son for over a year, to visit him a couple of times—no doubt in the hope that she would be able to persuade him to accept the proposal. His mother, worried about his health, urged him to accept the offer and recited the names of the friends and relatives who agreed with her position. The one name conspicuously missing was Avital's. Anatoly was not surprised.

The bond between them was so strong that they felt they lived inside each other's minds. Avital knew he would make his own decision, and he knew she would accept whatever he chose to do. "Please think about it for a while," Ida implored him.

"There's nothing to think about," he replied. He felt that the slightest compromise with his Soviet captors would detract from, perhaps even endanger, the great victory of the spirit he had already won.

Moreover, Anatoly told his mother, he himself would set a condition for his release: he would agree to unburden the Soviets of their continuing embarrassment if those who fabricated the charges against him—the government, KGB officials, and agents such as Lipavsky—were punished. Since that was hardly likely, he would not sign the request for his release.

It was true that the statement did not include any admission of guilt. He was not asked to request a pardon or to make an apology—it was only a simple sentence asking for his release on the grounds of health. But Anatoly knew it would be distorted to seem much more than that. "In the Soviet Union," explained an intimate friend who agreed with Anatoly's position, "everyone knows that they think one thing, write another, and say a third." Everything that had been done to him for the past six years, Anatoly said, was illegal. "On what basis should I appeal? Any appeal would be inappropriate." Anatoly was convinced that the Soviets would in the end decide according to their own interest, without regard to letters of appeal. His signature would have been read as an appeal for a pardon; it would imply that he had done something wrong, that there was, after all, some foundation to the charges for which he had already spent hard years in prison.

The Americans were ill-equipped to understand Shcharansky's character, his refusal to make any deals with the Grand Inquisitor. He had developed an extraordinary internal strength that enabled him to withstand the KGB pressures under interrogation and the harsh conditions of his imprisonment. Anatoly had learned to survive, to preserve his intellectual and emotional life, which nurtured him in the punishment cells and enabled him to cope—on two occasions—with the very real possibility of his own imminent death. Willpower and self-discipline had helped him to face down the fear and the horror, and he had maintained his equilibrium. Now, having endured extreme psychological and physical rigors, he was confident that he could take whatever they threw at him. He was very much his own man. And from his point of view he had won the battle: the captive, not the captor, would dictate the future course of the war. Anatoly tried to explain this to his mother, to tell her that he had transcended the man he was before his arrest, that he had broken through the spider's web of Soviet deception and would not retreat.

But Kampelman and the other Americans involved in the negotiations were deeply disappointed by Anatoly's decision, and there was consternation in the White House. Some officials mistakenly placed the blame on Avital and the people who surrounded her, for Avital had of late grown very militant in her demands for the release of all Jews in the USSR. Nevertheless, they continued to press for Anatoly's unconditional release.

As her own religiosity grew, Avital became increasingly

involved with religious activists. In Israel, she was now almost exclusively surrounded by members of the Mercaz Harav Institute. In America, she worked most closely with New York rabbi Avraham Weiss, an outspoken ally of Gush Emunim (Bloc of the Faithful, the religious-nationalist group that spearheaded most settlements in the territories) and defender of individuals within that movement who committed violent actions against West Bank Arabs. (The rabbi himself disavowed all violence.) Weiss became the leading activist on behalf of the Shcharanskys, accompanying Avital on many of her trips and managing what became known as the Shcharansky Fund, which helped pay for Avital's worldwide struggle on behalf of her husband. He continually clashed with the establishment groups by demanding more militant actions than they deemed wise or necessary.

Disagreements were not confined to the Jewish organizations and activists around Avital. Within the Reagan administration, there was always some difference of opinion about the ultimate wisdom of highlighting the Shcharansky case. Some experts on the National Security Council and elsewhere actually felt that the more attention the administration paid to the Shcharansky affair, the more concessions the Soviets would eventually demand for his release. "Every time the president sees Avital," one U.S. official said, "the price goes up." But despite the view that it would be best to keep the case out of the headlines, it was always high on the Reagan administration's agenda. In the end, the school of thought that considered a high-visibility profile to be more effective won the day.

The U.S. government's role in the entire Shcharansky affair was pivotal in terms of the kind of charge that was made against Shcharansky and the length of the prison sentence, as well as in his eventual release. The Shcharansky affair was simply "a thorn in everybody's side," according to David Shipler of the *New York Times,* who was Moscow bureau chief in the midseventies and a friend of Anatoly's. In order to improve Soviet-American relations, it had to be resolved. "It was always there. At every bilateral meeting that took place, Shcharansky's name was mentioned. I believe that eventually this did have an effect."

IN THE YEARS that Anatoly spent in prison, the Soviet leadership changed from Brezhnev to KGB chief Yuri Andropov to Konstantin Chernenko to Mikhail Gorbachev. The hopes for obtaining Anatoly's release appeared to increase with the accession of power by Gorbachev, who was extremely young by Soviet leadership standards, image-conscious, and apparently more open to compromise than his predecessors. Moreover, it was now quite obvious to Soviet policy makers concerned about President Reagan's Strategic Defense Initiative, "Star Wars," that it would be beneficial to make some gesture in order to influence American public opinion on arms control and on bilateral relations in general. Reagan's decision to raise the Shcharansky matter personally with Gorbachev at their November 1985 summit meeting in Geneva was extremely significant in setting the stage for Shcharansky's final release. United States government experts agree that the earnest behind-the-scenes efforts of a few American congressmen, lawyers, Jewish leaders, and others were only sideshows to the real action—"window dressing," as one official put it.

The American official most directly involved in arranging the details of Shcharansky's release was Mark Palmer, a deputy assistant secretary of state. The career diplomat, who in effect had been assigned the Shcharansky portfolio, came to be widely credited in Washington with playing the key role in obtaining his release. Part of the complex deal being worked out with the Soviets was that American officials would not embarrass the Kremlin by publicly taking credit for obtaining Shcharansky's freedom. The administration agreed, hoping that similar deals involving other dissidents could be arranged in the future.

It did not seem plausible that Gorbachev would agree to Shcharansky's release in the period just before or after the November 1985 summit, since this might be construed as Soviet weakness. In the late summer of 1985, there were rumors that the Soviets were about to open the doors to a new wave of emigration and might also free Shcharansky or another well-known prisoner of Zion. Much of the optimism appeared to originate with officials of the World Jewish Congress, whose president, Canadian magnate Edgar Bronfman, had just returned from a trip to Moscow. Bronfman and his top associates, in off-the-record comments to American Jewish and Israeli leaders, said that the Soviets had promised to begin a process to improve relations with world Jewry. They believed the Kremlin would make good-will gestures before the Geneva summit. There was a growing feeling that Gorbachev was interested in reforming the Soviet system and that this might include a more rational, human approach to the Soviet-Jewry issue, if only in order to secure Western financial credits and the high-technology equipment the USSR so desperately needs.

There were also indications that the Soviets, who have long sought a role in the Middle East peace process, might be weighing a renewal of diplomatic ties with Israel. Speculation about an imminent easing of curbs on Soviet Jews increased following a secret meeting in July 1985 between the Soviet and Israeli ambassadors in Paris, and a brief but cordial meeting at the United Nations between Prime Minister Shimon Peres and Soviet Foreign Minister Eduard Shevardnadze. A New York Jewish newspaper claimed that a Moscow-Israel airlift of fifteen thousand Soviet Jews would take place in the first half of December, just after the summit. In November, the Soviets agreed to release longtime refusenik Ilya Essas, who had become a religious leader among Soviet Jews. But there were no indications that Anatoly's release was in the cards. In October, Gorbachev, in an interview with the French Communist newspaper *L'Humanité,* insisted that Shcharansky had been involved in espionage and was therefore a special case among imprisoned Jewish activists. However, World Jewish Congress leaders who returned to Moscow in December noticed that for the first time mention of Shcharansky's name no longer elicited angry harangues and charges that he was a spy. Yosef Begun, imprisoned for teaching Hebrew, had replaced Shcharansky as the number-one villain.

In the weeks before the summit, refuseniks in Moscow told a correspondent from the *Jerusalem Post* that they thought the Kremlin would not release large numbers of Jews except in exchange for some major concession from the United States. There was little support for Avital Shcharansky's stated position that the United States ought not to compromise on lifting American trade barriers until the Soviets freed all 400,000 Jews who had received official invitations from relatives in Israel but were afraid to use them. Although Avital's stand might be rhetorically satisfying, several refuseniks said, it would not bring about the desired results.

"The United States is going to have to offer increased trade in items the Soviets need—computers and advanced Western technology—in order to win increased Jewish emigration and the release of the prisoners of Zion and the long-term refuseniks," said Lev Blitshtein, a refusenik close to the Shcharansky family. Blitshtein, a former chief administrator in the Ministry of Meat and Dairy, had been "in refusal" for ten years, kept from his wife and children who had been permitted to go to America. They had signed divorce papers in order for her to leave the USSR. In the shabby, run-down apartment where the family once lived together, the walls were bare except for a poster of Israeli soldiers conducting a prayer service. "Despite the pain I feel every day at being separated from my family, I consider myself the luckiest man in the world that I was able to get my wife and children out of this country, to a place where they could build a better life," he said.

Leonid Shcharansky, who was visiting Blitshtein, viewed the accession of Gorbachev and the upcoming summit as promising developments in the struggle to obtain his brother's release. Noting that his brother had served more than half of his thirteen-year sentence, he said the Soviets might free Anatoly as a gesture of goodwill at the time of the summit. He emphasized that it was important not to get sidetracked—for example, by focusing on new restrictions and harassments that Anatoly was being subjected to in prison—and to work only for his release.

Leonid did not think that putting the focus on Anatoly's release eclipsed the struggle to free other prisoners of Zion and refuseniks. In any case, "freedom for Anatoly Shcharansky, the man who has more than any other inspired the movement, has to be given top priority."

The reverence that Leonid felt for his brother was not confined to the family. Alexander Lerner, one of the world's foremost experts in cybernetics and one of Anatoly's closest friends despite a thirty-year difference in their ages, had painted several portraits of Tolya in the years before and after his imprisonment. One showed Anatoly's face reflected in the light of a menorah, the holy Jewish candelabrum, rendering him as the spirit of Jewish resistance and regeneration. Lerner, like Leonid, felt that the upcoming summit was a golden opportunity for obtaining Tolya's release.

In chilly Geneva, as the summit was about to open, Jewish students from all over Europe held a "Free Shcharansky" rally in front of the ornate National Theater. Two goats were paraded across the square in front of the theater to dramatize the "scapegoat" status of Soviet Jews. The gulf between the activists and the establishment American-Jewish and Israeli organizations became apparent at a Geneva press conference, where Edgar Bronfman urged Jews to avoid expressing anti-Soviet sentiments during the summit. But he conceded that despite Soviet hints that a process was under way to ease tension between world Jewry and the USSR, there had as yet been no evidence of the Kremlin's willingness to ease the plight of Soviet Jews.

Avital was also in Geneva for the summit, where she tried unsuccessfully to deliver to the Soviet mission a letter to Mrs. Gorbachev, appealing for her help in freeing Anatoly. Avital and her aides were later arrested by Swiss police because demonstrations had been outlawed for the duration of the summit. Lawyer Irwin Cotler, with the help of the U.S., Canadian, and Israeli governments, managed to have her released after a few hours.

At the summit talks themselves, President Reagan raised

Shcharansky's name during a private meeting with the Soviet secretary-general. For over an hour, Gorbachev listened to Reagan's views on the issue of human rights. Reagan focused on Soviet Jews and talked about Anatoly. According to U.S. officials, Gorbachev "hardly responded to any of the things the president pushed—on emigration or anything else. He didn't come back, as Gromyko had done on earlier occasions, by saying 'I don't want to talk about it.' He was simply silent." But the Reagan message clearly had gotten through.

IN THE CHAIN of events that finally led to Anatoly Shcharansky's freedom, the West German government also played a crucial role. In the spring of 1985, East Germany's special representative for humanitarian affairs, lawyer Wolfgang Vogel of East Berlin, approached his regular contact in Bonn, Ludwig A. Rehlinger, secretary of state at the Federal Ministry for Intra-German Relations, and told him: "I have a special mandate to negotiate Shcharansky's release."

For years, the two men had been holding ongoing talks on the question of "humanitarian affairs" between the two Germanys, which are broadly defined to include the release of political prisoners from East Germany and the exchange of intelligence agents from both sides. Vogel's sudden announcement was made during the course of one of these regular meetings in the ministry offices along the Bundesallee thoroughfare. Vogel made it plain that the "Eastern side"—in this case meaning the Soviet Union—was seeking an adequate quid pro quo in exchange for Shcharansky's liberty. To the West Germans, it was immediately clear that this meant the release of Eastern European agents. But the deal they came up with was turned down by the Soviets—

for reasons known only to the Kremlin leaders. Thus, the spy swap that finally came about in June 1985 did not include the most famous prisoner in the USSR. Instead, twenty-five Western agents were traded for four East Bloc spies imprisoned in the United States. The exchange took place at the Glienicke Bridge, a little-used iron span over the Havel River dividing East Germany and West Berlin—the crossing to Potsdam, sixteen miles away. At the same site in February 1962, the American U-2 pilot downed by the Soviets, Francis Gary Powers, walked to freedom past Soviet superspy Rudolf Abel, a KGB colonel of Jewish origin who had been caught spying in the United States. Vogel had arranged that deal too.

Wolfgang Vogel, a debonair Communist East Berlin millionaire born in Silesia in 1925, has been the key figure in virtually every East-West swap since the Powers-Abel exchange. A confidant of and troubleshooter for East German Communist party chief Erich Honecker, Vogel has acquired a reputation as a master of delicate international business.

According to a former high CIA official, individuals like Vogel had moved into the area of international diplomacy known as "flesh peddling" because it was "too messy" for governments to handle. Huge sums of money, usually paid by West Germany to East Germany to obtain the release of prisoners, have passed through Vogel's hands. Vogel has also defended Nazi criminals in East Germany.

Involved in unofficial American contacts with Vogel over Shcharansky was Rabbi Ronald Greenwald, the ambitious, hard-driving Brooklyn man who, besides being a local Orthodox leader, was also an international commodities trader with Republican party links. They met on several occasions in Vogel's elegantly furnished offices and periodically discussed the Shcharansky case over a span of eight years. The American was impressed by Vogel, terming him "a humanitarian." But it appears that once Vogel got the go-ahead from the Kremlin on a Shcharansky deal, there was no longer any need whatsoever, if there ever had been, to work through such back channels. Vogel spoke directly with the American embassy and negotiated exclusively with his old trading partner, Rehlinger, though Greenwald did continue to meet with him.

In July 1985, a month after the big spy swap on the Glienicke Bridge, Vogel was back in Rehlinger's office, saying that his mandate to negotiate Shcharansky's release had been renewed. Bonn officials believed that the West would have to pay a hefty price if the deal was to win approval of the Soviet leadership, but the precise nature of the price had them stumped. The Kremlin had demonstrated that its concern was not with the number of spies exchanged or their importance. All that Rehlinger could do at that point was to reiterate that the West German government would be glad to do anything possible to secure Shcharansky's release. Vogel also contacted U.S. Ambassador Richard Burt at the embassy in Bonn to make him aware of the renewed efforts to reach a deal.

In the ensuing months, Rehlinger and Burt met periodically to exchange information and coordinate their positions. However, it was not deemed necessary to set up a joint American–West German negotiating team.

At that time, West Germany was holding only one Soviet spy, Yevgeny Semlyakov, a Russian computer specialist who was considered small fry. In order to satisfy the Kremlin's minimum requirements, a multinational "package deal" had to be arranged. The Americans said that they would be willing to include a number of Eastern European agents in the proposed exchange.

Vogel was the sole negotiator on the Eastern side, representing the interests of the USSR, Poland, and Czechoslovakia, as well as his own country. He had known Rehlinger for over twenty years, and the two men were familiar with each other's aims and negotiating tactics. They wasted no time getting down to business, presenting each other with lists of names of agents whose release they wished to obtain. But it was a laborious process, with bureaucratic delays caused each time a name was added or deleted. A major sticking point as far as the Americans were concerned was that Anatoly, convicted on trumped-up espionage charges, should be set apart in an exchange of real or suspected spies from East and West. Some kind of formula would have to be worked out. Apparently, the Soviets never insisted that Shcharansky be flown first to the United States, as had been the case when the two main figures in the 1970 Leningrad trial—Kuznetsov and Dymshits—were freed.

In December 1985, shortly after the Geneva summit, Vogel told Rehlinger that his mandate to negotiate Shcharansky's release was still valid. Talks resumed, with a break during the Christmas holidays. The final round of negotiations took place on January 23, 1986, at the Gaspinger Hof Hotel ski resort in Geros, in the Austrian Tirol, where Rehlinger was vacationing. He was joined there by Vogel, U.S. Ambassador to East Germany Francis J. Meehan, and Olaf Grobel, an aide to Ambassador Burt. Rehlinger, concealing the identity of his visitors from the hotel management, held the meeting in a suite adjoining his room. The negotiators worked throughout the day on the release of the prisoner of

Zion and the exchange of spies, taking only one break, for lunch. In the late afternoon, they finally agreed on the list of names, and the time and place for the exchange: Glienicke Bridge on Tuesday morning between ten o'clock and noon, February 11, 1986.

There was still one possible snag. Two days after the meeting in Austria, Vogel flew to the United States to talk to two of the spies on the list: husband and wife Karl and Hana Koecher, who had passed CIA secrets to Czechoslovak intelligence. Since they were American citizens, they could not be expelled against their wishes. However, Vogel had no trouble persuading the Koechers to go along—they agreed readily to the exchange, and everything was set to go. The Koechers, Semlyakov, and two other spies held in West Germany—Jerzy Kaczmarek of the Polish secret service and East German security agent Detlef Scharfenot—would be traded for Shcharansky and three persons held by East Germany: Czechoslovak Jaroslav Jaworski, West German Dietrich Nistroy, and East German Wolf George Frohn.

The rumor mills were working around the world. In January South African President P. W. Botha suggested that Pretoria might release black nationalist leader Nelson Mandela as part of an East-West swap that would include Shcharansky, Andrei Sakharov, and a South African soldier captured in Angola. Pretoria's position had been conveyed to the Kremlin months earlier by World Jewish Congress president Bronfman, who encouraged the Kremlin leaders to pursue the possibility of a trade with South Africa for Anatoly. Although Israel was reportedly involved to some degree in efforts to have Mandela included in an exchange of prisoners, it all came to naught—as was evident from Vogel's offer, the Soviet leadership had long before made up its mind about when and how to release Shcharansky. The Israeli ambassador to Bonn, Yitzhak Ben-Ari, was notified only a few days before the exchange was to take place.

The real story was leaked, apparently by the KGB, to *Bild,* the daily newspaper published in Hamburg, which published its international scoop on February 2, 1986.

In Israel, the prime minister's office declined to comment on the reports, but official sources confirmed that there was definitely "indicative information" that an exchange was about to take place.

It was evident to some experts that Gorbachev, from an internal standpoint, wanted to clean the slate before the huge Soviet Communist Party Congress convening at the end of February and to preempt the worldwide pro-Shcharansky demonstrations planned by Jewish organizations. Zbigniew Brzezinski believed that the decision to release Shcharansky was based on the Soviet hope of influencing American public opinion on disarmament issues, and possibly included a probe for some Soviet-Israeli dialogue on the Middle East conflict.

ANATOLY HIMSELF was unaware of the agreement reached in Austria, even the day before his release. In December, he was in the prison of the Perm labor camp in the Ural mountains, serving his second punishment of the year for protesting the revocation of his mail privileges. On Christmas Day, he was taken to the camp hospital, injected with vitamins, and treated for his heart problems. The fattening process had begun again, as it had in 1984. Within one month he gained twenty-two pounds.

Anatoly imagined that the authorities were priming him for a visit by his mother and brother, even though his latest punishment had included revocation of visiting rights until 1987. But his only visitors were four KGB men, who appeared at the hospital on January 27, 1986 and ordered him to dress. As they drove him away, Anatoly took a last look at the soldiers patrolling on the other side of the electronic fence, the border between the labor camp and "the big camp," as the political prisoners called the Soviet Union. His escort boarded a plane with him. A few hours later, he was back in Moscow's Lefortovo Prison, where his ordeal had begun nine years earlier. The KGB men had given no hint of what was in store for him—further punishment, or a visit from his family.

On Monday morning, February 10, Anatoly was reading German classics—Goethe, and a book by the eighteenth-century poet Friedrich von Schiller—when the same four KGB agents came in and handed him a pile of old civilian clothes. "Get dressed," one of them said. This had never happened before, and Anatoly understood at once that something extraordinary was about to happen. He donned the ill-fitting clothing, gathered up his books, and followed them out of the cell.

A black Volga whisked him once again through the familiar streets of Moscow directly to the main airport. A warmed-up plane was waiting for them. As Anatoly got out of the car, one of the KGB men took his books from him and said he would not be permitted to take them aboard. Anatoly insisted on taking just one of the books, the tiny volume of Hebrew Psalms that had been Avital's gift. The KGB man refused. Anatoly lay down in the snow, declaring that he would not move until they gave it back. Although he could not help thinking that he was about to be freed, Anatoly continued his battle with the KGB to the end. The four agents cursed and threatened, but finally returned the book of Psalms. Anatoly entered the plane, his excitement mounting. Minutes later they took off. Judging by the sun, he knew that they were flying westward. He could smell freedom. Anatoly asked no questions for two hours, until he realized that they must be crossing the Soviet border; then he demanded an explanation from one of the stony-faced intelligence agents. Finally, one of the KGB men said that he was empowered to declare that the Supreme Soviet of the Soviet Union had deprived Shcharansky of his Soviet citizenship for his conduct. "As an American spy, you are being expelled from the Soviet Union."

"First of all," Anatoly replied, "I am deeply satisfied that thirteen years after I asked you to deprive me of my Soviet citizenship, my demand has been met." He denied that his human rights activities involved any form of spying, and urged the secret service agents to join him, to leave Russia, and live in a free society, as he was about to do. He expressed the hope that the Soviets would acknowledge that he was "absolutely innocent." He had been cruelly and unjustly punished, serving nine terrible years in prison for acting as a Jew, a Zionist, and a guardian of human rights. This had nothing to do with espionage or any of the other crimes he was falsely accused of, he told the agents, adding: "And I am sure that this activity was very useful—not only for those people whom I was defending, but also for the country which I have the good fortune to leave now. Because the problem of human rights concerns everybody, and that's why you too should leave this society which condemns such concern."

Then he turned away from them to read from the volume that had sustained him, opening to a well-worn page:

Psalm 133, the blessing of unification with his brethren in restored Zion, a song of ascent. As the plane began to descend through the clouds, Anatoly looked out the window and asked the agents what country they were in. The KGB men said they didn't know. His first thought was that they were in Holland or Switzerland and that he would be seeing Avital in a few more minutes. But when they landed, he saw signs indicating that they were in East Germany and felt immediate disappointment, knowing that Avital would not be there.

The KGB men told him to get off the plane without them—for diplomatic reasons, they were prohibited from accompanying him onto East German soil. "Do you see that car out there?" said the KGB man in charge, pointing to a dark vehicle parked on the tarmac. "You will walk straight to it, agreed?" "You know I never make agreements with the KGB," Anatoly said. "If you tell me to go directly to the car, I will go some other way." The KGB man responded that that could be dangerous for him. "We shall see," Anatoly said. Descending from the plane, he followed a zigzag route to the car, where an East German government official and an interpreter awaited him.

He asked where he was. They said East Berlin, and then fell silent. It was a tense, Kafkaesque scene, Anatoly thought. To break the ice, he said that as a Jew, Berlin had always aroused mixed feelings in him—but that now it meant freedom. Anatoly told them that he had been reading Goethe and Schiller that morning in his prison cell and never imagined that he would be free in their land a few hours later. He asked the driver to describe the sights along the way as they drove toward Wolfgang Vogel's office. The Shcharansky charm melted the two men, who entered into a lively exchange with their charge.

At Vogel's luxurious office, American Ambassador Meehan, who had helped arrange the swap, told Anatoly that he would remain in East German custody that night and the next morning, and that he should avoid any confrontations with his East German hosts. The rebellious Shcharansky decided to go along with the ambassador's request, since this time it wasn't the KGB he was being asked to obey. Meehan described the procedure set for the next morning: Anatoly would walk from East Germany to West Berlin, the border between them being the middle of the bridge. Then he would be taken by the Americans to the airport, flown to Frankfurt and from there to Israel.

After drinking a toast, Anatoly was taken to a villa for the night, which he shared with the released Czech, Jaworski, who had been sentenced in 1981 to twelve years in prison for helping East Germans flee to the West.

In the morning on that Tuesday, February 11, Anatoly realized a cherished dream: for the first time in nine years, he drank a real cup of coffee. He declined breakfast: "Just give me another cup of coffee," he said.

From the villa, he was taken directly to the snow-covered Glienicke Bridge, accompanied by Ambassador Meehan and Vogel. At American insistence, Anatoly was to be released half an hour before the exchange of convicted or suspected spies, to underline the fact that he was not a Western agent. On the West Berlin side, Ambassador Burt and Rehlinger drove up to the bridge in a black limousine and walked up to the border—a four-inch-wide white line painted across the roadway, from which the snow had been brushed away.

The bridge is located in the forested Wannsee district of southwestern Berlin, the neighborhood where Nazi leaders held the infamous January 1942 conference to plan the systematic extermination of European Jews.

Hundreds of journalists and cameramen on the West Berlin side were kept back from the bridge. At a few minutes before 11:00 A.M. Anatoly appeared, wearing a black fur Russian hat and an overcoat that was far too large, flanked by Meehan and Vogel. He brimmed with excitement as he strode across the white line and into the West, smiling and shouting, "No wall!" He was greeted by Burt and Rehlinger. The latter said: "Welcome, Mr. Shcharansky. I'm very glad to see you *here*."

"When will I see my wife?" Anatoly asked. "You'll have a pleasant surprise in Frankfurt," he was told.

Rehlinger was astonished at the energy and wit the released prisoner displayed as the limousine sped off for Templehof Airport and a short flight to Frankfurt in a U.S. plane. Burt and Rehlinger told him about the negotiations that had led to his release. Anatoly told them anecdotes about his life in the prison camp, with no trace of self-pity. Studying Shcharansky, Rehlinger was reminded of childhood friends. He had been born in 1927 in the Tiergartenviertel (Zoo Quarter) of Berlin, where a large part of the population was Jewish. In Anatoly, he recognized what was typical of many Jews he had known: a mixture of intellect, toughness, and spirit. He was not a man to be broken by a totalitarian regime. In fact, Shcharansky gave Rehlinger a sense of why the Jews had not broken during the last two thousand years.

In Moscow, Ida Milgrom and Leonid were informed by an American reporter that Anatoly was safely in West German hands. "Tolya is free, Tolya is free!" exclaimed his mother, her tears flowing.

At the giant U.S. airbase in Frankfurt, Avital waited anxiously. She had become increasingly tense and nervous in the days before the release was confirmed. She had heard such rumors periodically during twelve years, and all had proved false. To protect her privacy, friends told the press a few days earlier that she had secluded herself in a religious kibbutz in northern Israel to escape the media. Other sources said she was already in West Germany. In fact, Avital was in Jerusalem the whole time, until she was flown to Frankfurt in an Israeli executive jet at 5:00 A.M. on the day of Anatoly's release.

At the airport, she told one of the Israelis waiting with her that she was apprehensive about her husband's physical condition after all he had endured. But as he descended from the plane, she saw that he was wholly himself, with the joy of life still written all over his face. She ran to him and fell into his arms. They embraced for a long time in silence. Finally, he pulled his head back to look into her tear-drenched face. With his characteristic feel for the great one-liner, Anatoly grinned and said: "Sorry I'm late."

The crowd of German, American, and Israeli officials greeted him exuberantly, and Israeli Ambassador Ben-Ari handed him an Israeli passport to replace the laissez-passer issued by the Communists. Anatoly hugged the envoy and asked if the passport were really legal, since there was no photograph of him in it. It would do, the ambassador said. In the VIP lounge, Anatoly was left to spend thirty minutes alone with Avital, the wife who had proved, like Odysseus's Penelope, to be good and wise and faithful to her wedded love.

When they emerged and were served refreshments, Avital remained tense. She urged Anatoly not to drink coffee, but he would not be denied and relished every swallow. The Israeli doctor who had accompanied Avital on the Westwind plane examined Anatoly to see if he was fit enough for the four-and-a-half-hour flight to Israel and the welcome that awaited him there. After the doctor gave his approval, Ambassador Ben-Ari surprised some bystanders when he told Anatoly that he would now face a difficult time: while he was imprisoned, the ambassador said, the whole Jewish people had stood behind him; but now that he was free, various groups would try to pull him to their side. Straight-faced, Anatoly said he thought he could take it. Indeed, to all these seeing him for the first time, as well as those who knew him, Anatoly Shcharansky appeared a man capable of handling just about anything that fate threw at him.

Anatoly and Avital's twelve-year struggle was finally over; they were together at last and bound for home.

7

Homecoming

On board the white Westwind executive jet, a steward produced a bottle of Israeli wine and the passengers drank a toast: "Lehayim!" to life. In addition to Avital and Anatoly there were Avi Maoz, Avital's ubiquitous aide from the Mercaz Harav yeshiva, and the Israeli doctor who had traveled to Frankfurt.

The pilot set the plane on autopilot and joined his celebrated passenger for a few minutes. To his surprise, Anatoly was remarkably well-informed about Israeli aircraft. In *Pravda* he had read about the Kfir jetfighter and even the supersophisticated Lavi warplane that Israel was developing.

Anatoly's interest in the plane and its flight path prompted the pilot to invite him into the cockpit. For a few minutes he held the copilot's controls as the jet pierced the darkening sky, leaving southern Europe and heading out over the Mediterranean.

His first sight of Israel came on the radar screen. For some minutes after the pilot pointed out the coastal contours, Anatoly did not take his eyes off the green phosphorescent image. Then the pilot announced that they would be landing shortly, and Anatoly returned to his seat beside Avital. For the first time since crossing the Glieniecke Bridge that morning, he retreated into himself.

Sitting in silence, he stared out the window. The long

journey was almost over; the hope that had sustained him for the past twelve years was about to be realized. He squeezed Avital's hand as if to reassure himself that she was flesh and blood and not the stuff of dreams.

The plane banked, and beneath the wing a glittering necklace of light shone through the darkness. The plane flew low over a city pulsing with light. "Tel Aviv," someone said. Anatoly craned downward. The woman who, for twelve years, had never stopped talking, pleading, demanding, even carping, had no words for this moment. Avital grasped Anatoly's hand and watched him as he peered, rapt, through the window.

They touched down. Anatoly embraced his Avital, as he called her—it was always "my Avital" and "my Tolya"—and then turned back to the oval window, watching as the plane moved past ranks of stationary aircraft and a waiting ambulance toward a reception area. In the center of the reception area members of the Israeli cabinet were lined up in semidarkness. Beyond them, journalists, photographers, and technicians from Israel and dozens of Western media organizations had taken up positions on the mobile airplane stairways provided for the purpose.

The light fog was not dense enough to hide from Anatoly's view a small grove of graceful palms growing incongruously in the middle of the tarmac. If he needed a sign that he had indeed left behind him the cold of the Russian winter, the palms provided it.

As the pilot cut the engines, Avital held Anatoly back. She had called ahead to her brother Michael, asking him to get decent clothes for Anatoly. Like the Ethiopians who had arrived a year earlier from disease-ridden refugee camps,

Anatoly was dressed in refugee's clothing, his torn pants held up by a piece of twine.

Michael, tall and lanky, crossed the tarmac carrying a white plastic shopping bag. In it were light gray pants, a belt, a blue shirt, and a dark-brown sweater jacket. In the rear of the plane, under Avital's watchful eye, Anatoly shed the clownish, threadbare trousers and shirt and put on the new clothes. It took barely two minutes. Avital straightened his jacket collar like a veteran wife and the two walked hand in hand down the short corridor to the open doorway.

The cabinet members, a well-drilled platoon, had aligned themselves to the left of Prime Minister Peres, having been through this exercise often enough before. Suddenly Peres broke ranks: he walked toward the plane door, followed closely by Vice-Premier Yitzhak Shamir.

Anatoly descended a single step and disappeared from view as he and Peres tumbled into a long embrace, clinging like long-lost brothers. Then Anatoly turned to Shamir and they too embraced, as warmly if not as long.

When he stepped back, Anatoly could smell on the damp, chilly air the wintertime aroma of Tel Aviv at Ben-Gurion Airport: the smell of jet fuel mingled with the sweet-and-sour harvest scent of the surrounding orange and grapefruit groves. Anatoly did not wear the skullcap worn by religious Jews; nor did he kiss the ground as many had done.

The ministers had held back from intruding, but as Anatoly and Shamir ended their embrace they surged forward, jockeying politely for position. Anatoly stepped forward and began shaking hands, as Interior Minister Rabbi Yitzhak Peretz recited the traditional prayer: "Blessed art Thou, Our Lord, King of the Universe, who resurrects the dead."

Squinting into the floodlights, Anatoly could discern the crowd of newsmen waiting behind the barricades. He waved and moved toward them, clasping his hands over his head and calling out in Hebrew "*Hakol beseder*"—Everything's all right. His eyelids were red and his face pallid, but his eyes were dancing with emotion informed by a nearly tangible intelligence. There was no bitterness or self-pity, no defeat nor even exultation in Anatoly's expression; his was the face of a man at peace with himself, one who knew all along that this day was coming. Something began to stir in the ranks of the reporters, who had covered many such scenes before. Some found to their surprise that they had tears in their eyes.

A journalist representing one of Israel's Orthodox newspapers had clambered up the side of one of the stairway ramps for a better view. He began to sing "*Heivenu Shalom Aleichem*"—We have brought peace unto you. By the second line his thin solo had become a chorus as one by one the hardened newsmen succumbed to the moment and to Anatoly, and joined in.

Anatoly's escorts were steering him toward a bus that would carry him and the cabinet members to the terminal building. But he was drawn to the singing. Peres and Shamir moved up to join him and Anatoly put his arms around their shoulders, as if he were about to start an impromptu hora with Israel's leaders. Instead, he raised his face and let the song wash over him.

"He's so short," said someone in the crowd, a comment echoed many times. Israelis who had for so long heard of Shcharansky as a moral giant expected to find him a Goliath in stature as well. His diminutive size was as surprising as his apparent good health.

Clutching Avital's hand, Anatoly joined in the singing, peering about as he did so, seeking familiar faces. When he saw one, he smiled, waved, and nodded.

Again he raised his hands over his head in a boxer's victory salute; then, sensing Avital's hand seeking his, he traded the boxer's pose for the lover's and resumed their handclasp.

Avital, dressed in a wool skirt, sweater, and high-heeled gray suede boots that made her a head taller than her husband, moved through the scene as if in a trance. Her shyness and alternating tears and smiles contrasted with her beaming, self-possessed husband. Moving with him through the crowd of dignitaries, she introduced him to a few of her strongest supporters among Israeli politicians, who included Knesset members Geula Cohen and Rabbi Haim Druckman, as well as the chief rabbis of Israel.

And all the while, they held hands. They moved together without strain, her pull of the arm to meet a minister or his toward the crowd of journalists and supporters always gentle, yet firm, accepted by the other with trust.

For the few brief moments they became separated Anatoly was drawn into the circle of ministers while Avital hovered at the edge. Someone approached her and it took her a moment to realize she was being spoken to. She thanked the politician who was congratulating her but she looked past him, toward her husband; and as soon as Anatoly seemed to be trying to step out of the crowd she went to him and took his hand.

SYLVA ZALMANSON had carried a small transistor radio to work that day, putting it on her engineer's drafting table to listen to the news bulletins about the prisoner exchange.

Avital had been on Sylva's mind for almost a week, ever since the first reports of Anatoly's impending release. The heavy-set woman with the ready laugh made sure to be home in time to see the live broadcast of the arrival ceremonies. The two women had been friends for almost three years in the seventies, when they and their husbands had shared a common fate. Both Anatoly and Edward Kuznetsov were in prison, while their wives campaigned in the West for their release. Shcharansky and Kuznetsov shared a passion for intellectual honesty and a determination to reach their Jewish homeland, but they were different men for all that. Tolya could lightheartedly force a KGB man to pay half the cost of their shared taxi; Kuznetsov's hatred left no room for humor.

Kuznetsov came to the Jewish emigration movement already a veteran of the Soviet prison system: he had spent seven years as a convicted dissident before his 1970 arrest in the Leningrad conspiracy. When they met in 1969, Sylva Zalmanson found him charismatic, "with a halo around his head as he spoke so beautifully, so eloquently, so forcefully."

Originally sentenced to death for his role in the abortive hijack attempt, Kuznetsov saw his sentence reduced in response to internal and external protest to fifteen years, including nine in prison under a strict regimen—the hardest time one can do in the Gulag.

By the time she met Avital, Sylva had been free for three years and had become a veteran campaigner, combining hunger strikes in front of the United Nations and Jerusalem's Wailing Wall with meetings with U.S. officials, European politicians, celebrities, and journalists. She took it upon herself to coach the shy young wife of Shcharansky; and under her tutelage Avital learned much about power politics and the proper care and exploitation of celebrated support- ers. Charlie Chaplin had been one of Sylva's conquests: after hearing of her campaign he had arranged a Canadian visa for her imprisoned husband. But the visa had expired long before Kuznetsov was freed.

"In Hebrew," Sylva recalled as she watched the airport arrival scene, "the word for grateful is literally prisoner of thanks. We *were* prisoners. Only our husbands were in prison while we were at cocktail parties in Washington. It made us feel awful. We were in this terrible position, and it was like playing a role, and it was terribly uncomfortable, at least for me." She and Avital spent hours on planes together, talking about the dreams they had in common. A home, a husband, a child—those were the stuff of their dreams.

Edward was freed in a May 1979 "spy" swap as or- chestrated, as complicated, and almost as well publicized as the one that freed Anatoly. Sylva chose to recede from pub- lic view. She had what she wanted, and she'd paid the price in advance. She was happy at last.

But Kuznetsov was a hard man when Sylva first knew him, and nine years in the Gulag had not softened him. Al- most from the moment he came home, Sylva knew it would not be easy for them. Edward was uncomfortable with her affection; the tension between them was visible to all who saw them together. He had always dominated in their rela- tionship; but now, in public, he was snapping at her and pulling away from her touch.

Within a few months Edward had begun to grow rest- less. His ambitions and skills as a writer found no scope in

Israel; there was no outlet for his Russian, and though he tried his hand at journalism in English and Hebrew translation, he didn't feel satisfied.

On a lecture tour abroad, a few years after his liberation, Kuznetsov met a young woman who fell in love with him. He was not averse to the relationship. Soon afterward he received an offer of a job as a broadcaster for Radio Liberty in Munich, which broadcasts to the Soviet Union the very kind of anti-Soviet message that Kuznetsov thrived on. He jumped at the opportunity.

He left Sylva behind in Israel, with a dozen photo albums showing Sylva demonstrating for his freedom, Sylva with former Prime Minister Menachem Begin, and Edward, gaunt and shaved bald, arriving in Israel. He also left behind a three-year-old daughter, Anat, who had his Asian eyes, high cheekbones, and strong will.

Sylva survived, buoyed by her joy in Israel and her love for the little girl Edward had given her. Within a few years, she had a good job as an engineer, a nice house in the suburbs south of Tel Aviv, and a thriving social life.

On the day of Anatoly's homecoming, she listened to the radio broadcasts and hurried Anat, now six, through a supper of fried eggs and avocado on toast. Then the two of them sat on the gray tweed sofa in front of the television to watch the evening events.

As she watched, she explained to the child who Anatoly Shcharansky was and a little bit more about Kuznetsov. Anatoly's arrival was a searing reminder of her own husband's homecoming. "From the moment they stepped out of the plane," she would say, "holding hands, always holding hands, I was jealous. For us, for Edward and me, it was much much different.

"You see, the important thing for all of us is that they survive together, that their relationship works out. They are like a living legend, a romantic couple, like a prince and a princess in a legend. If they can make it together, then it will mean that dreams do come true. Even for me. And yes, for Kuznetsov, too."

IN THE FIRST-CLASS LOUNGE at Ben-Gurion Airport, a table was laden with sandwiches, fruit, and cold drinks. Peres had scheduled a telephone call to President Reagan. While they waited for the call to go through, he asked Anatoly if he wanted something to eat.

"No, nothing," said Anatoly, "except some nice black coffee."

A television in the corner of the room was broadcasting the scene in the lounge, as an Israel Television crew moved through the room. "Look," someone said, "you can see yourself on television." Anatoly shook his head: "I only want to look at my Avital." They sat on a sofa holding hands and whispering together as they waited for the phone call.

Peres spoke first, thanking the president for his efforts to free Anatoly. Then he handed the phone to Anatoly.

"Dear Mr. President," Anatoly said without hesitation, "I am under strong stress right now, sitting between our prime minister and my Avital. And that's why you shouldn't be surprised if my speech isn't smooth.

"But there are things which I feel myself obliged to tell you. First of all I know how great was your role in this greatest event of my and my wife's lives, enabling me to join my people today in Israel, and of course we both are very deeply grateful to you for this.

"Secondly, and obviously as you know very well, I was

never an American spy, but I had wide contacts with many American politicians, journalists, lawyers, and other public figures as a spokesman of the Jewish national movement and the Helsinki group movement. And that's why I know very well how deep is the concern of all of your people with the problems of human rights all over the world and I know what a great role is played by your country in these problems."

He asked Reagan to "tell all your people about our deepest gratitude to your people and your country for everything they do for human rights in the world and for Jews who want to emigrate in particular."

Avital too thanked Reagan, but her emotions overwhelmed her and her message of thanks was brief, wishing the president "health and strength."

From the next room came the sounds of singing from some fifty Mercaz Harav yeshiva students and another fifty prominent Soviet emigrants, as well as scores of political leaders and journalists, who had gained admission to the ceremonies.

"Mr. President, you probably can hear the voices," said Avital, "the voices of happiness here in Israel. All my nation, all my people—they are very happy and we believe this is only the beginning of the exodus from Russia. And we hope that you will assist us, like this time, in this effort."

She was crying now, as she had been off and on since Anatoly's plane had landed at Frankfurt.

Somebody asked Anatoly what the president said to him. He smiled. "He said some nice things about my character. . . . I don't think I should repeat them. And he said he hopes I continue in my efforts. He promised that he and his people will continue in their efforts on this issue and," he added with a smile, "he wished me mazel tov."

ABSORPTION MINISTRY HALL at Ben-Gurion Airport—bursting with journalists, politicians, Soviet-Jewry activists, former prisoners of Zion, and yeshiva students—had never witnessed anything quite like Anatoly's arrival. One of the posters that decorated the hall featured a picture of Anatoly taken in the days when he sported thick muttonchop sideburns. Somebody removed it before the night was over, taking it home as a souvenir of the history he or she had witnessed.

Michael Gilboa, a broadcaster for Israel Radio's Russian-language program, was moved by the occasion, but also disturbed as he worked the hall, interviewing former prisoners of Zion like Yosef Mendelevich and Hillel Butman, who had spent years in the same prisons as Anatoly.

Gilboa's report of Anatoly's arrival was to be broadcast to the Soviet Union via shortwave that night, in the hope that Soviet jamming equipment wouldn't prevent thousands of Russian Jews from hearing it. But did the occasion, Gilboa wondered, warrant such a festival?

Before Anatoly, there had been other prisoners of Zion who had spent as many years in Soviet jails and suffered no less, but whose arrival had not caused such public celebration. There had been no such welcome for Mark Nashpitz, who had endured a five-year exile in Siberia. His term had ended in 1979, but he was not allowed to leave for Israel, return to Moscow, or resume work as a dentist. He moved to a town sixty miles from Moscow where he found employment making artificial floral wreaths. Despite his continued semiexile, he remained active in the emigration movement. In 1985, his parents, living in Israel, wrote to the wife of the Soviet leader, Raiza Gorbachev, to appeal for an exit visa for their son. To their astonishment, she sent them a postcard, acknowledging receipt of their letter; and shortly thereafter, Nashpitz and his family received exit visas. They arrived in Israel in October 1985, without any fanfare, almost unnoticed by the press.

Anatoly, still gripping Avital's hand, followed Peres and Shamir to a hall where the waiting crowd was already bathed in the heat of klieg lights.

On the way he saw *New York Times* correspondent David Shipler, his friend from the heady days in Moscow when Anatoly was the crucial link to both the dissident movement and the emigration movement.

Anatoly reached out to Shipler, and the two men embraced, Shipler towering over Anatoly. But there was no time for conversation. The crowd around Anatoly pushed forward, sweeping him along with them. But he managed to whisper into Shipler's ear, "It's so good to see one of my criminal contacts."

A hail of colorfully wrapped candies rained down on the couple's head as they entered the hall. The prime minister's bodyguards tensed, then relaxed. The rhythmic flashing of the photographers' bulbs gave the room a surrealistic feeling, and Anatoly again had to squint into the bright lights, searching the room for familiar faces.

Avital pointed out a slim man in the crowd. "Hillel Butman," she said. Anatoly smiled and nodded at him. The two men had communicated with each other for close to a year in Vladimir and Chistopol prisons. But this was the first time they had ever set eyes on each other.

After Absorption Minister Ya'alov Tsur had handed Anatoly his I.D. card, Peres rose to speak. He heaped praise upon Avital. "She fought like a lioness," said Peres. "No place was too far away, no person a stranger, no opportunity too small. She went from place to place, from person to person, pursuing real or imaginary opportunities. She fought as a Jewish woman and as an envoy of her people."

Avital blushed, raising her hand to her face only to have Anatoly, in his pride—though knowing, he was to say in days to come, very little of all that she had done for him during the years they were separated—reach over to pull it down.

About Anatoly, Peres said, "For twelve years he was alone and ailing, with no one to turn to. Yet his Jewish pride and his Zionist belief was like a rock. This is the heroism of one man, alone, with a spirit that faced a superpower. The body can be imprisoned, the spirit cannot."

Shamir's message was directed at Moscow: "You let us have Anatoly today. It is a holiday for us. It will not impeach your prestige to open the gates and allow all our people out. It will serve your interests, we are sure," said Shamir, his voice trembling.

As much as the praise that was heaped upon her, something else was embarrassing Avital. It was evident to all who watched them. She was uncomfortable with embracing in public, and she stiffened visibly when Anatoly tried to put his arm around her, or nuzzle her neck. Religious Jews refrain from public displays of affection between husband and wife, and at one point Avital pulled back from Anatoly, who was obeying, with obvious enjoyment, a photographer's request that he hug his wife. Then Avital leaned toward him, whispering in his ear. Anatoly smiled and nodded and took her hand.

They listened to the two politicians' speeches, but Anatoly was also interested in everything that was going on around him. His gaze shifted from Peres to the sea of faces in the room to Avital's face, which appeared to interest him more than anything else. For long moments he would ignore the speeches, the crowd, and the photographers to gaze at her moist brown eyes.

She clung tightly to his arm. When he mopped his forehead with a handkerchief, complaining about the heat, she unzipped his jacket. Again her tears came suddenly, and she wiped them away with a white handkerchief.

Anatoly was the last to speak. A decade earlier, he had conducted press conferences, in front of no more than a handful of reporters crowded into tiny book-lined Moscow apartments or in the open spaces of public gardens. Now he faced a throng of journalists and supporters, most of whom he had never met.

Some of those in the room, like McGill University law professor Irwin Cotler, were eager to hear whether the man whose cause they had taken up with such fervor still advocated linking the human rights and Jewish emigration movements.

Geula Cohen, a right-wing member of the Israeli Parliament, listened to Anatoly's speech with her eyes closed in a kind of private reverie, nodding her head in a slow rhythmic beat to his voice as he searched for words to describe the world he had left behind.

Anatoly stepped up to the podium, adjusting the microphone to his height like a professional. He began by apologizing for his Hebrew, which was at first halting but from the start eloquent, rich with idiom. "In any case," he said, "there are certain events in a person's life which are impossible to describe in any language."

Often he leaned toward Avital, who moved her chair to be next to him at the podium, to ask her for a Hebrew word. For years the face she had shown the public had been flushed with sorrow, her eyes somber, her mouth tight with her inner pain. Now, for the first time in years, the public saw her smiling, even laughing. As suddenly as her tears would come and go, so would the smile.

As the speech progressed Anatoly appeared to develop confidence in his Hebrew, and the pace of his words quickened.

"I don't know very much about what went on all those years I was in jail, outside the Soviet Union. Twelve years ago I said to Avital on our parting, 'I'll see you soon in Jerusalem.'

"But my way here became as long and as hard as the *Galut* [the exile from Israel], because in these years the pharaohs of our time decided to announce a new conspiracy of Jews, from Russia and other countries, against the regime. I know how deep was the hatred of the KGB, and how strong their determination not to allow this day to come.

"The very fact that this day has come," Anatoly said, "is a strong indication of the justness of our cause. This successful struggle was possible because Jews everywhere in the world understand that the fate of Jews in any country is their fate, too.

"What unites us is the strength and independence of Israel, our homeland. We Soviet-Jewish activists have nothing against the Soviet regime. But we do have a spiritual link with our homeland and nothing can sever that link.

"I am in shock, we are in shock, Avital and me, from the rain of compliments, no, the hail of compliments—which doesn't make the work any easier.

"But the compliments must go to all those who struggle for human rights, who continue the struggle, to all those Jews who are standing up to the Soviet authorities, demanding their right to emigrate to their homeland.

"We made no conspiracy against the Soviet Union. We made a conspiracy of the entire nation with our homeland, our state.

"You know, I dreamed many times while in prison of arriving in our land and there my Avital would be waiting for me. But in my dream, whenever we began to embrace . . . I would wake up in my cell. But I must add that in my dream I never saw as many people as I saw when it finally came true."

As Anatoly finished his speech, the singing broke out again, but he quieted his supporters, saying he wanted to continue in English. Although he had no notes, he made the same speech in English as he had in Hebrew, almost word for word.

"On this happiest day of our lives," he said, "I am not going to forget those whom I left in the camps, in the prisons, who are still in exile or who still continue their struggle for their right to emigrate, their human rights."

Leaving the reception hall, *Los Angeles Times* correspondent Robert Toth, to whom the KGB said Shcharansky passed "secrets," and Irwin Cotler talked about the Anatoly they had just seen.

Cotler, who had never met Anatoly, was brimming over with contagious enthusiasm about him. "I was encouraged by the speech reaffirming Tolya's commitment to human rights as well as Zionism," he said. It was Anatoly's human rights activism that had so enchanted Cotler in the beginning, when he first heard about the case. Like so many others, Cotler wondered how Anatoly's commitment to human rights would fit in with the politics of the religious nationalist Gush Emunim, which had so warmly adopted Avital.

Toth felt that it was hard to predict the effect of prison on Anatoly and wondered, too, how Shcharansky would react to what Cotler called the "xenophobia" of Gush Emunim. If Tolya was still the same man he had known in the early and midseventies, said Toth, then it was unlikely that he would be pleased by some of the things he would soon be hearing from the people who were closest to his wife.

As they walked toward the public rally, to which Gush Emunim settlements had sent busloads of religious youngsters, the two men encountered another, different group of religious Jews. These few black-garbed ultra-Orthodox men held a large placard warning against "Mormon soul-snatching" in Jerusalem. The Mormons were building a university campus in the Israeli capital, and many religious Jews feared that the sect's members would try to convert Jews. One of the demonstrators said he knew nothing about Shcharansky's efforts on behalf of religious freedom for Seventh Day Adventists, Baptists, and other churches in Russia. Such ecumenism would be frowned upon by these people.

"I want to believe," said Cotler as he passed the placard, "that prison has only strengthened him, not changed him."

THERE WERE SEVEN thousand people crowded onto the wide lawn in front of the airport terminal. The official organizer was the Public Council for Soviet Jewry, but most of the people in the rally were from the settlement movement that had been spawned at Mercaz Harav, the yeshiva that had assigned Avi Maoz many years before to act as Avital's aide de camp. They were mainly young people, singing folk hymns like "A Yisrael Hai" (The People of Israel Live), which Gush Emunim had appropriated as a kind of anthem. As they sang the songs, many of which are based on biblical passages, they danced the hora, a folk dance that originated in Russia.

The crowd spilled off the lawn onto one of the airport streets that weave through the terminal. Many had come with children, toddlers carried on the shoulders of their parents. Dozens more held placards. One asked, in English block lettering, "And what about Sakharov?" but most were written in Hebrew, calling for freedom for all prisoners of Zion. Israeli flags waved at the top of long poles hoisted by hefty teens; and religious men and women sang and danced in separate circles, skullcaps flapping on the heads of the boys and men, skirts flaring around the legs of the girls and women. Mendelevich pointed out during his speech later on that "only one community, the religious nationalist community" had come to the airport to greet Anatoly.

The cheer that went up when the Scharanskys, accompanied by Peres and Industry Minister Ariel Sharon, climbed on the stage, was deafening. Behind barricades set up by the police, the crowd pressed forward, reaching out toward the couple. Anatoly waved and cheers suddenly seemed to double in their intensity. But it was when Avital smiled to the crowd, shyly waving into the lights and the darkness beyond, that the cheers and applause reached their full pitch.

After a few words from Peres, Anatoly rose to speak. At the official reception he had spoken with metaphor and irony, aiming his language at a select crowd. Outside in the chilly night, he chose a simpler, more emotional tone.

"Brothers and sisters," he began, Avital at his side; "during those difficult years when I was in jail, during those years when I heard not a word from anybody, there was not a single day that went by, not a single moment that passed, in which I did not feel a connection with you all."

The cheers and applause again were overwhelming, and Anatoly had to raise his arms for silence. "Even when I was in solitary confinement," he said, "I sang the song, 'How good it is to be together, as brothers' [from the Book of Psalms]."

The first voices to begin singing the hymn came from the front row of the barricade between the stage and the crowd. When Anatoly joined in, the song spread quickly. He raised his arms, at first hesitantly, and then with enthusiasm, conducting the singers. The accordionist and folk singer who had earlier led the crowd in song picked up the tune. The singing lasted several long minutes, dying down only when Anatoly beckoned Avital forward to make her own speech.

Her message contained an element of partisan politics that delighted the crowd. "Just as Natan has arrived, so will all the Jews, from the Soviet Union, from America, from Europe, from everywhere. I call on the government," she declared, turning to the prime minister, "to protect our entire country, not to give up one bit of it, so that all these Jews can build the country." Peres, whose Labor Party advocates territorial compromise, smiled stolidly.

The remark earned her huge applause, even greater than was received by her husband.

While Anatoly had been an abstract figure—a face on a poster, a cause—she had been real, and not only real, but also one of them. Her dark, beautiful face was memorable and much admired; Avital's face appeared on as many posters as her husband's. In her conservative brown dresses, boots, and sweaters, standing on street corners in European capitals with a sandwich board bearing Anatoly's picture or coming out of presidential offices, Avital projected a self-denied sensuality that was her own charisma.

At the close of her speech, Avital, holding a large, white-and-blue skullcap, pressed it into Anatoly's hand.

He looked at it, and then at her; he spoke softly in Russian and seemed to hold it out to her. Avital took the *kippa* from his hand and placed it firmly on his head. The crowd went wild.

THE SHCHARANSKYS' DRIVER was no ordinary chauffeur; he was Avraham Burg, a young religious politician on the opposite side of the political spectrum from Gush Emunim. The son of Dr. Yosef Burg, the longest-serving cabinet minister in Israel, Avraham was one of the few leaders of the "Peace Now" movement who wore a *kippa*. Peres had named him his adviser on Jewish Affairs when the Labor Party premier took office in September 1984. Burg had become deeply involved in Soviet Jewry.

Burg and the Shcharankys were accompanied to Jerusalem by a two-car police escort and another two dozen cars carrying TV camera crews, Mercaz Harav activists, and other well-wishers. Burg drove fast, reaching one hundred miles per hour on the straight stretch between the airport and the

Judean hills. The police cars bracketed them, maneuvering constantly to prevent any others from getting too close.

As they passed Latrun, Burg explained to Anatoly that it was the site of a critical battle with the Jordanians in the War of Independence. He pointed out the Latrun Trappist monastery, in an olive grove on the left.

The pace slowed as they entered Sha'ar Hagai—The Valley's Gate—the winding road that leads up to Jerusalem. Burned-out husks of supply trucks, destroyed while trying to break the siege of the Jewish half of Jerusalem during the War of Independence, lay scattered along the roadside. Anatoly had heard of those rust-red monuments and was excited to recognize them. Wild almond trees lined the road. In the car beams their blossoms looked almost like a covering of snow, though they presaged the coming of spring in Israel.

Anatoly sat close to Avital in the back of the car. Their heads, though barely visible to the following cars, were recognizable by the blue-and-white *kippa* still on Anatoly's head.

At the entrance to Jerusalem, admirers from the nearby Mercaz Harav yeshiva lined the street. Burg sped past them without stopping.

Anatoly had asked for a short tour of the city, so Burg drove across town to Mount Scopus. From there, they looked down on the Old City and on the northwestern half of Jerusalem.

"I described these scenes to Anatoly in many of my letters," said Avital.

They crossed a spur from Scopus to the Mount of Olives. Here Anatoly got out of the car and walked to the edge of the parking lot overlooking the city. He asked Burg to point out some landmarks, but only the most extravagantly lit buildings could be distinguished in the foggy night. The most prominent were the two domes of the Islamic shrines on the Temple Mount, one gold and one a silvery-colored lead. Burg pointed out the King David Hotel, just beyond the Old City walls on the western side of Jerusalem.

"Ah, that's where the British had their headquarters," said Anatoly, referring to the last years of the British mandate four decades before.

For a few minutes the small group stood in the misty night air, looking down on the twinkling lights of the city. They stood atop an ancient Jewish cemetery; across a valley was the Old City. Beyond that, on hilltops across the horizon, rose the new city of Jerusalem.

"Take me to the wall," Anatoly said.

MEN AND WOMEN cannot approach the Wailing, or Western, Wall together; each sex has its own section, the men's part being larger than the women's. Thus for the first time since his arrival in the West, Anatoly was separated from his Avital. As he stepped onto the wide plaza in front of the wall, Anatoly was rushed by a great crowd of yeshiva students. At first his face registered distress as they pressed in on him; but then they hoisted him to their shoulders and bore him forward, blowing on shofars as they went. In front of the wall the young men put him down, and policemen moved in, shouting, "Give him some room!"

Anatoly walked up to the wall. He kissed it three times and then he pressed his face frontally into its stone bosom. His eyes were closed, his lips moved, but nothing could be heard over the roar of the crowd. Then he brought out a tiny prayer book—the one Avital had given him, the one he'd fought so hard to keep. Holding it close to his face he opened without hesitation to Psalm 133 and began to recite: "How good it is and how pleasant for brothers to live together. . . ."

When he turned away from the wall he was again raised onto the shoulders of students as the crowd sang a cycle of songs. The sound wafted over the plaza and into the heights of the rebuilt Jewish Quarter, its edge crowded with onlookers.

Avital watched from the women's section, where she herself was serenaded by women singing "Woman of Valor."

The couple was reunited near Burg's car. Until then Anatoly had shown no sign of fatigue, though he had not slept since his arrival in East Berlin the day before. Suddenly he seemed exhausted. Burg drove out of the walled city and headed for the quiet northwestern neighborhood of Kiryat Moshe.

Welcome home drawings made by the neighborhood children were taped to the corridor walls leading to Avital's fourth-floor apartment. One showed Anatoly flying away from a burning prison toward the shining city of Jerusalem. Another portrayed him standing where he had just stood, at the wall; his figure loomed disproportionately large beside the other men and even beside the wall itself.

On the door of their apartment was a note containing the text of a telephone message from Mila Volvosky of Moscow, whose husband had just been sentenced to three years imprisonment for his emigration activities.

"There are no words to express what we feel in our hearts," said the note. "Anatoly's release is the fulfillment of our prayers. Your heroism, Anatoly, continues to give us strength. We hope that soon your whole family will be together in the holy land."

Avital had invested very little time or effort over the years in decorating the flat. The style and substance were strictly functional: a sofa, a couple of chairs, a table, and bookshelves filled with religious tomes and works on Soviet Jewry. Her filing cabinet was a series of shoeboxes crammed with the thousands of letters she had received over the years from friends, supporters, and admirers. Some handmade curtains were her only homemaker's effort. *Without Anatoly*, the flat seemed to say, *this is not a home.*

Before they went to sleep, long after three in the morning according to some curious bystanders who waited outside the apartment until the last light was turned off, Anatoly phoned friends in Israel and his family in Moscow.

In the Soviet capital, Ida Milgrom and Leonid had listened all day to the news on the BBC. The release was not reported on Radio Moscow. Their conversation with Anatoly was short. "It is like a dream," he told them, "like a dream."

THE WORLD was clamoring at their door. Reporters and photographers were begging for access. Telegrams from prime ministers and presidents, from celebrities and ordinary people captivated by the romance of their story, piled up in a mailbag in a corner of the living room. Israeli politicians who hoped to recruit Anatoly tried to make contact through Soviet immigrants they had helped.

For years Avital had responded to messages left on her answering machine with an immediacy motivated by hope that the messenger had word of Anatoly. On their first day together, she turned on the answering machine and did not touch the phone. For these first twenty-four hours, she insisted, there would be no intrusions.

Avital made her first meal for her husband, a delayed wedding breakfast. Anatoly ate a salad made of the splendid Israeli vegetables in season—tomatoes and cucumbers, green and red peppers, avocado, and lettuce, with a dash of fresh lemon juice. He tried a kiwi fruit for the first time in his life and had some fresh-squeezed orange juice. All day long he drank coffee.

With the journalists gone and the street returned to a semblance of its normal quiet self, Anatoly was able to go out onto the balcony to sun, a pleasure denied him for nine long years in prison. Occasional passersby would wave to him or shout out greetings, and he waved back, savoring, he said later, the love he felt from everybody he encountered in the country.

One of his first acts his first day was to contact the Finnish Embassy to start the formal application process for the emigration of his mother and his brother and family.

Their only visitors during the day were Avital's brother, the Ben-Yosef family, with whom Avital had lived for much of her time in Israel, and Dr. Mervyn Gottesman, a leading Israeli cardiologist who was Menachem Begin's personal physician, and who gave Anatoly a preliminary physical examination. Gottesman found that Anatoly was suffering from lesions of the heart, but pronounced his patient remarkably healthy considering all that he had endured.

Despite Avital's desire to keep her husband at home and the journalists at bay for the first twenty-four hours, by the end of his first day in the country Anatoly had agreed to be interviewed on Israel Television's prime-time news program.

On the show he had his first view of his mother since she had visited him the previous year. Ida Milgrom and Leonid had been filmed by a British television crew in Moscow, reacting to Anatoly's release. As he watched his seventy-nine-year-old mother say that for the first time in years she was able to fall asleep without any fear for her son, Anatoly grinned broadly. He told an interviewer that he had already filled out the application for her release and that he "understood" that the deal to free him also included exit visas for his family.

Pressed already about his place in the bitterly divided Israeli political spectrum, Anatoly was circumspect. He had much to learn about Israel, he said; when he had learned enough he would have things to say. Of one thing he was certain: "The Communist Party will not be able to recruit me."

Avital sat with him in the television studio. She listened carefully to every word and helped him out with his Hebrew, which, less than twenty-four hours after the airport arrival ceremony, already seemed improved. When the interviewer asked him about his feelings concerning Avital's religious beliefs and how that would affect their relationship, she listened tensely. But his answer seemed to please her.

"I want to learn about our religion," he said. "About me and Avital—I think we feel that we never have been separated, that we never have been apart. We are resuming our relationship exactly where it left off."

The TV interviewer's questions about their relationship did not surprise Anatoly. He had read much speculation in the Israeli press about the pressures on their relationship; her religious beliefs and his secular views. Some columnists had the bad taste to speculate on whether the marriage would last, noting she had become religious while he had not. Others worried that she would turn him religious. Still others conjectured that Shcharansky might be "hijacked" by right-wing nationalists, who had so warmly embraced Avital. One columnist even wrote that it might be harder for Anatoly to withstand the pressures on him to become religious or to join Gush Emunim than it had been to withstand the KGB.

In the coming weeks he had answers for every question, for he was unafraid to say that he did not know, that he still had to learn. He scoffed at those who dared suggest that Avital was pressuring him to become religious, and he laughed about all the speculation. "I learned long ago that where you have two Jews, you have three opinions. So in Israel, with four million Jews, there are many millions of opinions," he said.

Those who had expected Anatoly to follow in the footsteps of his former jail mate Mendelevich by quickly joining the religious right wing were sorely disappointed. So was Vice-Premier Shamir. Anatoly turned down an offer from him to be the keynote speaker at the Likud's national convention, which was to be held a few weeks after his arrival. It was a considerable honor, but Anatoly politely declined.

He did not appear in public again, after the Western Wall reception, wearing a *kippa*. He emphasized in interviews that while in prison, his knowledge of his Jewish heritage had helped him stay emotionally fit. Although he did not follow all the commandments, Anatoly said, he did feel strongly about religion.

THE SHY, BEAUTIFUL GIRL whom Anatoly had loved in Moscow had matured into an outspoken woman with strong political opinions of her own. When once, during an interview, he described Israeli politics as a "nightmare," Avital frowned.

Afterward, Anatoly told a friend in the studio, "I think Avital doesn't like my answer."

"For you it's a nightmare," Avital interjected.

"Well," he replied, "I answered for myself."

Mark Nashpitz was one of the few of his friends from Moscow who managed in the first days to get past the yeshiva students' protective cordon. They had last met during Nashpitz's Siberian exile, ten years earlier. Members of the yeshiva were in the living room when Nashpitz entered.

"This is an old friend," said Anatoly to the yeshiva students. "Would you excuse us?" The others left the room and the two former Muscovites talked for a few minutes.

"Have you become religious?" asked Nashpitz.

"I'm Jewish," he replied.

A few days after his arrival, Anatoly slipped out of his apartment to pay his first social call. It was to his old friend, Alexander Lunts, living in the Ramoth quarter of Jerusalem.

Lunts was astonished at Anatoly's adjustment. He had known many people who had been imprisoned in the Gulag, including some very strong people. Every one, without exception, had emerged with visible signs of stress that took months, even years, to recede. But except for his prison pallor, Anatoly seemed exactly as he knew him ten years ago. His humor, his alertness, and his self-possession were intact. Lunts was astonished, too, at his old friend's command of Hebrew.

Shortly after he arrived in Lunts's apartment, the telephone rang. Lunts lifted it to find Michael Sherbourne on the other end of the line.

"Can you tell me how to reach Anatoly?" Sherbourne asked.

"Just a minute," said Lunts. He handed the phone to Anatoly.

"Hello," he said.

"Who is this?" asked Sherbourne.

"Don't you recognize me?"

"Ulanovsky?"

"Who?"

"Ulanovsky?"

"Don't you know anyone else besides Ulanovsky?" Anatoly teased.

"Who is this?"

"You claim to have spoken with me hundreds of times, and you don't recognize my voice?"

With a loud exclamation, Sherbourne embraced his old telephone contact across three thousand miles.

MEANWHILE, THE LIBERAL LEFT, which watched the right wing's courtship of Shcharansky through the jealous eyes of an insecure suitor, was comforted by a televised statement in which Anatoly said that he intended to continue his study of Arabic, which he had begun in prison, so that he could understand Israel's large Arab minority. "I think it would be useful," he said, "because, whether we want it or not, there are many Arabs in Israel and we must, from time to time, try to talk with then. Maybe then there will be a little less shooting."

He had two dreams, he told another interviewer. First, to see the rest of the Soviet Jewry reach freedom; second, to see Israel living in peace with its neighbors. He said that he was relieved when he saw that there was no barbed wire dividing Jerusalem, because in *Pravda* Jerusalem is always described as a city under internal siege.

At dinner with Israeali President Chaim Herzog, who hosted the couple at the presidential mansion, Anatoly said that he would like to visit Israeli prisons, to compare them with Soviet prisons.

IN ADDITION TO ITS own vigorous local media, Israel has the third largest foreign press corps—after Moscow and Washington—in the world. And everyone—local and foreign and those flown in especially for the occasion—wanted a piece of Anatoly. Anatoly took them on like a worker in an auto plant, dealing with an implacable assembly line. Yet, he managed to give each a custom interview different from all the rest.

It was like the old days in Moscow, when he crammed into twenty-four hours a normal week's load of meetings and phone calls. If he wasn't sitting with a reporter, he was on the telephone or in a television or radio station being interviewed for foreign media organizations. He cooperated with anybody whose request managed to filter through the net of volunteers who manned the Shcharansky phone and guarded their front door. His only complaint was that he didn't have enough time for everybody.

Avital did not appear happy about it. As far as she was concerned they were on their honeymoon.

But Anatoly could not refuse Shipler or Toth, though among some in Anatoly's circle of friends from the days in Moscow were still critical of Toth for signing a KGB-prepared statement that he could not understand. Once those interviews were promised, how could he turn down the American television networks, or the major European networks, or the news magazines, or other major dailies, or. . . .

Avital gave him one week. After that, they would go on vacation.

The next six days were burdened with a schedule so tight, complex, and crowded that to some he had barely fifteen minutes to give. He gave close to a hundred interviews.

Avital sat with him on the sofa in the living room or at the small dining table that once had been covered with newspaper clippings or correspondence. She sat there, looking unhappy about it.

Sylva Zalmanson had said of Avital that "every public statement she makes takes a price from her." The reporters pried deeply into their relationship. She had long ago convinced herself that once Anatoly was free, they could lead a normal life and she would no longer have to expose her feelings to strangers. As long as Anatoly was imprisoned she was ready to pay the price to keep his name in the consciousness of the West. But now he was beside her and still the price was being paid. She had dreamed of days alone with Anatoly, making him breakfast, sitting with him alone and at ease, in a room with more signs of her homemaking than only a few curtains. "It is my greatest ambition," Avital told friends, "never to travel again."

Many of the questions still dealt with the effect on their relationship of Avital's acquired religiosity. Anatoly dealt lightly with the questions. "People," he joked, "are trying to figure out whether I will end up with a *kippa* or she end up without a kerchief." Eventually, after continual exposure to insensitive personal questions, Anatoly showed irritation.

Anatoly would say that it was love that motivated him. Love of freedom, love of Avital, love of Israel, and the love he felt he had received in return. At a press conference held in a Jerusalem hotel ballroom barely forty-eight hours after his arrival in Israel, he said that "meeting so much love here from everybody . . . really makes our position very difficult. But at the same time it inspires us very much."

Love, for him, was coupled with responsibility. Love had given Avital the strength to take it upon herself to set him free. Now love meant not only thanking all those who had helped to free him, but also explaining to the world, through the free Western press, what *his* struggle had been all about. He spoke often about the love between him and Avital, between them and their country, and he talked about the responsibilities entailed by such love.

In a *London Times* interview he described the years apart: "The time was not stolen from us. The time is stolen if you do not know what you have lived those years for. The time is stolen when you find out nothing about the world and about yourself. The time is lost when it was of no help to those around you. But during that time I could test myself and find out about myself and also Avital, and I, we, lived a real life—*real*, with real, deep feelings. And I also discovered that the most important feeling is—let's not use big words— love itself.

"That's what all this means to me. So those years were not lost. To start thinking about what if Avital and I had lived those years together in Israel?—It's impossible. Such things were not meant to be. Believe me when I say it simply. Those long years apart were truly worth living. It was a hard period, but also responsible and impressive, for both of us."

Anatoly had another love in his life, as Avital was to find out. Ever since he began his career as a spokesman in

Moscow he'd had an ongoing affair with the Western press. He admired the rules of the profession as it is conducted in democracies, perhaps because they were so different from those his father had been forced to obey as a Soviet journalist. And as that love was mutual, it spawned a mutual responsibility. At the Hilton Hotel ballroom press conference, Anatoly spoke directly of the responsibilities as, in a few words, he reviewed the meaning of the relationship between the Western press and the Soviet Jews and dissidents who relied on them.

It was evident as he spoke that he had also learned, during his years of struggle, the power of a truth clearly spoken.

"It's quite clear to the Soviet authorities that people who can send words of truth to the public opinion of the world are criminals; that is one of the reasons, of course, that I was arrested," he said. "You journalists are interested in freedom of information because it is the necessary condition for your work. And we Soviet Jews who are struggling for our right to emigrate, we who are struggling for human rights in the Soviet Union, are interested in freedom of information because it is the necessary condition of our survival or existence."

He did not censor himself, quickly squashing speculation that the Soviet authorities would allow his family to leave Moscow if he agreed to remain silent in the West. "As soon as the Soviet authorities feel that I am being more cautious because I don't want to make trouble for my relatives, my relatives will have no chance to leave the country and there will be a long silence."

A few months before his release, his brother Leonid told a *Jerusalem Post* correspondent in Moscow that "if the Soviets ever decide to free Tolya, they will hold us here. It is their way to split families. They would keep us here as a form of revenge and as part of an effort to keep Tolya from making a lot of noise in the West."

In the weeks after Anatoly's release, American newspapers several times published reports that Anatoly subsequently denied: about pressures from Washington not to speak out or promises that he wouldn't comment on prison conditions or Soviet repression. The Americans, he said, had never asked him to keep a low profile after his release. "I think they know it's illogical to ask me such things," he said.

In a way, the small man with the toothy grin was suddenly a potential wild card on the international scene. Zbigniew Brzezinski, national security adviser to President Carter, told the *Jerusalem Post* that "whoever recommended Shcharansky's release to Gorbachev probably has had his ass kicked." The Soviet authorities, he said, clearly underestimated Anatoly's sheer resilience and propaganda skills. "He wasn't broken, he wasn't cowed. He has a knack for saying things extremely effectively and he's obviously a crusader. I suspect that the Soviets underestimated that."

Nor did Brzezinski believe Anatoly would simply melt into the crowd like other well-known refuseniks after they reached the West. "This guy, I don't think he will."

Indeed, Anatoly had no compunctions about describing in detail the horrifying conditions of Soviet prison life; how the KGB tried to break prisoners through isolation and psychological pressures, combined with the raw physical conditions of cold and hunger that prevented sleep and weakened the spirit. Within two months of his arrival in Israel he had provided the West with a detailed report on Soviet prison conditions.

The reports of his plans for an American trip coincided with rumors in Washington that the Soviets were trying to persuade U.S. diplomats that such a trip would help neither relations between the two superpowers nor the cause of Soviet Jewry. But Anatoly denied that there was any pressure on him to cancel his trip and insisted on keeping up public pressure—including his own statements—as part of the overall effort to open the gates of the Soviet Union.

"And the fact that the KGB were made to release me without getting any concessions proves that our struggle can really be successful," he said. "I was an optimist when I started participating in this movement thirteen years ago. I was an optimist during my trial; and I am very optimistic now about the fate of Soviet Jews who are struggling to leave.

"I have always said what I think and I am not going to stop now."

If Anatoly was reticent about his place in the Israeli political spectrum, he left no doubt as to where he stood on other political questions. A past activist in the emigration movement, Bar-Ilan Professor Moshe Glitterman denigrated Anatoly's importance to the emigration movement and described him in the major Hebrew-language daily newspaper *Ma'airv* as a "human rights activist and not a Zionist." Anatoly responded sharply.

"What kind of argument can be made that I am not a Zionist? From my point of view Zionism is the struggle for the right of Jews to have their own country, for the struggle of Jews in other countries to emigrate there."

Some people, he said, believed that Zionists should not speak about the human rights of other people. But his participation in the Helsinki Watch Group was "a natural continuation of my activities as a Jewish activist." By this activity, he said, he was confident that he had contributed both to Jews who sought to emigrate "and to other people who are seeking their freedom."

His release had coincided with a flurry of reports about a possible release of imprisoned African National Congress leader Nelson Mandela, and Anatoly was asked about the imprisoned black leader.

He would rejoice, he replied, in the freedom of political prisoners everywhere, whatever their beliefs. But it was necessary to distinguish between his case and Mandela's. The ANC leader "was either calling to violence or was using violence." Linking the two cases could enable the Soviets to mislead people about the Jewish and dissident movements in the Soviet Union, which are strictly nonviolent.

"Dissidents like Andrei Sakharov and others never called for any violence. Our only battlefields were small apartments in Moscow where we held our press conferences."

ANATOLY KEPT his word to Avital: six days after the first interview, they left the Kiryat Moshe apartment for their long-delayed honeymoon.

They headed north to the hills of the Galilee and the Golan Heights for their quiet walks, staying for some time in a religious settlement and for a while in a small hotel in Safad, the home of Jewish mysticism.

Anatoly went swimming every morning in Lake Kinneret and spent much time hiking and reading. Twice he went to the naturally heated springs in Hammat Hagader, on the Jordan-Israel border, not far from the lake, but he stopped after reporters discovered him there. Slowly, in the generous Middle Eastern sunlight, his pastiness gave way to a healthy pink glow. In the evenings he watched the half-hour news broadcast. His Hebrew was not quite good enough to follow it all, but Avital was there to help with translations.

Midway through their three-week honeymoon, the Shcharanskys were joined for three days by Alexander Lunts. He and Anatoly toured the Galilee and the Golan Heights by day, shifting easily as old friends do from comments on the passing scene to recollections of their Moscow years. These leisurely, unprogrammed outings with a close friend, far from the limelight, were a balm for Anatoly. Lunts was a veteran nature lover who regularly hiked the land. He found Shcharansky weak and short of breath as they climbed mountain trails, and he slowed his pace to accommodate the younger man.

Arriving at dusk one day at Banias, one of the headwaters of the Jordan River, the pair walked past a busload of soldiers preparing to return to their base from an outing. Despite the dimming light, the soldiers recognized Shcharansky immediately, and he was soon surrounded by young men asking him to pose for a picture with them. A Yemenite woman from a nearby bus approached and asked, "Is this for Ashkenazim (Jews of European ancestry) only?" Anatoly laughed and drew her in for a photograph.

At a lookout point near Mount Hermon, a young kibbutznik with two girls in a pick-up truck approached and said that the girls would like a photograph with Anatoly.

"Sure," Anatoly said. "Be glad to."

"The thing is," said the kibbutznik, "I don't have a camera."

Lunts took the picture on his own camera, and promised to send it.

Anatoly and Avital were spotted walking hand in hand through the narrow arched alleyways of ancient Safad, high in the hills of the Galilee; and Anatoly was photographed cavorting in a hotel swimming pool, a look of incredulous delight on his face.

Except for a brief flurry of reports claiming that Anatoly's health had suddenly deteriorated, the press left them alone. During their vacation, Anatoly failed to attend a scheduled benefit dinner at which he was to be the guest of honor. Avital notified their hosts that he was too ill to attend. Reports circulated that Anatoly was unable to sleep, that he had difficulty walking; one report that gained widespread acceptance was that he had suffered caffeine poisoning, due to overindulgence in that long-denied luxury. However, once they returned from vacation, Anatoly resumed his public appearances, looking much fitter than he had upon arrival.

Every Friday morning after his return, Anatoly walked in the woods around Jerusalem with Lunts. In deference to Avital's Orthodoxy, he did not make these outings on the Sabbath, but spent that day at home with her. Avital, never much of a cook or for that matter much of an eater, was delighted to prepare food for Anatoly, to fuss over what he ate and wore. If she didn't, he certainly wouldn't; his head was elsewhere.

For the first time in a decade he began reading up on cybernetics. It was not clear to him whether he could return to his profession or whether fate had obliged him to assume some more public role. In any case, he told friends, he would like to obtain the newest wonder of the West, a home computer, to indulge his interest at least as a hobby. His memory had always been a marvel, and though he claimed it had been badly affected by his prison conditions, this was not discernible to those who had known him in Moscow. A computer expert who knew Shcharansky well reckoned that a man of his intellect would have no trouble returning to the field, despite the length of time he'd been away and the advances made while he was in prison. But clearly Anatoly had other options.

Besieged by offers from book publishers, he reached an agreement with International Creative Management, one of the largest talent and literary agencies in the world, for a contract that would handle all his future book and lecture-tour plans.

The pressures imposed by the media receded after they returned from vacation, and they could begin making plans.

They started to think about where they would live. The Kiryat Moshe flat had been loaned to Avital to serve as an office for her campaign. Jerusalem is a city of well-defined neighborhoods, and Anatoly wanted to see them all before they decided where they would make their home.

Avital understood that they would not be able to shut the door behind them wherever they lived. The reporters knocking on the door had been replaced by Soviet Jews looking to Anatoly for leadership, information, comfort, and help about relatives and friends left behind. Friends from the days in Moscow would come by to sit and talk, about the past and about the future.

Anatoly felt immediately at home in Israel. The land-

scape and climate enchanted him, and if the political atmosphere reflected fire and brimstone rather than milk and
honey, he was perhaps more suited by temperament to the
former than to the latter.

For nine years he had been locked away from the world
and assured by the KGB that he had been forgotten. He had
emerged to discover that his private struggle for sanity and
freedom had become a world epic. Ahead of him lay the
realization of the dream that had sustained him throughout
years of isolation: a life with Avital in the land he had always called "ours."

ON HIS FIRST night in Jerusalem, Anatoly had stood upon
the Mount of Olives, looking down on the lights of Jerusalem. It was a foggy, chilly night, and the streetlamps of the
city were haloed by the mist.

His driver said, "Relax, Anatoly. It's all over now."

Anatoly smiled and, without turning his head from the
view, said with satisfaction, "No; it's just begun."

Epilogue:
Washington
and Moscow

Shcharansky in the United States

Anatoly and Avital, having been forcibly separated for so long, were determined never to part again. But in the first week of May 1986, barely three months after his liberation, Anatoly flew to the United States—without Avital. His visit could not be delayed, for he had a message to convey and the means to convey it; he also had many people to thank. Avital was advised against accompanying him for a reason that could only have made their parting more bittersweet: she was carrying their child. The longest-awaited, most fervently desired child in the modern history of Israel, and everyone had a stake in this one: the activists who struggled for years to free Shcharansky, the politicians who kept him on the agenda, the media people who followed Avital's campaign and publicized her private suffering—all felt, if not a father's pride, at least an uncle's.

The good news, rumored for weeks but strategically released the day after Anatoly's departure for the United States, served to stoke up an already warm reception. On his arrival at Kennedy International Airport in New York, Anatoly was met by hundreds of young Jews, students from Hebrew schools and institutions who had waited since dawn in the hope of a few words from their hero. Anatoly's eyes lit up when he saw the crowd and the signs saying "Welcome." "I want to speak to them," he protested repeatedly, as he was propelled along two rows of burly New York City policemen; when they hustled him into a black stretch limousine he objected, saying in Hebrew, "What's going on? I want to talk to them."

That morning Anatoly and members of his party, which included Alexander Lunts, Avi Maoz (who was not, after all, "shut out"), and recently freed refuseniks Isai and Grigory Goldshtein, attended a gathering in the elegant east-seventies penthouse of Anatoly's new agent, Marvin Josephson, head of International Creative Management. It was immediately evident that the factional rivalry for Shcharansky's favors which had deluged him in Israel—where he was almost as closely besieged by politicians as he had been by the KGB in Moscow, except that in Israel his followers were constantly quarreling among themselves and appealing to him for judgment—would dog him here as well. One activist leader rather grumpily said that "Anatoly has fallen into the hands of the big shots. . . . He'll be packaged and sold."

Some people, feeling themselves at least partially responsible for Anatoly's release, were quick to assume responsibility for his behavior as well. When the leader of a major American Soviet Jewry organization urged Anatoly, as "a guest in our country," not to talk about the Jackson Amendment, Alexander Lunts snapped back: "What are you talking about? That's what he went to prison for!"

After a round of interviews with the editorial boards of the four major New York newspapers, Anatoly went off for the weekend to the Riverdale home of the orthodox maverick Rabbi Avi Weiss, who according to Avital had been the most helpful of her American supporters. Anatoly spent a quiet weekend with the Weiss family in their modest brick home, around the corner from Weiss's synagogue, the Hebrew Institute of Riverdale, which had served as Avital's American headquarters. On Saturday morning Anatoly strolled around the comfortable Bronx neighborhood, telling Weiss that he couldn't believe this was New York City. One thing disturbed the former Moscovite, however, and after failing to make sense of it himself he asked his host, "Why do all these people run through the streets?"—for though he looked, he saw no sign that they were being pursued. Rabbi Weiss repressed a smile and explained. "It's called jogging. People do it for enjoyment." Anatoly looked amazed. "In the Soviet Union," he said, "we exercised for health, not for pleasure."

Anatoly declined to attend Saturday morning services, but in the evening he came to the synagogue and addressed an overflow audience of a thousand people, most of whom watched on video screens placed outside the building. He sat on a chair that had been unoccupied for nine years, ever since Anatoly was first arrested, when Weiss had placed a sign on it that read, "Reserved for Anatoly Shcharansky, Prisoner of Zion." In a display of ecumenism rare among the orthodox, Rabbi Weiss invited a number of other activist rabbis, including some from the Conservative and Reform streams of Judaism, to share the limelight. He spoke, praising the other rabbis, praising Avital: "Blessed is the people who has a woman of valor like Avital." But the thrust of his speech, and of Anatoly's which followed, was that though something had been accomplished, much more remained to be done. "There can be no 'business as usual,'" he said.

Anatoly was visibly moved. In his address to the congregation he said that the KGB had striven to convince him that he was already forgotten; when he learned of demonstrations on his behalf they scoffed and said, "Students and housewives: you think they can help you? You are in our hands." They were wrong, Anatoly said, for those students and housewives proved stronger than the KGB. "Nothing is impossible when you feel connected to your people and your land."

On Sunday, May 11, Anatoly was the guest of honor at the annual March for Soviet Jewry. Three hundred thousand people, the largest crowd ever, turned out for the event. Shcharansky's appearance gave new impetus to what many felt had been a flagging movement. Anatoly urged the crowd to support the application of economic and political pressure to the Soviet Union in order to bring about compliance with the Helsinki accords, particularly but not exclusively the clause regarding the right of emigration. That policy, embodied in the Jackson Amendment, had proved its efficacy and ought to be an element in every contact with the USSR. Anatoly then remembered his gentile dissident friends, as he did in every speech I heard him give. "As a Zionist and a Jew, I support universal justice, the call from Sinai. We must never forget Sakharov and Orlov, who raised their voices for Soviet Jewry."

His activist bent was obvious during the next day's private meeting with one hundred leaders of Jewish organizations and a group of some of the wealthiest Jews in the United

States. Without criticizing any person, Anatoly deprecated the pragmatic course supported by such leading policy makers as World Jewish Congress president Edgar Bronfman, who visited the Kremlin a number of times and whose organization hinted in late 1985 that the Soviets were prepared to airlift thousands of Soviet Jews to Israel. American Jews should beware of KGB tricks, Anatoly said; there should be no "quiet diplomacy" conducted between Jews and the Kremlin. Let the U.S. President pursue a double policy, alternating between quiet diplomacy and publicity; the Jews of America needed to be single-mindedly active and noisy in pursuit of their goal. Anatoly called for a demonstration of 400,000 Jews if Gorbachev visited Washington. Beside him on the dais, smiling, sat Rabbi Weiss.

ON HIS FIRST morning in Washington, Anatoly received a standing ovation from almost two hundred senators and congressmen in the Capitol Rotunda. He was wearing a suit and tie, for the first time in twenty-one years. Later, when he emerged from the White House with Secretary of State Shultz, he was asked what Reagan had told him in the meeting that had stretched to forty minutes. Anatoly said he could not speak for the President but could only relate what he told Reagan and what his impressions of the President were.

"We were speaking about the best ways of dealing with the Soviet Union, and I was surprised how deeply President Reagan understands that system." He said he was "very encouraged" by what Reagan had told him. "Quiet diplomacy, from my point of view, can help only if it is supported by strong public pressure, strong public diplomacy."

The Refuseniks After Shcharansky

"AND THE RUSSIAN SOUL IS A DARKNESS—FOR
MANY, A DARKNESS."

—The Idiot

The Kremlin's release of Anatoly Shcharansky was cause for great celebration among Russian Jews—he was "Refusenik Number One," in the phrase of Lev Blitshtein, a Moscow Jew who is a friend of the Shcharansky family. "We loved him; we wanted him to be free." Anatoly's close friend, Ida Nudel, who has suffered Siberian exile and many other torments in her fifteen years as a Jewish activist, also felt "the greatest joy" when she heard of his release on the Voice of America. But a terrible sadness underscored the rejoicing among the many thousands of Jews who wish to emigrate from the USSR. For the times have changed, and not for the better. The USSR in the mid-1980s is much tougher, much more Stalinistic than it was in the 1970s. That, at least, is the view of many of the refuseniks whom I visited in late May and early June 1986 on a trip to Moscow, Leningrad, and Kishinev.

In 1979, a year after the trials of Anatoly Shcharansky, Ida Nudel, and Vladimir Slepak, the Kremlin was still allowing a significant number of Jews to emigrate—about fifty-one thousand in that peak year. In March 1986, a month after Shcharansky's release, only forty-two Jews were allowed to leave the vast empire that stretches across nine time zones. The Helsinki accords state that "Everyone has a right to leave any country, including his own"; but both this guarantee and the Universal Declaration of Human Rights, which the Kremlin also signed, are honored here more in the breach than in the observance.

The Soviet authorities seem much quicker to use repressive measures today than they were during the Brezhnev era, and the country's laws have been toughened to allow prison authorities to double or triple prisoners' sentences at will. Although he was under constant surveillance for three years before his arrest in 1977, Anatoly Shcharansky was, by today's standards, relatively "free". In his day, the KGB stopped a good many activities, such as the planned seminar on Jewish life in the USSR, but did not break up *all* meetings. Today, it would be impossible for seventy Jews to gather in an apartment for a lecture on Jewish history or any other subject.

Most of the Jews who applied to emigrate are déclassé now. Their grandparents were craftsmen, merchants, farmers. Their parents were engineers, scientists, doctors—fifteen years ago, 10 percent of Soviet scientists and doctors were Jews. But they themselves work as stokers, night watchmen, garbage collectors.

If the Soviet regime is different, so is the generation of Jews seeking emigration. In the two decades since the renewed emigration movement started, sparked by the consciousness-raising trauma of the Six-day War, children have grown up "in refusal"; families have been torn asunder. Grandparents, parents, wives or husbands or children have emigrated. Many members of the younger generation have immersed themselves in their Jewish identity, becoming observant Jews. They speak Hebrew in their apartments, on the subway, in the streets. They regard themselves as Israelis held captive in a strange land, where Jews have lived for two thousand years in exile, where anti-Semitism remains endemic and virulent.

When the Chernobyl disaster was made known to the

Russians, after the storm of publicity in the West, rumors began spreading among some of the common people. A Jewish engineer was responsible, they whispered, probably a refusenik on his way to Israel. Officially, no such libel was even hinted at; but without the atmosphere created by the constant anti-Jewish and anti-Israel campaign in the official media, such slanders could not grow. Posters sold in corner shops depict Zionists as tools of the CIA, in drawings reminiscent of the Nazi era.

Among some Jews who were active for years in the emigration movement, I heard other stories about Chernobyl, which was once a Jewish *shtetl*. According to two refuseniks in Moscow, a pamphlet about the Chernobyl (or Chernyopol) *shtetl* was published in *samizdat* just a few weeks before the nuclear disaster. The author, Mikhail Furman, was one of two survivors of the massacre of thousands of Jews in Chernobyl by the Nazis and their Ukrainian helpers. The postwar town of Chernobyl, which means "black field" in Ukrainian, was said to have been built over the mass grave of these slaughtered Jews. Coincidentally, the first refusenik arrested in the wake of the nuclear accident was Boris Chernobylsky, whose name indicates where his family comes from.

On May 24, 1986, Chernobylsky, a refusenik for ten years, went to Pushkin Square in central Moscow with his wife and three children. They held up a sign: "Let us go!" Immediately, militiamen arrested them. Boris was held for fifteen days, and warned that he would face prison the next time.

IDA NUDEL, the best-known Soviet Jew among people in the West, managed to elude her KGB shadows for a few days in early June 1986, emerging suddenly among friends in Leningrad for the first time in years. It was an act that reflected both defiance and desperation. The woman who is considered the soul of the Jewish emigration movement remains obsessed with the desire to live in Israel, and though she is as selfless as ever—aiding prisoners of conscience, sheltering evacuees from the Chernobyl region—she feels that she cannot wait any longer. The Jewish people and the Israeli government must somehow rescue her immediately, or she will not survive.

The release of her close friend Anatoly heartened her even as it fed her own desperation to get out, as I learned in a ten-hour talk with her, the first such interview she has managed to give in many years. She talked deep into the "white night" (in June in Leningrad, the sun still shines at midnight, a strangely disturbing phenomenon that disrupts one's equilibrium and sense of time). The interview took place in a boxy little apartment inside a vast gray complex of hundreds of identical flats, one of the hives that surround the great Soviet cities and house millions of worker bees. Our host, checking for surveillance, frequently parted the curtains to look out the window, which was clouded with salty residue from the Baltic sea air. The KGB men, most of whom look as if they belong in a "B" spy movie, were not yet in evidence—it took them one whole day to pick up her trail again.

Nudel and many other Jewish activist leaders are concerned that the entire movement, though revitalized by a new generation of refuseniks, may be in jeopardy, as the Soviet regime continues to pursue a neo-Stalinist line on the "Jewish question."

This diminutive woman, whom her friends describe as "the complete city person," has been living in semiexile in the small rural Moldavian town of Bendery since her release in 1982 from four years of Siberian exile. She is a cosmopolitan soul among simple, provincial people, many of them Jews who are too afraid even to talk to her. At age fifty-five, her bespectacled face is a map of where she has been and what she has gone through: cracked country lips, a furrowed, intelligent brow, black hair streaked with gray, penetrating Gloria Swanson eyes, and an aura that alternates between massive strength and obvious vulnerability.

She is a warm, inspiring, and seemingly indomitable figure, yet the wear and tear of Soviet persecution is evident. It is the nature of secret police to be cruel, but the KGB has surpassed itself in its unrelenting hounding and torment of the frail refusenik, who suffers from a diseased heart. "I cannot wait any longer," she says. "Take me out. I want Israel now!"

About a month before her visit to Leningrad, she had tried unsuccessfully to leave Bendery for a trip to Tbilisi to say good-bye to her close friends Isai and Grigory Goldshtein, the long-time refuseniks who had finally obtained permission to go to Israel. She got as far as the Kishinev airport, where a militia detective pointed his umbrella at her and commanded his men: "Take this woman!" As they hustled her into a waiting car, they told her, "Keep silent!" (As Nudel remarked later: "Everything in the Soviet Union must be kept quiet.") They warned her that trying again would not be in her best interest. Nevertheless, the next morning she boarded a bus from Bendery. A green Volga packed with KGB men trailed the bus until it reached the town limits. They flagged it down. Local militiamen, who towered over the small woman, wrestled her out of the bus. "Big, strong men—it would be funny, if it weren't so sad," recalled Nudel, who, like Anatoly, has an eye for the elements of farce within tragedy.

Ida Nudel is also an actress, with a dramatic voice and manner; and in the view of those who know her, she is a seer who looks deeply into her own soul, drawing upon a treasure of self-knowledge. Throughout the course of our conversation, a wide range of emotions played across her face, ranging from intense concentration to melancholy to joy. She smiles broadly, and the silver crowns of her teeth reflect the light.

Leningrad, the "Window on the West" built by Peter the Great, is the city of Pushkin, Dostoevsky, and of course the Communist deity, V. I. Lenin. The inner city, much of it built by the architect Rastrelli, has a Venetian quality. But to Ida Nudel and the other refuseniks, it is a precinct of hell—there's *nothing* quaint or redeeming or "European" in the evil empire; and the dirtiest word in their vocabulary is socialism. Only Israel, or their dream of Israel, is beautiful in their eyes. Thus the great Russian culture leaves them untouched. Ida, as a teenager, had read Pushkin and Lermontov to the Soviet nation on the radio. And then suddenly, at age seventeen, she wasn't a Russian any more. Early on, she came to believe that the ancient history of the Jews of Russia was over, that the long exile was over, that the Jews had to leave Russia forever.

One of her favorite ballads, by the late Vladimir Visotsky (the USSR's Bob Dylan), is about an animal surrounded by hunters, and the "red line" around him. "He knows, through the milk of his mother, that it is forbidden to cross that line," Nudel said, as she recalled an episode from her Siberian exile. An article had appeared in the local press about the Zionist enemy that mentioned Ida Nudel as one of the foremost villains. The next day, as she walked through the woods on her way back to her cabin, she was followed by five men. She could hear them talking about her, but blocked out their actual words. "I could only hear them on an animal level—I listened to their tone, to know whether they were really angry or not. Visotsky's song repeated in my heart all that day, because it was my own situation. If you are followed, you feel hounded. This feeling applies to all who are surrounded and persecuted. These men were angry about this woman with the clever eyes . . . but they didn't attack me. I didn't turn around. Just kept walking, until I was out of the woods."

In Siberia, she was under constant surveillance throughout her four-year term. When she was released in March 1982, she had the legal right to live in Moscow or anywhere else she chose, and to be registered there—all Soviet citizens must be registered in the town or city in which they reside. But Nudel, like her friends Anatoly Shcharansky and Vladimir Slepak (the latter received a five-year term in exile at the same time that she was sentenced to four years for "anti-Soviet activity"), was regarded as a primary Enemy of the People.

When she returned home to Moscow after the rigors of Siberia, the authorities gave her seventy-two hours to get out. They never said how long the ban would last. She tried to register in seven towns outside the sixty-mile zone around greater Moscow. She thought she would get permission to live in Struniwo near Alexandrov, where her friend Mark Nashpitz had settled after his Siberian exile; but despite his efforts to help, she was expelled. After four days in the town, the police and KGB came, took the book of registration from the home in which she was staying, and threatened the woman who owned the house, as well as her son. "Why are you registering this terrible woman?" one KGB agent asked, as he removed Nudel's name from the book.

Wherever she went it was the same. Every four days, the KGB reviews the registration lists in every hamlet of the USSR; and every four days, Ida Nudel was expelled. "I began to understand how popular I was with the KGB," she said. She tried again, this time in the Baltic republics, where she had some cousins—in Riga, for example. But she was in a limbo that lasted half a year. And she felt like a hunted animal. "I went to Tartu in Estonia, where a friend I helped in prison camp now lives. He wrote to me and said he would try to get me registered there. I had no registration stamp in my internal passport, the document that all Soviet citizens over age sixteen must carry." That was the mark, or non-mark, of Cain.

"I only had my friend's post-office address, and I arrived late at night in the little town. I was very weak from my exile, and carried a very heavy suitcase. I was absolutely exhausted, suffering from heart disease and carrying that suitcase, which was bigger than I am. I went to a rooming house, and the clerk gave me a registration card; then she asked to check my passport. When she found that I wasn't registered, she said, 'You're not registered anywhere. How is that possible? Get out of here right now or I'll call the militia.' Without waiting, the woman, who had gone very pale, went out to call the police. I left immediately, walking to the bus station. It was closed, and there was no place to wait. I walked very slowly to a little square with benches, feeling absolutely exhausted and very depressed. Some people were lying on the benches. I watched the police come by and roust them, shouting at them to move on. The police roust homeless people, the drunks and whores who are at the bottom of society—in prison, they're called 'ex-intelligentsia.' I went with some of them and found a place to rest. I was numb. But I couldn't stand it among them after half an hour, and didn't know what to do. That's what it means not to have registration, not to have that stamp in your internal passport. I told myself in my heart that never again would I go to a town where I didn't know someone to give me shelter. . . .

"This incident was just one of many that exhausted my soul. A human being is really very limited in his power. I have a very painful heart condition, and stress makes it worse. It hurts most at night when I lay in bed, especially between 3 A.M. and 4 A.M."

She didn't know where to go, but she knew where not to go—the Ukraine, virulently anti-Semitic, was dangerous for a well-known refusenik. She tried again elsewhere in the Baltic states, the three countries annexed by the Soviet empire in the World War II era. But the KGB warned prospective hosts—including the father of former prisoners Sylva and Israel Zalmanson—that she would never be allowed to register there. Finally, after six months of wandering around the Soviet Union, she received an invitation from a man, Moshe Lieberman, in Bendery, Moldavia, who had sent her packages while she was in exile. Somehow, he managed to have her registered in the town of 100,000. Nevertheless, after four days she was pushed into a police car and brought before the town's police chief, a big man who shouted and stamped his feet, demanding to know how she had managed to register in his town.

"I just sat there as he ranted at me, waiting until the storm subsided. Then I said, 'Look at you. You're a man.

You have a gun. You have many aides here who can kill me.
Why are you shouting?' My manner, and my spirit, were
my only weapons. 'Why are you afraid of me?' I asked him.
He was no fool. He calmed down and turned toward the
window. A big, very strong man who had shouted hysteri-
cally at a small woman. But I had bested him and he knew
it, and he let me go."

Bendery has been limbo. "I don't live there spiritually.
I don't live in the Soviet Union in my spirit. I wish the Russian people well, but I want all Jews to understand: it was
our fate before to live here. But now we have a country of
our own, at last."

There are some eight thousand Jews in Bendery: tailors,
shoemakers, craftsmen, whose children are teachers or engineers. There are forty refusenik families, but Nudel has
contact with only two of them—the Liebermans and the
Royaks. Everyone else is afraid.

She lives with her collie dog in a peasant hut of two
small rooms. It took two years to make it livable: piping in
cold water, bringing in electricity. When she first settled in,
Nudel thought that she would be able to change the lives of
her Jewish neighbors by applying her formidable energies to
the task. "I tried, and so did these two families—they were
born there, they knew the town. I organized a Hanukkah
celebration, including a musical show and a talk on Jewish
history. The kids dressed up in blue and white and held candles while I told them something of the story of our people.
It was a very simple show, and the kids were very happy.
Then the police came and frightened the thirty people there,
telling them what the consequences would be at their places
of work. It's harder for the Jews of small towns. After that
day, when I met people who had been at the celebration,

they pretended not to know me. I understood. It was the end of my short career in Bendery. I could do nothing. I kept trying, but it was fruitless. I don't stop with one disappointment; I'm too stubborn and devoted to my ideas. I tried for two years to influence the people there. But they are afraid. They are simple people, and they have reason to be afraid."

A great gulf separated Ida Nudel from the local Jews of Bendery. She was a famous person, with supporters around the world—in Siberia, she got twelve thousand letters from people in fifty-one countries. She knew she had the sympathy of many more people. "I'm safe, secure in my heart. But the Jews of Bendery don't have this inner security." They did not feel that anyone in the West was at all interested in their fate, and they did not want to get involved with the "troublemaker." Since Nudel was not allowed to travel, she was virtually isolated. Actress Jane Fonda visited her in April 1983—even the Kremlin could not refuse her—but when former vice-presidential candidate Geraldine Ferraro attempted to visit Nudel in 1985, she was denied permission.

She has continued to write and send packages to the refuseniks imprisoned by the Soviet regime on trumped-up charges. Her efforts to keep up-to-date on their conditions of servitude have gone on undiminished. There is no more important work in the Jewish movement, according to other refuseniks. Information is the only weapon the Jews have. And the prisoners are at the forefront of the movement. When Ida found that a prisoner was ill, she would send telegrams to doctors, get the information to refusenik circles in Moscow or Leningrad and thence to the West. She has received hundreds of letters from prisoners, and one of her dreams is to publish a book of these letters. "They tell it all. They give you an idea of their inner lives, how their Jewishness has evolved and how it changes." She has never stopped being involved.

But she feels she has lost touch with the day-to-day developments in the movement. "I was exiled, and am exiled still. They punished me severely by cutting me off. I don't know the young refuseniks, but I have some understanding of the situation." (In the next few days in Leningrad, she visited many of the new generation of refuseniks, along with veteran movement people. The KGB was right behind her.)

"I do know that the Jewish soul is awakening here again. There is a special spirit of dignity and identity. Part of it is a reaction to the malicious anti-Semitism that is vented in the newspapers and on television. The young Jews feel it. Years ago, Jews had to suppress their wounded hearts. But now—in the big cities, because the situation is different there—you can see that Jewish people are more dignified and proud, speak openly about being Jewish. It's especially true of youngsters between the ages of twelve and fifteen, when you become your own self. Some children feel only guilt when confronted by the anti-Jewish venom on television, but I think most will choose to pursue their Jewish identity. It's a new life, unusual, fantastic! All of us, Russians as well, lead a double life in the Soviet Union, a secret life. Now these young Jews totally reject the colorless, anonymous Soviet life. Their Jewish identity makes life suddenly so interesting."

She believes that the movement's continued growth and success in achieving repatriation depend entirely on the West. "Otherwise, the movement will be lost. People in the West must protest against every persecution, against every attempt to suppress our movement. No one can understand just how powerful our movement can be, if we get support from the West."

Like most of the refuseniks I interviewed, Ida Nudel spoke glowingly of President Reagan. (When she told Jane Fonda how much she admired Reagan and hoped for his reelection, the liberal actress put her finger to her mouth and whispered "Shhh—the intellectuals would never understand that.") Nudel urges a tough, no-nonsense line when dealing with the Kremlin. Referring to the Helsinki accords, Nudel said in a statement strikingly similar to Shcharansky's in New York, "The Soviets signed it. They agreed to fulfill it. If they don't, how can the United States trust their word on more complicated agreements? Helsinki is the key and always will be. The West must not sign any accords on arms or anything else until the Soviets show a willingness to abide by the Helsinki agreement."

She thinks that the Kremlin would strongly resist any attempts by the West to abrogate the agreement due to Soviet noncompliance with the human rights questions, which include the basic human right to emigrate. "You can say to the Soviets, 'If you don't want to fulfill the accords, then take back your signature.' But they'll never take it back because the first and second parts are so important to them—so the demand must be, 'Then fulfill the third basket.' " (The political aspects of the accords recognize Soviet hegemony over Eastern European territories. The third basket concerns human rights.)

"The Soviets never do anything without testing the waters first. They throw a bone to see how the dog will react. The West pretty much kept silent when the KGB put Sakharov on a plane [sending him to exile in Gorky]. If there had been a strong, universal reaction, the Soviets would have given in. Something similar occurred when they decided to cut off emigration. It started in Kharkov in the Ukraine, when they decreed that only people with immediate relatives abroad would be allowed out. When the West responded with silence, they applied this rule to the whole USSR.

"You must understand, it's like a different planet here. . . . After Chernobyl, it has become obvious that our life on earth depends on making this society more open. Otherwise, tomorrow, nobody knows what will happen. If emigration is open, this society will change."

She advocates a high-pressure campaign in the West, in complete agreement with the approach pursued by Anatoly Shcharansky. "We were together for many years. We shared opinions on many things. Because of our common understanding, we were very close. He understands my place in the movement—as a former prisoner, he understands." Like Shcharansky, Nudel was deeply involved with the dissident movement, the Helsinki Watch Group led by Yuri Orlov, Alexander Ginzburg, and others. "I was with the Helsinki people, and know them better than some Jews. I agreed entirely with them. Shcharansky was absolutely right when he stressed the connection between the Jewish movement and the dissident movement. If you don't think like the authorities, you are a dissident. If you're not loyal to the system, you're a dissident. . . .

"I think only how to escape from this place. I've gone through thousands of clashes with the KGB. What more can I say? Take me out. I cannot wait any more."

And yet, in her mind, she has made a "Schindler's list" of who should get out first, and her own name is not at the top. "I daydreamed that they asked me, 'Who goes out?' I thought about it a lot." Her list begins with the twenty-one prisoners of Zion, the ailing Uri Edelshtein, and Yosef Begun, and the others: Moshe Abramov, Yevgeny Yakir, Yaacov Levin, Nadezhda Fradkova, Zachar Zunshyne, Alexander Cholimyanskiy, Yosef Zissels, Yaacov Rosenberg, Leonid Shrayer, Mark Nepomnyaschiy, Natan Vershubskiy, Leonid Volvosky, Yosef Berenshtein, Roald Zelichonik, Vladimir Brodsky, Vladimir Lifshits, Bezalel Shalolashvili, Alexei Magarik, Lev Shefer. Then come the people who have served in prison or in exile, like Vladimir and Masha Slepak and herself. Then refuseniks with boys approaching army age and families with three children or more, and the most active refuseniks. Then come the rest of the refuseniks, followed by the remainder of Soviet Jewry.

What can people in the West do? "Rally public opinion," Nudel says firmly; "press for government declarations, make films and write books, send letters to refuseniks and to the Soviet government. Deluge them. Approach French, German, and Japanese businessmen who trade with the Soviet Union, get each one to ask for one person, one family. It has to be done on a personal level. If the businessman works at it, he'll succeed. You need very devoted people, you need many people like Isai Goldshtein. Make a film. Make people understand the situation. Make posters. Make it so you laugh and cry. The Soviets are very sensitive. They're afraid of being laughed at."

She speaks with semi-professional authority when she suggests making a film. When Nudel was in Siberia, she and Yevgeny Tzirlin made a stirring film about her life there that has been seen around the world. She wrote the scenario, which he translated into English. "We worked all day, shooting film in my very little room where I lived with my dog. It was very cold, the snow blowing and churning out-side. I said, 'Zenya, if we lose this moment, we are both fools. Stand up and get to work.' The weather was so mis-erable that no man or beast braved the outdoors. We shot film all day. In the last scene, I sat on my cot and looked into my soul. I turned my face to the camera and looked directly at my future audience, and I said, 'If you forget us, all this suffering is in vain.' "

Tzirlin left the next day and managed to smuggle the film to the West. "Months later, I started getting letters from England. 'Ida, it's not in vain.' Five thousand people in a London church saw it, and many wept. Now, it's seven years later. I'm very, very tired. And I say it again. 'If you forget us, all this suffering is in vain.' "

"WE'RE LOSING hope," said Lev Blitshtein, who has been a refusenik for twelve years. He lives alone in a dark, run-down Moscow apartment. His wife and children are in America. "This is an iron country," he says, shaking his head. "We see no change with Gorbachev."

Blitshtein, who over a decade ago was a high official in a ministry dealing with food distribution, is not allowed to join his family because he allegedly possesses "state se-crets"—about meat, one supposes. The Soviets have denied visas to as many as forty thousand Jews for this reason, or simply because "it is not in the Soviet interest."

There are said to be 400,000 Jews ready to pack up and leave the Soviet Union in a day. No one doubts that most of the remaining Jews would soon follow once the gates were open. According to the official Soviet census, there are just over two million Jews in the Soviet Union, but Jewish activ-ists say the number may be as high as four million—many intermarried Jews prefer to list their nationality as Ukrainian or Russian rather than Jewish. And of course, there are assimilated Jews who identify with Russia, with the Communist Party, even with the KGB. A couple of years ago on a Moscow street, Blitshtein ran into the notorious Dr. Alexander "Sanya" Lipavsky, whose treachery led to the arrest of Anatoly Shcharansky. "Lipavsky was not the first traitor to his people; nor will he be the last," says Blitshtein.

Like many of the refuseniks, Blitshtein listened eagerly to Voice of America radio reports about Shcharansky's visit to the White House and Congress in early May. He agreed with most of what Shcharansky said, but favored some flexibility in easing U.S. trade restrictions if the Soviets allow more Jews to emigrate. "The Soviets are desperate for trade. If you give nothing, you'll get nothing."

THERE IS A strong inclination among the refuseniks to report exactly and precisely on their situation. Since information is their main weapon, exaggeration can only undermine their cause. Natasha Khassina, a Moscow computer programmer until she was deprived of her work, is among the most rigorous in presenting facts. In the case of Uri Edelshtein, the twenty-eight-year-old Prisoner of Zion who was seriously injured in prison camp in December 1985, there had been reports in Israel and the West that the injuries were inflicted by fellow prisoners or by the prison authorities themselves. The truth is that, though he was put to work in a precarious place, there was no evidence of a deliberate attempt to injure him.

"Uri fell. It was an accident. We must never exaggerate the truth," Khassina says. "Uri's wife, Tatiana, just visited him in the hospital. He needs two more operations, problematical urethra surgery. But although the Soviets have promised to give him proper medical attention, this has not yet happened."

Edelshtein was arrested in August 1984, six years after his first application to emigrate. He studied Hebrew and Jewish history and observed the Sabbath, until the KGB stormed his apartment one day and "found" drugs. He was sentenced to three years. It was the first of many such plants on Jewish activists, for the KGB has decided to incarcerate them on criminal charges, hoping to quiet protests in the West. The latest case was that of Alexei Magarik, a twenty-eight-year-old Hebrew teacher, considered one of the best in Moscow. His wife, Natasha Ratner, also a young Hebrew teacher, has a seven-month-old baby. Alexei was known as a good organizer, which probably brought him to the notice of the KGB. On March 14, 1986, when he was returning to Moscow from a visit to a friend in Tbilisi, his satchel was confiscated. Later, he was told that six grams of hashish had been discovered in his tobacco pouch. At his trial on June 6, he received the maximum three-year prison sentence (a minimum term is unheard of)—in spite of the fact that two Jewish friends in Tbilisi testified that they packed his suitcase and there were no drugs or contraband of any kind in the suitcase. Trumped-up charges seem to be the KGB's latest gambit.

THERE ARE THREE young men among the refuseniks who may be arrested at any time. One of them is Albert (Haim) Burshtein, twenty, of Leningrad, whose parents have been refuseniks since 1980. The family lives in one of the innumerable massive housing projects. Albert, who speaks fluent English and Hebrew, has been most diligent in gathering information on prisoners and their families, and on other refuseniks. Interrogated frequently by the KGB, he responds to them defiantly. Recently his fifty-year-old father, Edward, was pulled in and told that he faced charges under Article 190 (slander of the Soviet state), which carries a three-year term. "But your son Albert, he is a *real* troublemaker—he'll be charged under Article 70 (propaganda against the Soviet state)," they threatened. This article carries a term of seven years in prison followed by five years in internal exile. The KGB did not like the youth's uncompromising attitude, nor his open struggle for Jewish rights.

Young Burshtein is one of many of the new generation who has become religious. Although he has perhaps naïve ideas about Israel, where he wants to build his life, he is correct and realistic about one thing. "Almost all the support we get is from Jews in the United States not from Israel." Yet he believes in Israel. After one arrest, he shouted at the KGB men: "I am a citizen of Israel, and Israel knows how to protect its people." Although the Burshteins' phone has been cut off for some time, Albert manages to talk every week to volunteer activist Pamela Cohen, the dynamic head of the Chicago chapter of the Union of Councils for Soviet Jews. He also communicates regularly with Lynn Singer, head of the Long Island branch of the Union of Councils, who has been struggling for Soviet Jews for over fifteen years.

Albert appears extremely articulate, tough, and mature for a twenty-year-old, and he has steeled himself for the worst. He knows what the Soviet Union is all about: his grandfather and many other members of his family were among the millions murdered under Stalin, who is, incidentally, admired by a growing number of Russians—one sees portraits of Stalin on a large number of trucks and vans.

Albert was first arrested by the KGB for his Jewish activities when he was fifteen. His most recent arrest, late in 1985, was for "stubbornly demanding an exit visa to Israel." At seventeen, he became religious after studying with a *baal tshuva* (penitent) who is a follower of the Brooklyn-based Lubavitcher rebbe. "It was my appreciation of how to be a Jew." He often talks Hebrew to his friends as they walk in the streets of Leningrad. "I am a Jew and a citizen of Israel," he says. It is a remarkable phenomenon—large groups of young Russian Jews speaking Hebrew, living as if they were already in Israel, thinking only of "repatriation." (In recent years, there has been increased emphasis on the idea of repatriation to the home country—Israel—rather than on reunification of families, which the Soviets, despite their official acceptance of the right of family reunification, have ignored.)

Despite an official warning from the KGB that he faces imprisonment for many years, Albert continues to act as a conduit of information, helping veteran prisoners, gathering information on new ones, carrying on with the crucial work that Ida Nudel and Natasha Khassina have been engaged in for many years. These women are his heroes, along with Anatoly Shcharansky, Prisoner of Zion Yosef Begun, and Roald Zelichonik (who is serving a three-year term). When Anatoly paid his visit to the United States in May 1986, Burshtein and his friends sent a message to him via Lynn Singer in New York: "You inspired us, and we are happy for you." That message, and the legends about Shcharansky, were in his mind when the KGB men brought him to KGB headquarters near the Neva River. They gave him a paper, saying: "You are officially warned that you are engaged in slandering the Soviet regime . . . passing information abroad that was later broadcast by Israel Radio." Albert said: "First you have to prove that it was slander." As the KGB agents manhandled him, his chief interrogator said: "We'll do just that, at the trial."

The next day, his mother came to the headquarters. They told her that if her son didn't talk to foreigners and re-frained from any more phone calls, the whole family would be released in a year. On behalf of her family, she refused the offer.

Ida Nudel, who corresponded with Burshtein for a long time and met him for the first time in early June in Lenin-grad, believes he may be a prime target now. "If they want to excite the Jewish world, maybe they'll hit this boy—you never know what their goals are."

BORIS DAVIATOV, thirty-five, of Leningrad, whose crimes in-clude the organizing of a private exhibit of refusenik art, is another Jew who faces prison. He has been effective in reg-ularly bringing together young Jews: socializing is an im-portant part of the movement, and boy often meets girl in an apartment in which Jewish history is taught, music is played, artwork displayed, Hebrew recited. Boris has long been a driving spirit in such groups, disseminating Israeli literature, staging plays about Hanukkah or Masada, and otherwise furthering Jewish culture.

The KGB broke up one of these meetings in 1984 and interrogated forty youths, trying by intimidation to induce them to accuse Boris of anti-Soviet actions. They warned him in September 1985 to stop his activities. On an earlier occasion, he was interrogated after writing a letter to Ana-toly Shcharansky in prison. The very act of writing to a traitor, the KGB said, was "anti-Sovietic."

Ida Nudel has praised Daviatov's efforts. Nudel fears he will be arrested because his name is virtually unknown in the West—she believes him particularly vulnerable because he speaks only Russian and is therefore limited in his contacts with Western visitors who could publicize his case. His wife is pregnant with their second child, and her anti-Israel parents, like Avital's, have remained vehemently opposed to his Jewish activism. Nudel believes the campaign for they threatened refuseniks must begin *before* they are arrested.

IN MOSCOW, Misha Shipov is the third young man who faces imprisonment. His grandparents are memorialized in the Museum of the Revolution downtown, where Kommosol Communist Party youth are brought to see the relics of the Bolshevik enterprise. The display card, however, doesn't mention the end of Yitzhak Abramovich Shipov's revolutionary career. Although he was big in the Central Committee, he was blotted out by Stalin in 1938. Misha, lean and handsome at twenty-nine, is an electrician in an art gallery. In May, the KGB took him from work and brought him to the notorious Lubyanka Prison in central Moscow.

During his years as a refusenik, he has been interrogated often by the KGB. He wrote to the Supreme Soviet and to the Foreign Ministry in Jerusalem, declaring that he was an Israeli held against his will in the USSR. (His brother, Sasha, lives in Jerusalem, where he is one of the leaders of the Soviet Jewry Education and Information Center.) The KGB again called him in and warned him. "You're making your position worse . . . you could get out, but not this way," his chief interrogator said. "You will go instead to Siberia." But Misha refused to sign any of the papers thrust in front of him. He felt he was nothing more than a hostage, held by agents who could never be persuaded that they were acting like terrorists.

At a Saturday night gathering in Moscow, Shipov sat holding a radio to his ear, trying to discern the midnight Voice of America news broadcast through the jamming, as other refuseniks present talked about the extraordinary growth of religious observance among them. Everyone seemed to take it for granted that he would soon be put away for a few years.

WHEN THE VIPS from the West go to Moscow and want to see some refuseniks, they invariably begin with Professor Alexander Lerner, who has been denied a visa for over fifteen years. Lerner was once one of the USSR's leading scientists, a member of the prestigious Academy of Sciences. He lives in a comparatively plush apartment near the university, a huge, bristling Stalinist-era edifice rising above the Moskva River.

When he joined the Jewish movement years ago, it was a very significant event; he lent his dignity to the refuseniks and contributed greatly to the cause. In the 1977 *Izvestia* open letter by the KGB agent Lipavsky, Lerner was named as the chief conductor of the Zionist conspiracy in which Shcharansky was only a violinist. But Lerner, now in his mid-seventies, was already too old and too well known to be tried. Shcharansky was chosen in his stead.

Lerner is still there, and whenever Senator Ted Kennedy goes to Moscow, he visits Alex Lerner to find out what is happening with the Jews. But some of the refuseniks say it is the wrong address. Lerner is now regarded by a number of leading activists as "a professional refusenik." He himself balks at the idea of ever carrying a placard demanding his release. "I would never do something like that," he said; "my role is to talk to congressmen and journalists, to explain the situation." He no longer reapplies for emigration.

LEONID SHCHARANSKY, Anatoly's brother, did not choose the refusenik way of life that was fated to be his. His wife and children are not Jewish. He himself was assimilated. But when Anatoly was put on trial following the Lipavsky slander, it was Leonid who talked to the correspondents, repeating almost verbatim the day-to-day testimony at the trial. And it was he who comforted their aged mother, Ida Milgrom.

Leonid and his family are still waiting for an exit visa. They applied on March 27, 1986, six weeks after Anatoly's release, but by June, there had been no answer of any kind. It was understood by some that when the United States engineered Anatoly's release, his family would also be allowed to emigrate. "I know Anatoly raised it, along with many questions, when he spoke with Secretary of State Shultz and President Reagan during his trip last month," Leonid said, at a friend's apartment in Moscow. "They promised to get an answer."

Charm seems to run in the Shcharansky family, and Leonid has an easy-going, warm personality; but he feels uncomfortable, buffeted by the winds of fate. "I had never considered emigrating, even during Anatoly's refusal years. But when my wife and I saw what this nightmare was all about, we decided to leave." He worries, however, about being the brother of a world-famous personality. "I want to be myself, not 'Anatoly's brother'; it may be a bit difficult to live close together."

Leonid, a hydraulic engineer and computer programmer, had to leave his work because of Anatoly's activities; he now does physical labor, mainly electric wiring. His closest friends are refuseniks, and he feels kinship and a great respect for Natasha Khassina. "She's very rational, and we see things the same way."

Although he doesn't relish living in his younger brother's shadow, he feels extremely close to Anatoly and proud of his character and intellect. "I knew from childhood that he would do something great—I waited for him to do something tremendous. And then it happened." Leonid's wife, Raya, is also very attached to Anatoly, but shares her husband's apprehensions about their future in Israel. Leonid believes in a supreme being, but chafes at the strictures of religion and resents those who wish to impose their rituals on others. The Shcharanskys have two boys, Sasha, fourteen, and Boris, eleven months.

"Fate is moving me to Israel," Leonid concluded. "I'm not in charge of my own destiny. That is a strange feeling."

FOR YEARS, the KGB has used army duty as a weapon against the refuseniks, as Anatoly revealed in his 1976 report to the Helsinki Watch Group. But the situation has worsened. Before 1980, according to Evgeny Lein, a veteran leader among the activists in Leningrad, hardly any sons of refuseniks were being inducted. "But then emigration stopped. Now the KGB uses the threat of induction to silence the fathers of teenage boys." Evgeny's youngest child, Alexei, was seven when his mathematician father first applied to emigrate in 1978. Now he's rapidly approaching draft age.

The Soviets have severely punished Jews who have been sent Israeli citizenship and have refused to serve in the Red

Army. In 1980, Gregory Geishis and Simon Shneerman were sent to prison for two-and-a-half-year terms. When Shneerman got out, he was still of draft age; the Soviets tried him again and sent him back to prison. According to Lein, there was not enough support from abroad for these victims. "Resistance to the draft stopped from that moment, when other boys saw that nobody in the West really paid enough attention. From that time, the children of refuseniks have been going to the army, which makes the refuseniks more quiet. They take away your sons. It's a very effective KGB tool. We decided, when the time comes, that our son will go; but we will protest, fight, inform people, create publicity."

Dr. Lein and his wife Irina, who has a Ph.D. in chemistry, both lost their jobs when they applied to emigrate. He now tutors students in mathematics and physics. Life has been a struggle ever since. They have frequently been arrested and manhandled by the KGB, their children were expelled from school, and Lein was imprisoned for a year. Martin Gilbert wrote about the Leins in *The Jews of Hope*, and the *New York Times* ran an editorial appealing to the Soviets to allow the Leins to go to Israel. Former Israeli president Ephraim Katzir and his late wife tried to visit the Leins in 1984, but were pulled away by the KGB just outside the huge housing project on Engels Prospect where the Leins live. All the attention may have saved him from further prison terms, but there has been no indication that the Soviet authorities will relent, or that they will even reconnect their telephone. Meanwhile, Lein keeps tabs on the latest tactics employed by the secret police, counsels refuseniks on legal questions, and comforts the families of prisoners.

Lein works with all of the various refusenik groups,

whether religious, cultural, or political. "We musn't struggle against one another," he says. "We have the KGB, and
we are all in the same boat."

ON THE DAY I visited Anya Lifshitz, whose husband Vladimir was arrested on January 8, 1986, under Article 190 (anti-
Soviet agitation and propaganda), she was saying good-bye
to her eighteen-year-old son, Boris, who was being drafted
into the army. Vladimir, forty-five, is a mathematician and
economist with a Ph.D., whose crime was to write about his
family's life in letters to friends in Israel, the United States,
and England. He was beaten in prison in February, suffered
a concussion and a broken nose, and spent ten days in the
prison hospital. The KGB had ordered the criminals in his
cell to "teach him a lesson." One month later he was sentenced to the maximum three-year term. A file was opened
on Anya for refusing to testify against her husband.

Anya was allowed to visit her husband in late May 1986.
He was still suffering the consequences of the beating and
had lost consciousness two days before the short meeting
with his wife. No doctor was treating him.

Anya and her eleven-year-old daughter, Maria (Masha),
are alone now. Boris was drafted at the insistence of the
KGB, despite a military medical commission's finding that
he was physically unfit to serve because of stomach ulcers.
Just before his departure, Boris said that he continues to
regard himself as "an Israeli kept here by force."

Anya, forty-one, a construction engineer before she became a refusenik, was in despair over what the KGB was
doing to her family. A refined and delicate woman, she came
from an assimilated family and never imagined that she would
be in such a situation. But as her friend Evgeny Lein said,

"She is a very strong person, and the family is united in spirit—they will persevere."

One of Anya's closest friends is Galina Zelichonik, whose husband, Roald (Alik), is another Prisoner of Zion, a Hebrew teacher who also is fluent in Japanese and English. He had been warned by the KGB to stop teaching Hebrew, and was later accused of leading a Zionist conspiracy. In August 1985, he received a three-year term for writing letters to the West. Galina, who is almost totally blind, is a Russian-Polish woman who converted to Judaism and keeps a kosher, traditional home. In May, she traveled two thousand miles to visit her husband in a Kazakhstan prison. Spouses are allowed two such visits a year, of up to three days. But Jews are rarely granted more than a one-day visit. She found him in extremely poor health. In March, when his blood pressure was 190/130, a group of doctors who examined him recommended that he be hospitalized. Now, two months later, his blood pressure was 220/130. Despite his medical problems, her husband spoke to her joyfully about Anatoly Shcharansky's release and the impact he thought Tolya would have on people who have never given Soviet Jews a second thought. "No other man can tell the truth like Tolya can," Galina said. "We are so happy that he is home and that he still shows his concern for all of us."

LOVE BLOOMS in the movement, but the KGB is a jealous guardian. In March 1986, Lev Furman, a veteran Leningrad refusenik in his forties and a close friend of Ida Nudel, met, wooed, and won twenty-six-year-old Marina, a Kiev refusenik, in Tbilisi, where they both went to say good-bye to the Goldshtein brothers. When Marina flew back to Leningrad, a KGB general, Zazslavsky, sat next to her. The general, former head of the KGB "Jewish department" in Leningrad, knew of their wedding plans. "We'll see to it that your husband won't be around when you give birth to your first baby," he said. "The fate of your first child will be terrible. It's our mistake that Furman is not sitting in jail. We'll take him after your wedding." Lev and Marina got married in June.

INA BEGUN, wife of Yosef Begun, the longest-serving and best-known Prisoner of Zion, believes the Soviets may continue to add years to her husband's sentence, to take revenge on a stubborn man who won't be broken. Dr. Begun, fifty-four, the Moscow-born mathematician and Hebrew teacher, has suffered three trials and punishments since 1977. He served over four years in exile in Siberia. Then, in October 1983, he was sentenced to seven years in prison and five years' exile in Siberia. The charge was "anti-Soviet propaganda."

Begun, an observant Jew, is uncompromising in his demand to wear a skullcap. Therefore, in April 1985, he was punished for breaking the dress code. He is now under strict regime at Chistopol Prison, where Anatoly was also incarcerated. "They say he is a 'negative influence' on other prisoners," says Ina, who lives in Moscow. "Under the new Soviet article, 188/3, the chief of the labor camp or prison now has the right to prolong a prisoner's term without limit. It's another way to bully prisoners. But it is impossible to change Yosef's nature, which is to be a Jew, to talk to prisoners, Jews and gentiles, about the Holocaust and its meaning. That's considered 'Zionist propaganda' by the Soviets, and they punish him for it."

She has not seen her husband since she and Baruch, his twenty-one-year-old son by his first marriage, visited him on

August 2, 1985. (His other, adopted son, nineteen-year-old Barak, studies at a yeshiva in Israel.) Yosef is not allowed visits, mail privileges, packages, or a normal diet. Ina is hoping to see him again in October—"if he's not still being punished."

The Soviet authorities have told Ina that she should influence her husband's behavior. But she knows he will not yield in any way. She fears he will soon go on a hunger strike, and that his poor health will deteriorate seriously. "He insists on observing Shabbat, festivals, and fasts. I won't tell him to compromise; I won't help them break his spirit. He needs my support, not advice to compromise. I only ask him to avoid the hunger strike. But for him, it's the only way to protest.

"Support from the West is crucial. It is the only way he can survive." She feels that Anatoly Shcharansky knows better than anyone the situation of her husband, "better than I ever could. I know there are many demands on Anatoly, but I would like to speak with him (but of course, they deny me any calls from overseas). I want to send my best regards to him and to congratulate him and Avital. I'm sure their happiness now is the reward for all her work and all his suffering."

THE SLEPAKS, Vladimir and Maria (Masha), have been leading Jewish activists for sixteen years and are, with Ida Nudel and Yosef Begun, the best known. Through the years, the Slepaks have been constantly harassed, imprisoned, exiled in Siberia. Their two grown sons were permitted to emigrate in the late 1970s. The Slepaks' "record" is very long; they have had many confrontations with the KGB, as they helped hundreds of Jews to get to Israel. In June 1978, they hung a banner from their balcony on Gorky Street, Moscow's main thoroughfare, saying "Let us go to Israel." KGB men, occupying neighboring apartments, poured boiling water over them and tore down their banner. They were then arrested and charged with "hooliganism."

In December 1982, they returned to Moscow after five years in Siberia. Two years later, they were once again refused exit permits, on the premise that Slepak's work as a radio engineer some fifteen years earlier had been "classified." (In April 1986, Soviet leader Gorbachev gave an interview to the French Communist daily *L'Humanité* in which he said that the maximum for such secrets to be a problem was ten years, and that no one would be denied the right to emigrate if he had had no access to state secrets for that length of time. Although Soviet television and radio reported the interview, they did not mention this remark. If it were true, thousands of refuseniks who have been denied the right to emigrate would now be allowed to go.)

By 1985, the Slepaks were thoroughly demoralized at the lack of public concern for them and began to feel that they were a lost cause. Now, in June 1986, they still feel little hope, although Anatoly's release has heartened them greatly. They spoke on the phone to their old friend on May 5, and Anatoly told them, "We are talking as if it were nine years before."

They learned from a visitor that their grandchildren had been at the huge march for Soviet Jewry in New York and that Anatoly had embraced them there.

The Slepaks, both around sixty, are in good health and keep in shape during the long winter by skiing. "We must be strong to see our children and our five grandchildren," says Masha, a warm and gracious woman.

They are not very active any more, though they are still close to their many friends in the movement. During the last Passover, they were invited to a small gathering of ex-Prisoners of Zion and family members of current prisoners. A KGB officer called them and warned them not to attend. "Of course, we went," Vladimir said. Their old habit of resistance has not been eroded. But they are tired, as Ida Nudel is tired.

"We cannot survive another sixteen years of refusal," Vladimir said. "The problem of Soviet Jews becomes uninteresting to the media and to readers. It's a terrible development. On all levels, Jews must repeat, Let my people go!"

"Jews musn't forget that there are other Jews," says Masha, "they musn't forget us."

THE JEWISH ACTIVISTS in Leningrad and Moscow are part of a large community of refuseniks who offer one another mutual support. It is much harder for refuseniks in most other Soviet cities and towns, where foreign visitors are rare and there are no Western journalists. In Kishinev, the provincial capital of Moldavia, the small community of refuseniks had not had a foreign visitor in years. Some of those refuseniks live in terror and *want* to be forgotten. One man, "X," answered his phone and said "X is no longer in the Soviet Union."

One meeting was arranged for me at 6 P.M. on a Saturday in a ramshackle house in the old part of the town, in the streets where Jews were massacred during the pogroms of the early twentieth century. As I walked down the unpaved road, I saw two cars staking out the house. I kept walking, circling back to Lenin Prospect, Kishinev's main street. As I passed the city market, a muscular man and a stunning woman, both wearing white T-shirts, smiled, took me by the arm, and said: "The KGB are at the house. We'll go somewhere else to talk." The woman's shirt was stenciled with Hebrew letters, reading *Am Yisraeli Hai*, the People of Israel Live. They introduced themselves: Lisa (Leah) Shneerman and Vladimir (Volodia) Zuckerman, a veteran refusenik and former Prisoner of Zion. We talked for a few minutes in a park, where we were joined by Lisa's husband, Simon, a long-time refusenik who, at age twenty-eight, had just completed his second prison term. He informed us that the KGB men had left, and we could go back to the house.

The Shneermans and their three-year-old daughter, Yana, live in a tiny room in the wooden shanty house that was built after the war by Lisa's parents, who brought up nine children there. Simon, who is on probation for a year, has to be in the house from 8 P.M. to 6 A.M. every day. The KGB comes often, at all hours of the night. During Passover, they woke the Shneermans constantly. (Half an hour after we entered the house, the KGB men surrounded it again.) Simon is a second-generation refusenik and went to prison twice for refusing induction. It would not be astonishing if the Soviets imprisoned him for a third time. Shneerman, like other refuseniks who have served time in Soviet prisons, expressed his great respect for Shcharansky and was certain that Anatoly would be the most effective spokesman possible for oppressed Soviet Jews.

Their friend Zuckerman, thirty-nine, is an engineer, divorced, whose eleven-year-old son lives with his mother in Israel. Volodia spent three years in Siberia for "anti-Soviet activity," getting out in 1984. He has not seen his son in nine years or spoken to him on the phone in over a year.

The dream of all three is to live in Israel, "our motherland," as Simon calls it.

Although there are thousands of Jews in Kishinev, the Shneermans and Zuckerman are virtually alone. "There's a circle of about fifteen refuseniks, but we are afraid of a lot of people," Lisa explained. "The pressure on refuseniks is much greater in a small town."

Shneerman played old tapes of songs by favorite Israeli singers like Naomi Shemer and Arik Sinai. They set out a feast in the tiny room and plied me with questions about Israel. No Israeli had been to Kishinev in six years, they said, but they get letters from Kibbutz Hazor and Kibbutz Mishmar Hanegev, and from some individuals. They have no words to tell how grateful they are for this contact. But what they want is visitors—it is vitally important to them.

Three hours later, the KGB men drove off and I could go on my way with nothing to worry about. No nightmare secret police for me; no knock on my door at midnight.

IT IS A BROAD movement, and there are hundreds of refuseniks who should be heard. Here are just a few of their voices:

    * Veteran activists Victor and Irina Brailovsky, of Moscow, in their fourteenth year of refusal, are still being turned down on the basis of "state secrets." The Jewish movement has never been so suppressed," he says. "It's absolutely another era, another epic. Friends who got out in the 1970s don't understand. Now, for instance, we would never talk about our activities. Punishment is much quicker and more severe."

    * Eliezer Jousefovich, thirty-seven, father of four, a

Moscow refusenik since 1980, turned down for "state se-crets" because of army duty fourteen years ago: "We try to be Israelis here, and Jews. The connection is strong. My wife Katya and I try to educate our kids as Israelis, no matter what the authorities do to suppress us."

* Moshe Furman, eighty, father of Lev, a Leningrad re-fusenik since 1974, a highly decorated war hero and career navy captain: "We are all growing older together in refusal, as the new generation of refuseniks grows up."

* Aba Taratuta, fifty, a long-time leader of the Jewish activists in Leningrad, known for his loyalty, sense of hu-mor, and dedication: "I heard Shcharansky on the Voice of America and agree 100 percent with him about the need to retain the Jackson–Vanik Amendment, and about every-thing else he said. It's amazing that he didn't lose his sense of reality after nine years in prison. Now we must struggle for the freedom of Yosef Begun and all the other prisoners."

* Alec Zilber, thirty-three, and his wife Marina, twenty-nine, of Gorky—artists who recently staged a demonstra-tion in Moscow with their seven-year-old son, Arseiny: "It's very difficult in school for the children of refuseniks. Ar-seiny is not a member of the Communist scout movement, so the other children taunt him. He was beaten in the pres-ence of the teacher, who simply turned her back on it. He came home bleeding around the eyes."

* Judith Ratner (Byaly), fifty-three, of Moscow, whose family has been waiting for nine years: "In the absence of emigration, we must fight for the people who *must* get out now, like Ida Nudel. The KGB is constantly warning us, threatening us. But every normal person understands our situation—that we must be allowed to go to Israel. We know

that people abroad are fighting for us, and we know that Anatoly Shcharansky will continue to be at the forefront of our struggle."

—LOUIS RAPOPORT,
June 1986